The Recipe Hall of Fame Cookbook

★

*Winning Recipes
from Hometown America*

Crusty Red Potatoes pg. 99

Originally a gesture of international friendship, the Statue of Liberty was given to the United States by France to commemorate the centennial of US independence. It has become a global symbol of freedom.

Best of the Best

★★★★★★★★★★★ ★★★★★★★★★★★

The Recipe Hall of Fame Cookbook

★

Winning Recipes from Hometown America

EDITED BY
Gwen McKee
AND
Barbara Moseley

Illustrated by Tupper England

QUAIL RIDGE PRESS
Preserving America's Food Heritage

Recipe Collection © 1999 Quail Ridge Press, Inc.

ALL RIGHTS RESERVED
Recipes reprinted with permission from the publishers,
organizations or individuals listed on pages 277-291.

Library of Congress Cataloging-in-Publication Data

The recipe hall of fame cookbook: winning recipes from hometown America /
edited by Gwen McKee and Barbara Moseley;
illustrated by Tupper England.
p. cm.
ISBN 1-893062-08-2
1. Cookery, American. 2. Cookery—Competitions—United States.
I. McKee, Gwen. II. Moseley, Barbara. III. Quail Ridge Press
cookbook series.
TX715.R285 1999
641.5973—dc21   99-23538
                                                          CIP

First printing: 53,000 copies, September 1999
Second printing: 53,000 copies, October 1999
Third printing: 51,000 copies, January 2000
Fourth printing: 27,000 copies, May 2000
Fifth printing: 30,000 copies, September 2000
Sixth printing: 15,000 copies, August 2001
Seventh printing: 25,000 copies, March 2002

Printed in Canada
Book design by Cynthia Clark
Cover photo by Greg Campbell

QUAIL RIDGE PRESS
P. O. Box 123 • Brandon, MS 39043 • e-mail: info@quailridge.com
www.recipehalloffame.com • www.quailridge.com

Contents

As the focal point of our government's Legislative Branch, the Capitol is the centerpiece of the Capitol Complex. In addition to its active use by Congress, the Capitol is a museum of American art and history.

★★★★★★★★★★ ★★★★★★★★★★

How do you judge a recipe and say, "This dish is so wonderful, it belongs in a category of its own—it should be in a Recipe Hall of Fame"?

This is the question we asked ourselves over and over. And answering that question—choosing the recipes for this book—was indeed a challenge.

Two decades ago, Quail Ridge Press began collecting and publishing the best classic and modern recipes from every corner of the USA. Our goal was to preserve America's food heritage by finding and sharing the best recipes from the best cookbooks from all over our country. Not an easy process, we researched the many customs and cultures and tastes—and cooking habits—of our nation. This effort has grown into a 28-volume Best of the Best State Cookbook Series with over 11,000 popular and proven recipes. (See page 304 for a complete listing.)

Over the years our readers have been asking us, "Which are the **Best** of the Best of the Best?" We have had letters, calls and e-mails telling us how one recipe was the hit of the family reunion, while another was the talk of a bridal shower, and another had become an established family favorite. Not surprisingly, many of them mentioned the same dishes which are often our own favorites, too. These recipes were clearly classics, a cut above any other . . . and timeless.

We began to realize that these special recipes did indeed deserve some greater recognition, and what better way to reach our goal to preserve America's food heritage than to honor these recipes with their own Recipe Hall of Fame. This effort ensures that these exceptional dishes so many people enjoy will always be available.

In choosing Hall of Fame recipes, we used several criteria. First, all the recipes selected are in our Best of the Best State Cookbook Series. So in effect they are already winners, since the recipes in these Best cookbooks have been chosen as favorites from each state.

The next criteria was simply taste. Then, very importantly, the recipe has to work for whoever prepares it. It has to come out right, so that when someone makes that recipe, they will want to make it again and again.

As we tested the many recipes, we considered another important criteria: Is this easy to make? After all, we live in pressured, fast food, "defrost-a-meal" times, and a good home-cooked meal is almost a luxury. It shouldn't have to be. Winning recipes should combine easy preparation, taste and appeal.

Another consideration was balance between courses such as appetizers, breakfasts, lunches, dinners, desserts, etc. So this is not only a collection of outstanding dishes and meals, but a book that serves a very practical purpose: putting great food on the table at any time, for any occasion.

Finally we asked ourselves, which recipes do *you* think are the best? With these criteria in mind, we asked the people who cook from these books, specifically our Best of the Best Club members, to pick their favorites. The votes have come in from cooks all over the country who have conveyed to us how they like to cook, what they get compliments on, and what their families and guests like to eat. Our survey results and the overwhelming response helped confirm that our choices were also our readers' choices.

So in the final analysis, we and our readers voted with our taste buds—the ultimate way to determine that a recipe is among the ***Best*** of the Best of the Best and "belonged in a Hall of Fame."

We are proud of these award-winning recipes and hope you will enjoy them as much as we do.

Welcome to The Recipe Hall of Fame.

Gwen McKee and Barbara Moseley
August, 1999

P. S. Please note that the title of each contributing cookbook is listed below the recipe along with the state name in parenthesis indicating the Best of the Best cookbook where the recipe appears. Beginning on page 277, you can find a list of the cookbooks who have contributed the recipes that are the first inductees into The Recipe Hall of Fame. Throughout the book we've added some of our own comments as "Editor's Extras." Other comments and notes that enhance the recipe's "flavor" are from the original recipes.

Beverages & Appetizers

★★★★ ★★★★

Welcoming Wine

A wonderful way to say hello.

1 (6-ounce) can frozen orange juice
  concentrate
1 (6-ounce) can frozen lemonade
  concentrate
2 cups cold water

1 fifth white wine
1 cup orange liqueur
1 (28-ounce) bottle carbonated water
Ice
Orange slices

Place frozen concentrates in punch bowl or large pitcher. Stir in 2 cups of cold water. Mix until smooth. Stir in wine and orange liqueur. Add carbonated water and ice. Stir gently. Top with orange slices.

To Market, To Market (Kentucky)

Plain People's Lemonade

Lemonade is a favorite beverage among Amish and Mennonite families. The Amish traditionally prepare lemonade by pressing sliced lemons to release the flavorful oils. However, this easy recipe with grated lemon rind seems to impart a similar flavor.

1½ cups sugar
1 tablespoon grated lemon rind
½ cup boiling water
1½ cups freshly squeezed lemon
  juice (from about 6 large lemons)

6 cups cold water
Ice cubes

In jar with tight-fitting lid, combine sugar, rind, and boiling water; shake until sugar dissolves. Add lemon juice; shake well. Chill. Before serving, add water and ice cubes. Makes 2 quarts.

Bountiful Ohio (Ohio)

French Mint Tea

Refreshing on hot summer days and good for parties.

3 family-sized tea bags
Enough water to cover well
Handful of fresh, clean mint

Juice of 4 lemons
1 (12-ounce) can frozen orange juice
2 cups sugar

In a pot bring to a boil, tea bags, water and mint. Cover and remove from heat. Allow to steep 30 minutes. Remove tea bags and mint by strainer. Add lemon juice, orange juice and sugar. Add enough water to make 1 gallon. Refrigerate. Yields 1 gallon or 16 (8-ounce) servings.

Southern Secrets (Tennessee)

Golden Anniversary Punch

1 (6-ounce) can orange juice frozen
  concentrate
1 (6-ounce) can lemonade frozen
  concentrate
1 (6-ounce) can frozen pineapple
  juice

1 (12-ounce) can apricot nectar,
  chilled
½ cup lemon juice
1 quart orange sherbet
2 large bottles ginger ale, chilled

Add water to frozen concentrates according to directions on cans. (If frozen pineapple juice is unavailable, use 1 large can of pineapple juice.) Add chilled apricot nectar and lemon juice. Just before serving, spoon in sherbet. To keep carbonation, carefully pour ginger ale down the side of the bowl. Makes 20-25 servings.

Lake Reflections (Kentucky)

Champagne Nectar Punch

The Best!

2 (12-ounce) can apricot nectar
1 (6-ounce) can frozen orange juice
  concentrate
3 cups water

¼ cup lemon juice
⅛ teaspoon salt
3 (V/b-quart) bottles champagne,
  chilled

Mix all ingredients except champagne; chill. Add champagne just before serving. Makes about 42 servings in champagne glasses.

What's New in Wedding Food (North Carolina)

Hot Perked Party Punch

9 cups unsweetened pineapple juice
9 cups cranberry juice cocktail
4½ cups water
1 cup brown sugar

4 cinnamon sticks, broken
4½ teaspoons whole cloves
¼ teaspoon salt

Combine pineapple juice, cranberry cocktail, water, and sugar in a 30-cup coffee maker. Place all other ingredients in basket. Perk a regular cycle. Serve piping hot.

Prairie Harvest (Arkansas)

Hot Buttered Rum

A Michigan cold weather drink.

1 pound brown sugar
½ cup butter or margarine, softened
¼ teaspoon nutmeg

½ teaspoon cinnamon
½ teaspoon cloves
Rum

Cream sugar and butter. Add spices to make base. In a 6-ounce mug, put 1 jigger rum and 1 heaping tablespoon of base mixture. Fill with boiling water. Base keeps in refrigerator for months. Make a batch of the recipe and place in attractive wine glass or mug; include recipe, and give as a gift. Makes 32 servings.

The Junior League of Grand Rapids Cookbook I (Michigan)

Cappuccino Mix

Not too sweet, nice to have on hand.

1 cup instant coffee creamer
1 cup instant Quik chocolate
⅔ cup instant coffee

½ cup powdered sugar
¼ teaspoon cinnamon
¼ teaspoon nutmeg

Combine all ingredients in blender until very fine. Store in air-tight container. Use 3 tablespoons mix to 8 ounces hot water. Makes about 3 cups dry mix.

Iola's Gourmet Recipes in Rhapsody (Great Plains)

Irish Cream

Irish Cream is an ideal after-dinner drink complementing good cuisine. This recipe is one of our favorites.

3 eggs
1 can sweetened condensed milk
1 cup brandy

½ pint whipping cream
1½ tablespoons chocolate syrup
¼ teaspoon coconut extract

Blend in blender. Put in bottle. Keeps 1 month in refrigerator.

Sparks from the Kitchen (Wisconsin)

★ **Editor's Extra:** Nice to serve over cracked ice in a stemmed glass. Also outstanding over ice cream!

Coffee Punch

Small jar instant coffee
4 cups sugar
4 cups boiling water

12 quarts milk
½ gallon chocolate ice cream
½ gallon vanilla ice cream

Mix coffee, sugar, and water. (This may be kept in refrigerator indefinitely.) Stir this mixture into milk and pour over ice cream when ready to serve. Serves 75.

Pirate's Pantry (Louisiana)

★ **Editor's Extra:** Delicious with a little spike of bourbon and/or a sprinkle of nutmeg on top.

Tex-Mex Dip

This popular recipe makes a HUGE amount. Have a Texas-size party!

3 ripe avocados
2 tablespoons lemon juice
½ teaspoon salt
¼ teaspoon pepper
1 cup sour cream
½ cup mayonnaise
1 package dry taco seasoning mix

2 cans plain bean dip
3 green onions with tops, chopped
3 medium tomatoes, coarsely
   chopped
2 (3½-ounce) cans ripe olives,
   drained and chopped
8 ounces Cheddar cheese, shredded

Peel, pit, and mash avocados with lemon juice, salt, and pepper. In separate bowl, combine sour cream, mayonnaise, and taco seasoning.

Spread bean dip on a large, shallow serving platter. Top with seasoned avocado mixture. Layer with sour cream and taco mixture. Sprinkle with chopped onions, tomatoes, and olives. Cover with shredded cheese. Serve chilled or at room temperature with round tortilla chips.

Company's Coming (Texas)

Annie's Mexicorn Dip

1 small can Mexicorn, drained
1 small can white corn, drained
1 cup grated sharp Cheddar cheese
½ cup sour cream
½ cup mayonnaise

½ cup green onion, chopped
1 (4-ounce) can chopped green
   chilies
1 teaspoon Lawry's seasoned salt
Garlic salt to taste

Mix the above ingredients well. Chill in the refrigerator 1 hour. Before serving, sprinkle on a little chili powder for decoration. Serve with big corn chips for dipping.

Gourmet: The Quick and Easy Way (Oklahoma)

★ **Editor's Extra:** Chopped olives or jalapeño peppers are zippy variations.

Dream Fruit Dip

My friends love this dip. It is great for parties.

12 ounces cream cheese
1 cup confectioners' sugar, unsifted
1 cup sour cream
1 (7-ounce) jar marshmallow creme

2 teaspoons vanilla extract
2 teaspoons almond extract
2 teaspoons cinnamon
2 tablespoons cognac (optional)

In small bowl of electric mixer, cream the cheese until soft and smooth. Add the confectioners' sugar and beat until well blended. Add the sour cream and the rest of the ingredients. Blend just until well combined. Place in a pretty bowl. Cover and chill several hours before serving. Just before serving, place in the center of an attractive large platter. Surround bowl with a variety of fresh fruits: bananas, strawberries, cherries, honeydew melon balls, cantaloupe balls, grapes, pineapple chunks, and apple slices.

Sweets...from Marina with Love... (Texas)

Hot Spinach Artichoke Dip

1 (15-ounce) can artichoke hearts (not marinated)
1 (10-ounce) package chopped spinach, thawed and drained
1 small jar pimento, drained and chopped or ½ cup diced red pepper

4 ounces mozzarella cheese, shredded
¼ teaspoon garlic salt
1 cup mayonnaise
1 cup parmesan cheese, grated
½ cup ripe pitted olives, chopped

Drain artichoke hearts and cut into small pieces. Add remaining ingredients and mix. Spoon into sprayed 1-quart glass casserole. Bake at 350° for 30 minutes. Serve warm with tortilla chips. Serves 12-20, depending on what else is served.

Chickadee Cottage Cookbook 2 (Minnesota)

★ **Editor's Extra:** Try adding a tad of hot pepper sauce.

 Minnesota is called the "Land of 10,000 Lakes." Of the state's 87 counties, only one—Rock County—doesn't have a natural lake.

★★★★★★★★★★★   ★★★★★★★★★★★

Too Easy Tamale Dip

Easy and very good.

2 (15-ounce) cans tamales
1 (16-ounce) can chili without beans
1 (8-ounce) jar picante sauce

2 (5-ounce) jars Old English cheese
1 onion, chopped

Chop the tamales and add rest of ingredients and blend. Put in fondue or crock and keep warm. Serve with anything "dipable." Serves 20 with other hors d'oeuvres.

Stir Ups (Oklahoma)

International Bean Dip

Best bean dip ever tasted.

1 (15-ounce) can refried beans
4 ounces cream cheese, softened
12 ounces sour cream
**1 bunch green onions, finely
  chopped**
½ (12-ounce) can Ortega salsa
1 (1¼-ounce) packet taco seasoning

**½ (4-ounce) can diced green chile
  peppers**
Dash oregano
Salt and pepper to taste
**1 cup grated Monterey Jack,
  Longhorn, or Cheddar cheese**

Combine all ingredients except grated cheese in ovenproof dish. Sprinkle top with grated cheese. Bake 1 hour at 300°. Serves 15.

Cook 'em Horns (Texas)

★★★★★★★★★★★★   ★★★★★★★★★★★★★

Texas Black-Eyed Pea Dip

Fills the bill for a New Year's party. Make ahead and reheat. A winner—from Athens, Texas, the Black-Eyed Pea Capital of the World!

¼ bell pepper
8 jalapeño peppers (or to taste)
2 stalks celery
1 large onion
1 teaspoon coarse black pepper
2 tablespoons Tabasco
½ cup catsup
1 teaspoon salt
3 chicken bouillon cubes

¼ teaspoon nutmeg
¼ teaspoon cinnamon
2 (15.5-ounce) cans black-eyed peas
1 cup canned tomatoes
1 teaspoon granulated (or chopped) garlic
½ cup bacon drippings
3 tablespoons flour

Chop finely the peppers, celery, and onion. Add the next 7 ingredients and bring to a slow simmer. Then add the black-eyed peas, the tomatoes, and garlic. Cook for 30 minutes. Blend together the bacon drippings and flour and heat with cooked mixture for 10 minutes. Stir well to prevent sticking. Serve hot with tostadas or Doritos.

Collectibles II (Texas)

★ **Editor's Extra:** Remember, the jalapeño seeds determine the hotness—I recommend no seeds.

Pizza Dip

Outstanding!

1 (8-ounce) package cream cheese, softened
1 (14-ounce) jar pizza sauce
⅓ cup onions, chopped

1½ cups grated mozzarella cheese
1 (6-ounce) can ripe olives, drained and chopped
2 ounces sliced pepperoni, chopped

Preheat oven to 350°. Press cream cheese in bottom of 9-inch glass pie pan. Spread pizza sauce over cream cheese and layer remaining ingredients in order listed. Bake at 350° for 25 minutes. Serve with light corn chips. Yields 8-10 servings.

Georgia On My Menu (Georgia)

Ácoma Pueblo, founded about AD 1100, is possibly the oldest continuously inhabited settlement in the United States. Perched atop a sandstone mesa that rises 357 feet above the valley floor, it is also known as Sky City. The location was chosen for protection from marauding enemies, but the incredible beauty of its panoramic view may have been an added reason. It is located 84 miles west of Albuquerque, New Mexico.

★★★★★★★★★★★★ ★★★★★★★★★★★★

Mock Oyster Dip

1 package frozen chopped broccoli
1 large onion, minced
8 tablespoons butter or margarine
1 can cream of mushroom soup

1 can mushroom stems and pieces, undrained
1 (6-ounce) roll of garlic cheese
Dash of hot sauce

Cook broccoli in water till soft (over-done); drain. Sauté onion in butter; add cream of mushroom soup, mushrooms and juice. Break up garlic cheese and add to mixture. Add hot sauce and broccoli. Mix well. Keep warm in chafing dish; eat with dipper potato chips.

Can also be served in patty shells or over noodles as a casserole.

Recipes and Reminiscences of New Orleans I (Louisiana)

Legendary Crab Rounds

Simple to prepare and absolutely fantastic.

1 cup mayonnaise
½ cup grated onion
1 cup shredded Cheddar cheese
6 drops Tabasco sauce
¼ teaspoon curry powder

1 (6½-ounce) can crabmeat, drained
2 French bread baguettes, sliced ½ inch thick

In medium bowl, combine mayonnaise, grated onion, Cheddar cheese, Tabasco, curry powder, and crabmeat. This may be made one day in advance. To serve, place mixture on bread rounds and broil until golden brown. Serve immediately. Makes 50-55 rounds.

Crème de Colorado (Colorado)

Texas Crab Grass

½ cup butter
½ medium onion, finely chopped
1 package frozen chopped spinach, cooked and drained

1 (6½-ounce) can crabmeat
¾ cup parmesan cheese, grated
Melba rounds or crackers

Slowly melt butter in heavy saucepan. Add onion and sauté until soft. Add spinach to onion mixture. Add crabmeat and cheese. Transfer to chafing dish and serve with Melba rounds.

Noted Cookery (Texas)

★★★★★★★★★★★★   ★★★★★★★★★★★★

Crusty Crab Points

6 ounces crabmeat
½ cup butter, softened
1 (5-ounce) jar sharp Cheddar
   cheese spread

½ teaspoon mayonnaise
½ teaspoon seasoned salt
½ teaspoon garlic powder
3 English muffins, sliced in half

When using canned crabmeat, drain. Combine all ingredients except English muffins with electric mixer. Spread on English muffin halves. Freeze for 1-1½ hours. Cut each muffin half into 6 wedges. Refreeze in plastic bags until ready to serve. Broil until golden brown and bubbly, about 5 minutes. Serve immediately. Makes 3 dozen points.

   Filling is also good on party rye, or leave the English muffin halves uncut and serve as open-faced sandwiches.

Honest to Goodness (Illinois)

Crabmeat Mornay

Outstanding!

1 stick butter
1 small bunch green onions, chopped
½ cup finely chopped parsley
2 tablespoons flour
1 pint breakfast cream (half-&-half)

½ pound grated Swiss cheese
1 tablespoon sherry wine
Red pepper to taste
Salt to taste
1 pound white crabmeat

Melt butter in heavy pot and sauté onions and parsley. Blend in flour, cream, and cheese until cheese is melted. Add other ingredients and gently fold in crabmeat. This may be served in a chafing dish with Melba toast, or in patty shells.

River Road Recipes I (Louisiana)

★ **Editor's Extra:** Fresh or canned crabmeat used to be the only choices. Now it is handy to keep pasteurized fresh crabmeat on hand for several weeks. Look for it in the refrigerated seafood section of your supermarket.

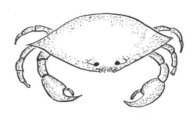

Crab Stuffed Mushroom Caps

1 tablespoon butter
¼ cup finely diced onion
¼ cup finely diced celery
1 ounce white wine
1 teaspoon salt
¼ teaspoon white pepper
½ teaspoon thyme
1 teaspoon lemon juice

4 ounces king, snow, or lump
  crabmeat
1 ounce heavy cream or half-&-half
¼ cup shredded baby Swiss cheese
½ cup bread crumbs
16 large mushrooms, stems removed
16 small, thin slices baby Swiss
  cheese

Preheat oven to 375°. Melt butter in medium skillet over medium heat. Sauté onion and celery in butter until tender. Add wine, seasonings, lemon juice, and crabmeat; simmer 3 minutes.

Add cream and shredded cheese; cook until cheese melts. Add bread crumbs. Spoon crab mixture into mushroom caps. Top with slices of baby Swiss cheese. Bake 12-15 minutes or until cheese is lightly browned. Makes 16.

Great Beginnings, Grand Finales (Indiana)

Crab or Shrimp Mousse

Made in a fish-shaped mold, garnished with lemon slices dipped in paprika and sprigs of parsley, our shrimp mousse is prettier than a picture in any magazine! Serve with candlelight and silver.

1½ cups chopped shrimp (crab
  or lobster may be used, about
  1 pound)
1 cup chopped celery
½ cup chopped bell pepper
2 tablespoons grated onion
1 teaspoon salt
3 tablespoons lemon juice

1 tablespoon Worcestershire
½ teaspoon Tabasco
1 can tomato soup
3 (3-ounce) packages cream cheese
3 envelopes plain gelatin
1 cup cold water
1 cup mayonnaise

Spray a 2-quart mold with cooking spray. Combine shrimp, celery, bell pepper, onion, salt, lemon juice, Worcestershire, and Tabasco. Mix well and let stand to blend flavors. Combine soup and cream cheese in double boiler. Heat and stir until cheese melts. Soften gelatin in cold water for 5 minutes. Add to soup mixture. Remove from heat and cool. When mixture begins to thicken, blend in mayonnaise. Stir in shrimp mixture, spoon into mold, and chill. Serve with crackers, or may be used as a salad served on lettuce leaves.

Cotton Country Cooking (Alabama)

Sea Island Shrimp Spread

Shrimply divine!

1 (3-ounce) package cream cheese
1 cup sour cream
1 (0.7-ounce) package Good Seasons
  Italian Dressing Mix

2 teaspoons lemon juice
1 (4¼-ounce) can shrimp, drained
  and rinsed

Blend ingredients. Let stand at least 4 hours before serving with crackers.

Gazebo Gala (Tennessee)

Mini Pizzas

Kids love to help you make these—and they love eating them, too!

1 package English muffins
1 small jar Ragu sauce
¼ pound sliced pepperoni

½ cup chopped onions (optional)
½ cup chopped olives (optional)
8 ounces shredded mozzarella cheese

Cut muffins in half. Spread sauce on muffins. Layer pepperoni and whatever you like, and top with the cheese. Place on cookie sheet and bake at 350° (400° for a crispier crust) for 10-12 minutes.

The Hagen Family Cookbook (Great Plains)

★ **Editor's Extra:** Try this on flour tortillas for a great crispy treat. Bake at 400° for 8-10 minutes.

Bacon Filled Cherry Tomatoes

Make these when you are alone, because your family will eat them faster than you can put them together! These were always a favorite when we catered parties.

1 pound bacon, fried and crumbled
¼ cup green onions, chopped
2 tablespoons parsley, chopped

½ cup mayonnaise
24 cherry tomatoes

Combine ingredients except tomatoes. Cut a thin slice off top of each tomato. With a small spoon or melon baller, hollow out tomato. Fill tomatoes with bacon mixture. Makes 24.

Country Classics (Colorado)

★★★★★★★★★★★   ★★★★★★★★★★★★

Smoked Chicken Pesto Quesadillas

If you really want to dazzle your friends, make this as an appetizer. The flavors meld beautifully. Be sure to make enough, because it goes quickly.

8 ounces pesto, homemade or good-
    quality brand
8 (8-inch) flour tortillas
1 (8-10-ounce) smoked chicken
    breast (or turkey), pulled into
    thin shreds

¾ pound provolone, or combine
    provolone and mozzarella, grated
Mazola oil

Spread 3 heaping tablespoons of pesto on each tortilla. Divide the chicken breast shreds over the pesto on each tortilla. Sprinkle ⅓ -½ cup of cheese over the chicken. Place another tortilla on top. Heat ⅛ inch of oil in a black iron frying pan and heat each side until golden brown and the cheese is melted. Serves 8-12 as an appetizer or can be used as a main course.

Lighter Tastes of Aspen (Colorado)

★ **Editor's Extra:** Try folding over a single tortilla—makes it easier to flip!

Tortillitas

1 (8-ounce) package cream cheese,
    softened
1 cup sour cream
5 green onions, chopped
1 (4-ounce) can chopped green
    chilies

1-2 teaspoons garlic salt
6-7 (12-inch) flour tortillas
Picante sauce

Combine all ingredients except tortillas and picante sauce. Mix until smooth. Cover 1 tortilla with about 3-4 tablespoons of the mixture, spreading to the edges. Place another tortilla on top of this and spread with mixture. Continue layering until tortillas and mixture are used, ending with a tortilla on top.

   Chill thoroughly and cut into squares. Spear with a toothpick and serve with picante sauce. Can be made a day in advance. Makes 35-40 tortillas.

Gateways (Missouri)

Smoked Salmon Dip

1 (6-ounce) can salmon
1 (6-ounce) package cream cheese,
  softened
¼ cup milk
2 teaspoons lemon juice

Several drops liquid smoke,
  to taste
⅛ teaspoon pepper
Dill weed, to taste

Finely chop salmon. Stir together with cream cheese, milk, lemon juice, liquid smoke, and pepper. Add dill and serve with assorted crackers or fresh vegetables. Makes 1½ cups.

Seasoned with Love (Wisconsin)

Sooner Salsa

A quick and easy salsa!

1 (16-ounce) can stewed tomatoes
4 medium tomatoes, chopped
3 small jalapeño peppers, chopped
  and seeded

⅓ cup chopped onion
½ teaspoon salt
½ teaspoon cayenne pepper

Combine tomatoes, peppers, and onion in food processor and process until desired consistency. Add salt and cayenne pepper; process again to mix. Store in refrigerator. Yields 4 cups.

Note: With jalapeños, keep as many or as few seeds as you wish; the more seeds, the hotter the salsa.

Cafe Oklahoma (Oklahoma)

Route 66, the fabled "Main Street of America," crosses Oklahoma for 392-plus miles. The "Mother Road" was in fact born in Oklahoma, as the road's architect, Cyrus Avery, lived in Tulsa. Travelers find neon-lit diners, drive-in theaters, mom-and-pop gas stations, and rustic trading posts along the route from Chicago to Los Angeles. Though it can now be an adventure to find, you can still "get your kicks on Route 66."

Vegetable Bars

2 packages crescent-shaped dinner
  rolls
2 (8-ounce) packages cream cheese
¾ cup mayonnaise
1 (1-ounce) package ranch-style
  dressing (original)

Black olives, chopped
Sharp Cheddar cheese
Choose your favorite vegetables:
  carrots, mushrooms, broccoli,
  cauliflower, red onion, green onion,
  radishes, bell pepper, zucchini

Preheat oven to 350°. Lay out rolls on jelly roll pan to make a crust. Bake in preheated oven for 8-10 minutes. Cool. Combine cream cheese, mayonnaise, and ranch dressing. Spread cream cheese mixture over crescent crust. Chop vegetables into small pieces. Press chopped vegetables and black olives into cream cheese mixture. Top with shredded sharp Cheddar cheese. Refrigerate at least 4 hours or overnight. Cut into bars to serve. Yields 48.

Cookin' in the Spa (Arkansas)

★ **Editor's Extra:** A jelly roll pan is a cookie sheet with sides. This also is pretty in a pizza pan.

Pepper Cheesecake

Must be prepared ahead. Put a big fresh red flower in middle or garnish with black olives and tomatoes.

16 ounces cream cheese, softened
8 ounces sharp cheese, shredded
1 (1½-ounce) package taco
  seasoning
16 ounces sour cream, divided
3 eggs

1 (4-ounce) can diced green chilies,
  drained
½ cup red bell peppers, diced
½ cup hot salsa sauce
16 ounces guacamole or avocado dip

Preheat oven to 350°. Beat cream cheese, shredded cheese, and taco seasoning until fluffy; stir in 1 cup sour cream. Beat in eggs 1 at a time. Fold in chilies and red peppers. Pour in greased springform pan and bake for 40-45 minutes. Cool for 10 minutes on wire rack. Combine remaining sour cream with salsa and spread on top. Bake for 5 minutes. Refrigerate overnight.

To serve, unmold and spread with guacamole or avocado dip. Garnish with fresh tomatoes, olives, or cheese. Serve with taco chips. Makes 20-25 servings.

Return Engagement (Iowa)

Hot Cheese in a Jar

2 pounds melted Velveeta cheese
  (do not substitute)
1 medium onion, grated or ground
1 (5.33-ounce) can evaporated milk
1 pint Miracle Whip salad dressing
  (do not substitute)

1 (8-ounce) can seeded, deveined
  jalapeño peppers, chopped fine
  (cut off stems)

Melt cheese in top of double boiler. Add onion, milk, Miracle Whip and peppers to melted cheese, and mix well. Pour into 6 (8-ounce) jelly jars. Cool, screw on caps, refrigerate. May be used as a cheese spread or let stand about 30 minutes at room temperature and may be used as a dip. Ingredients may be mixed in a blender, then added to the melted cheese. Yields 6 jars.

Note: The jars of cheese, tied with a ribbon, make nice gifts at Christmas, or at any time when something small would be appreciated. But remember, it must be refrigerated.

Cowtown Cuisine (Texas)

Homemade Boursin

The easiest, least expensive, most requested cheese spread you will ever serve.

1 (8-ounce) package cream cheese,
  softened
1 clove garlic, crushed
1 teaspoon basil

1 teaspoon caraway seed
1 teaspoon dill weed
1 teaspoon chives, chopped
Cracked black or lemon pepper

Blend cream cheese with garlic, basil, caraway, dill weed and chives. Pat into a round, flat shape. Roll all sides (lightly) in lemon pepper or cracked black pepper. Good to make a few days ahead or serve right away with assorted crackers.

The Country Mouse (Mississippi)

★ **Editor's Extra:** The above recipes are two of our all-time favorites.

★★★★★★★★★★★★★ ★★★★★★★★★★★★★

Plains Cheese Ring

Former First Lady Rosalyn Carter is given credit for making this addictive spread popular. It's said that it was one of Jimmy's favorites and was always on the Carter family's holiday table. It can be served with a meal, but also makes a great addition to the appetizer table. You will be pleasantly surprised at the way the unlikely ingredients interact.

1 pound sharp Cheddar cheese, grated, then allowed to soften	1 small onion, grated
1 cup chopped pecans	Black pepper to taste
1 cup mayonnaise	Dash cayenne
	Strawberry preserves

Combine all ingredients except preserves. (A food processor works well and eliminates the need to chop ingredients.) Place in ring mold greased with a little mayonnaise. Chill. When ready to serve, unmold. Fill center with preserves. Serve with buttery crackers. Serves 8-12.

Savannah Collection (Georgia)

Pineapple Cheese Ball

2 (8-ounce) packages cream cheese, softened	2 cups chopped pecans
1 (8½-ounce) can crushed pineapple, drained	¼ cup green pepper, finely chopped
	2 tablespoons onion, finely chopped
	1 tablespoon seasoned salt

In a medium bowl with fork, mix cream cheese until smooth. Stir in pineapple, 1 cup pecans, green pepper, onion, and seasoned salt. Shape into ball and roll in remaining nuts. Wrap in foil; refrigerate overnight.

To serve, place cheese on board, garnish with pineapple slices and cherries, if desired. Surround with assorted crackers.

Elvis Fans Cookbook (Tennessee)

World's Best Pimento Cheese

We had never liked pimento cheese until we ate it at Papa Robin's, a now-defunct restaurant in Jasper, Arkansas. Our re-creation of their marvelous pimento cheese:

4 tablespoons mayonnaise
1 (3-ounce) package cream cheese, softened
3 cloves garlic, chopped
Handful fresh parsley
Several vigorous shots of Pickapepper and Tabasco sauces

1 cup pecans
1 small jar diced pimentos and all juice
12 ounces extra-sharp Cheddar cheese

Purée till smooth in processor the mayonnaise, cream cheese, garlic, parsley, and sauces. Turn into a bowl. Now, in food processor, process just till coarsely chopped 1 cup pecans; add pecans and pimentos, with juice, to mayonnaise mixture. Now grate in food processor 12 ounces extra-sharp Cheddar cheese. Turn into bowl with remaining ingredients. Stir well to combine. Let stand, refrigerated, at least 1 hour. Even better the next day.

The Dairy Hollow House Cookbook (Arkansas)

Cheese Bennes

½ pound sharp Cheddar cheese, grated
¼ pound margarine or butter, softened
½ teaspoon salt

Pinch cayenne
1¼ cups sifted flour
½ cup benne seeds (sesame seeds), roasted

Cream first four ingredients together. Add flour and knead. Add seeds and knead. Form into four or five long, thin rolls. Chill in waxed paper several hours or freeze.

Slice rolls into "thin dimes." Bake at 350° for 10-15 minutes. If desired, sprinkle with salt while hot. Keep in tightly covered tin. Makes 10-12 dozen. Freezes well.

Charleston Receipts Repeats (South Carolina)

Beale Street in Memphis, Tennessee, is the birthplace of the blues. Memphis musicians include W.C. Handy, Jerry Lee Lewis, Charlie Rich, B.B. King, Al Green, and Elvis Presley. Nashville is the country music capital of the world. Called Music City USA, it is the home of the famous Grand Ole Opry, which is nothing less than an American institution.

Cranberry Meat Balls

An excellent blend of ingredients.

2 pounds ground beef
1 cup cornflake crumbs
1/3 cup dried parsley flakes
2 eggs
2 tablespoons soy sauce

1/4 teaspoon pepper
1/2 teaspoon garlic powder
1/3 cup catsup
2 tablespoons onion, chopped

In a large bowl, mix ground beef, crumbs, parsley, eggs, soy sauce, pepper, garlic powder, catsup, and onion. Blend well and form into small balls. Brown in oven at 400° for 15 minutes. Pour off grease.

SAUCE:
1 (16-ounce) can jellied cranberry
  sauce
1 (12-ounce) bottle chili sauce

2 tablespoons brown sugar
1 tablespoon lemon juice

While meat balls are baking, combine cranberry sauce, chili sauce, brown sugar, and lemon juice. Cover drained meat balls with sauce and bake, uncovered, at 300° for 15 minutes. Serve in chafing dish. Makes 80-90 meat balls.

Finely Tuned Foods (Missouri)

Sauerkraut Balls

These taste great!

8 ounces bulk pork sausage
1/4 cup finely chopped onion
1 (14-ounce) can sauerkraut, well
  drained and snipped
2 tablespoons bread crumbs
1 (3-ounce) package cream cheese
Garlic salt to taste
Celery salt to taste

Pepper to taste
2 tablespoons parsley flakes
1 teaspoon prepared mustard
Flour for coating
1/4 cup milk
2 eggs, beaten
Cracker crumbs
Barbecue sauce

In skillet, cook sausage and onion until meat is browned; drain. Add sauerkraut and bread crumbs. Combine cream cheese, garlic salt, celery salt, pepper, parsley flakes, and mustard and stir into sauerkraut mixture. Chill. Shape into 1-inch balls.

Coat with flour, dip into milk and eggs, mixed. Roll in crushed cracker crumbs. Deep-fry in hot oil until golden brown. Serve with barbecue sauce for dipping.

What's Cook'n? (Wisconsin)

Swedish Meat Balls

Meatballs are good served as hors d'oeuvres on toothpicks—with or without gravy, or as main dish with buttered noodles or rice.

½ cup minced onion
2 tablespoons butter or margarine
1 egg
½ cup milk
½ cup fresh bread crumbs
1¼ teaspoons salt

2 teaspoons sugar
½ teaspoon allspice
¼ teaspoon nutmeg
1 pound ground chuck
¼ pound ground shoulder pork

In large skillet, sauté onion in 2 tablespoons butter until golden. Meanwhile, in a large mixing bowl, beat egg; add milk and crumbs. Let stand 5 minutes; add salt, sugar, allspice, nutmeg, chuck, pork, and onion. Blend well with fork.

SAUCE:
2 tablespoons butter or margarine
3 tablespoons flour
1 teaspoon sugar
1¼ teaspoons salt

⅛ teaspoon pepper
1 cup water
¾ cup light cream

In same skillet, heat 2 tablespoons butter. Using 2 teaspoons, shape the meat mixture into small balls, about ½ to ¾ inch in diameter. Drop some balls into skillet, and brown well on all sides; remove to warm casserole; repeat until all meat is brown.

Then stir flour, sugar, salt, and pepper into fat left in skillet; add water and cream slowly; stir until thickened. If desired, pour gravy into casserole with meatballs and heat thoroughly. The gravy may be served separately, if desired. May be prepared the day before and refrigerated. Serves 6.

Cypress Garden Cookbook (Florida)

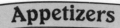

Sausage-Cheese Balls

These freeze before or after baking. Great for appetizers, served hot.

**10 ounces grated sharp Cheddar
  cheese**

**3 cups buttermilk biscuit mix
1 pound hot bulk sausage**

With hands, mix all ingredients. Roll into marble-sized balls. Freeze.
Bake while still frozen at 325° until toasted, about 20-30 minutes. Yields
100 balls.

Keepers (Texas)

The first two bells cracked while being tested; the third casting of what would
later be dubbed the Liberty Bell was hung in the tower of Independence Hall
on June 7, 1753. It was hidden in a church basement in Allentown from 1777
to 1778 to protect it from being melted down and made into cannons by the British. Rung
every July 4th and on every state occasion until 1835, the bell cracked as it was being tolled
for the death of Chief Justice John Marshall. The Liberty Bell was moved in 1976 to its pre-
sent location in a glass pavilion near Independence Hall, Philadelphia, Pennsylvania.

A chime that changed the world occurred July 8, 1776, when the Liberty Bell rang out from the tower of Independence Hall summoning citizens to hear the first public reading of the Declaration of Independence.

Momma Rogers' Melt in Your Mouth Butter Biscuits

This is the easiest ever to prepare! They are wonderful!

2 sticks real butter, softened   **8 ounces sour cream**
2 cups self-rising flour

Mix first two ingredients, then add 8 ounces sour cream. Drop by spoonful into tiny cup muffin tins or tartlet pans. Bake at 450° for 8-10 minutes. Do not grease muffin pans. Makes about 50 small bite-sized biscuits.

St. Paul Cooks (Tennessee)

Butter Dips

⅓ cup butter   **3½ teaspoons baking powder**
2¼ cups sifted flour   **1½ teaspoons salt**
1 tablespoon sugar   **1 cup milk**

Heat oven hot (450°). Melt butter in oven in oblong pan, 9x13x2 inches. Remove pan when butter is melted. Sift together flour, sugar, baking powder, and salt. Add milk. Stir slowly with fork until dough just clings together. Turn onto well-floured board. Roll over to coat with flour. Knead lightly about 10 times. Roll out ½ inch thick into rectangle 12x8 inches. With floured knife, cut dough in half lengthwise, then cut crosswise into 16 strips. Pick up strips in both hands and dip each strip on both sides in melted butter. Next lay them close together in 2 rows in same pan in which butter was melted. Bake 15-20 minutes until golden brown. Serve hot. Makes 32 sticks.

Variation: (1) Add ½ cup grated sharp Cheddar cheese to dry ingredients. (2) Add ½ clove finely minced garlic to butter before melting. (3) Sprinkle paprika, celery seed, or garlic salt over dips before baking.

High Hampton Hospitality (North Carolina)

Located in Asheville, North Carolina, Biltmore House is an elegant 250-room French Renaissance chateau built in the 1890s by George W. Vanderbilt. It is the largest private home in America. Surrounded by formal gardens, the 12,000-acre estate is a national historic landmark.

1990s Melt in Your Mouth Dinner Rolls

You had better double this one, as they disappear quickly.

1 package dry yeast	⅓ cup margarine
½ cup warm water	⅓ cup sugar
1 tablespoon sugar	Dash of salt (½ teaspoon)
1 teaspoon baking powder	2 eggs, beaten
1 cup milk	4½ to 5½ cups flour

Add yeast to warm water. Add 1 tablespoon sugar and baking powder. Let stand for 20 minutes. Meanwhile, scald 1 cup milk. Add margarine, ⅓ cup sugar, and a dash of salt. Cool. Then add eggs. Add flour and mix. Refrigerate overnight.

Roll out half the dough as you would for pie and brush with melted margarine. Cut 12 pie-shaped pieces. Roll each from wide end to pointed end. Place on cookie sheet which has been sprayed, and let rise. Do the same with remaining dough. Bake at 400° for 10 minutes. Makes 24 rolls.

Touches of the Hands & Heart (Ohio)

Popovers Fontaine

If you have never had the thrill of seeing a "runny" batter bloom into a large golden cloud, try this recipe. Popovers are definitely a Sunday morning breakfast treat. Serve with fried ham and scrambled eggs. Butter generously and top with honey or syrup.

3 eggs	1 cup flour
1 cup milk	½ teaspoon salt
3 tablespoons salad oil or melted butter	

Preheat oven to 400°. Lightly grease 8 (5-ounce) custard cups or an old-fashioned popover pan. In a medium bowl, with a rotary beater, beat until well combined the eggs, milk, and oil. Sift flour and salt into egg mixture. Beat just until smooth. Pour batter into greased custard cups, filling each half-full. Place cups on a baking sheet and bake 45-50 minutes, until golden brown. Serve at once. Makes 8.

The Ham Book (Virginia)

★★★★★★★★★★★   ★★★★★★★★★★★

Your Own Butter

Making butter is quite simple. Using the large chopper blade in your food processor, pour in a quart of cream and just let it go. It will become whipped and then just keep getting thicker and thicker until it finally separates. Put it all into a mixing bowl, squeeze the liquid (skim milk) from the fat with your (clean) hands, and there you are—a lump of butter. I have found that the best results occur if you let the cream sit in the refrigerator for a week before you churn it and then let it warm almost to room temperature.

The skim milk that's left is sweeter, more wholesome, and far more delicious than any I could buy in a supermarket. It could only be fresher if the cow were making it herself. That skim milk goes into soups, sauces, and custards, and no one knows that what they are eating is good for them.

WHAT TO DO WITH YOUR LUMP OF BUTTER:
Break it into 1-inch pieces and throw it back into the processor. This is the point where you make the butter into any fantasy that pleases you. I generally add about two tablespoons of fresh herbs and a little nutmeg, black pepper, and salt. Spin it just long enough to smooth the herbs and soften the butter into a "whip." You now have what is probably the most wonderful herb butter you've ever eaten.

After you learn the herbs, the rest comes easily. Ripe pears whipped into fresh butter, or blackberries, or maple syrup, or lobster meat. The possibilities are endless. Imagine whipping a handful of wild strawberries into your butter and squeezing it through a pastry bag onto French toast points that have been sautéed in Grand Marnier and dusted with vanilla sugar. That, and a cup of coffee, would be a wonderful way to celebrate the first morning of a romance—or the last.
Excerpt from James Haller's entire chapter on butter.

Another Blue Strawbery (New England)

Every year on July 4th, the Declaration of Independence is read from the same balcony it was first read from, the Old State House. Built in 1713, it is the oldest public building in Boston. The oldest wooden building in Boston is Paul Revere's House. It was nearly 100 years old when the patriot took his famous midnight ride to warn "every Middlesex village and farm" that the British were coming.

9-Minute Strawberry Jam

2 quarts strawberries **6 cups sugar**

Clean the strawberries; place in saucepan and pour boiling hot water over them. Set 1 minute; drain off water. Put on stove; bring to a boil. Boil 3 minutes, then add 3 cups of sugar; bring to a boil, boiling for 3 minutes. Add the remaining 3 cups of sugar; bring to a boil, cooking 3 minutes.

Set aside; let cool—sometimes overnight. This thickens as it cools. Pour into glasses the next day and seal with wax, or use seal-type lid.

Four Seasons Cookbook (Michigan)

Mrs. McKenzie's Wine Jelly

¾ cup water, room temperature **1 (25.4-ounce) bottle wine**
1 box Mrs. Wages Home-Jell **(Red, Sweet White or Rosé)**
** powdered fruit pectin** **4½ cups sugar**

In a large enamel kettle, using a wooden spoon, stir pectin into the water until dissolved. Bring to a boil over high heat; boil 1 minute, stirring constantly. Add wine, then sugar, stirring constantly, reducing heat to medium. Cook for 5 or 6 minutes to dissolve sugar. Do not boil. Remove from heat, skim with metal spoon as necessary. Quickly pour into hot sterile glasses. Cover with hot paraffin or use seal-type lids and rings. Chill before serving. Delicious with meats.

Note: For a milder flavor, add water to wine for total not to exceed 32 fluid ounces. A few drops of red food coloring added during final cooking stage enhances the color when using red wine.

Dixie Dining (Mississippi)

★ **Editor's Extra:** Deliciously made with rosé, the beautiful clear pink color of this jelly is as pretty as the taste is delicate.

Prosciutto-Parmesan Pull-Apart Loaf

Men love this.

¾ cup (1½ sticks) butter or margarine, softened
⅓ cup grated parmesan cheese
½ cup (2 ounces) coarsely chopped prosciutto
1 teaspoon freshly cracked pepper

¼ cup chopped fresh basil or ¼ cup chopped fresh parsley and 1 tablespoon dried basil
1 (1-pound) loaf Italian bread or French bread

Combine all ingredients (but bread) in a small bowl. With serrated knife, slice bread diagonally almost all the way through 12 times, at 1½-inch intervals; spread 1 rounded tablespoonful prosciutto butter between sections, using half of butter mixture. Turn loaf around so that ends are reversed; slice loaf diagonally almost all the way through 12 times, making diamond patterns of 1½-inch sections of bread. Spread with remaining prosciutto butter.

Preheat oven to 450°. Tear off a sheet of heavy-duty aluminum foil 5 inches longer than bread. Center bread on foil. Fold over long sides of foil to come halfway up sides of loaf and fold or crimp short ends of foil to secure. Heat 10 minutes or until crust is crisp and loaf is heated through. Makes 12 servings.

To heat on grill: Bring long sides of foil together over top of bread; fold together 1 inch of foil. Crease and continue folding foil until it fits loosely over bread. Repeat folding technique at short ends of foil. Place loaf, right-side-up, 5-6 inches from heat. Heat 8 minutes or until loaf is heated through.

Note: Although this claims 12 servings, I have gone through almost 2 loaves of this at dinner parties for 8 people.

Cook, Line & Sinker (Ohio)

The most accurate representation of Christopher Columbus' flagship, the *Santa Maria,* can be seen at its mooring on the Scioto River in downtown Columbus, Ohio. Costumed guides explain the life and hardships of the 15th-century sailors who explored uncharted waters half a world away from home.

★★★★★★★★★★★★   ★★★★★★★★★★★★★

Sausage Spinach Bread

This is one of those versatile recipes that can be made for many occasions. Serve it as an appetizer or as a bread.

2 loaves frozen French bread dough	**2 tablespoons chopped onion**
1 (10-ounce) package frozen chopped	**1 egg**
spinach	**10 ounces grated mozzarella cheese**
1 pound hot pork sausage	**½ cup grated parmesan cheese**

Allow dough to thaw. Cook spinach according to package directions. Drain well. Brown sausage and drain off fat. Add onion and cook until onions are soft. Beat egg. Add about half of it to the drained spinach and reserve the rest to brush over the top of the bread.

Working with one loaf of bread at a time, roll the bread out into a rectangle, about 9x13 inches. Spread half of the spinach, sausage, and mozzarella cheese over the dough. Sprinkle with half of the parmesan cheese. Roll up, jelly roll-style, starting on a long end, sealing all edges tightly so the filling remains inside. Place on baking sheet and pierce tops of bread loaves with fork a few times. Brush with beaten egg. Bake at 375° for 20 minutes or until brown. Serve hot. Repeat steps with second loaf. Makes 2 loaves.

Note: Most frozen bread loaves come two to a package. If not, simply save the extras in the freezer to be used at a later date.

Extra! Extra! Read All About It! (Louisiana II)

Baby Broccoli Muffins

Marvelous. These freeze very nicely.

1 (10-ounce) package frozen chopped	**1 stick margarine, melted**
broccoli	**¾ cup cottage cheese**
1 (7½-ounce) box corn muffin mix	**1 large onion, chopped**
4 eggs, beaten	

Preheat oven to 425°. Grease miniature muffin tins. Cook broccoli according to package directions. Drain well. In a large bowl, mix corn muffin mix, eggs, melted margarine, cottage cheese, onion, and drained broccoli until blended. Put in miniature muffin tins and bake 10-12 minutes. Yields about 5-6 dozen muffins.

Note: Dollop with sour cream and a tiny fresh broccoli floweret.

Unbearably Good! (Georgia)

Frenchies

Lusty crusty munchies. Better make plenty.

1 (6-roll) package French mini-loaves
1¼ sticks butter or margarine
1 teaspoon garlic powder
1 teaspoon Tabasco
1 teaspoon water
1 tablespoon parsley flakes
  (optional)

Preheat oven to 225°. Slice French bread into thin rounds (a generous ¼ inch). Melt margarine; add remaining ingredients. Brush both sides of bread rounds very lightly with butter mixture. Bake on 2 cookie sheets in preheated oven 40-50 minutes till dry, but not brown. Turn heat off and leave in oven 30 minutes or more (or overnight). Store in tin or cookie jar.

Note: If you freeze the bread first and use a knife with a serrated edge (or an electric knife), it will slice much easier and neater.

The Little New Orleans Cookbook (Louisiana II)

Jalapeño Cornbread

"Muy caliente!" they say in Spanish. This dish is hot, hot, hot! But great, if you're an aficionado of Mexican cuisine or just like super-spicy foods. Whether you're planning a fiesta or simply want something to wake up a plate of pinto beans, try this zesty cornbread.

3 cups yellow cornmeal
1 cup cream-style corn
1 teaspoon sugar
2 teaspoons salt
1 cup chopped onion
1½ teaspoons baking powder
1 cup vegetable oil
3 eggs
1¾ cups milk
½ cup chopped jalapeño peppers
1⅓ cups grated cheese

Mix all (in large mixing bowl) and pour into a 9x13-inch ungreased pan. Bake in a preheated 350° oven for 1 hour.

Note: If you're not familiar with the jalapeño pepper, be forewarned: These hot green peppers are not for people with timid taste buds. And don't be fooled by a can marked "mild" jalapeño peppers. Even the "mild" variety can make your eyes water.

Pow Wow Chow (Oklahoma)

★ **Editor's Extra:** This makes a lot, but halves easily for a delicious supper with veggies.

★ ★ ★ ★ ★ ★ ★ ★ ★ ★ ★ ★   ★ ★ ★ ★ ★ ★ ★ ★ ★ ★ ★ ★

Strawberry Bread

3 cups all-purpose flour
2 cups sugar
1 teaspoon ground cinnamon
1 teaspoon salt
1 teaspoon baking soda

4 eggs
1¼ cups Wesson oil
1 cup chopped pecans
2 (10-ounce) packages frozen
   strawberries, thawed

Preheat oven to 350°. In large mixing bowl, sift together flour, sugar, cinnamon, salt, and baking soda. Set aside. In small bowl, beat eggs and Wesson oil. Add pecans and strawberries. Add strawberry mixture to dry ingredients. Grease and flour two 9x5x3-inch loaf pans; pour mixture in loaf pans and bake at 350° for 1 hour. (Bake 45-50 minutes for smaller pans.) Yields 2 large loaves or 4 small loaves.

Foods à la Louisiane (Louisiana)

Best Ever Banana Bread

You'll never use another banana bread recipe after tasting this one.

1 cup butter or oleo
3 cups sugar
6 eggs
3 cups sour cream
4 teaspoons baking soda

2 teaspoons vanilla
4-5 bananas, mashed
1 teaspoon salt
5 cups flour

Cream together butter, sugar, and eggs. Mix sour cream and baking soda together in separate bowl and let stand until foamy. Add the rest of the ingredients to the above mixtures and mix well. Place into 4 greased and floured 9x5-inch bread pans and bake 50 minutes at 350° or until toothpick inserted comes out clean.

Marcus, Iowa, Quasquicentennial Cookbook (Iowa)

★ **Editor's Extra:** A good use of ripe bananas, this makes 4 loaves, so I often halve it. Okay to use Egg Beaters, low-fat sour cream and margarine—superb!

Peach Muffins

1½ cups flour
¾ teaspoon salt
½ teaspoon baking soda
1 cup sugar
2 eggs, well beaten
½ cup salad oil

½ teaspoon vanilla
⅛ teaspoon almond extract
¼ cup chopped almonds (optional)
1¼ cups coarsely chopped fresh
   or drained canned peaches

In mixing bowl combine dry ingredients; make a well in center of mix. Add eggs and oil, stirring only until dry mix is moistened. Stir in remaining ingredients. Spoon ⅓ cup batter into greased muffin tins; bake at 350° for 20-25 minutes, or until muffins test done.

Variation: For Peach bread, spoon batter into a greased and floured 5x9-inch loaf pan; bake at 350° for 1 hour, or until bread tests done.

Celebration (Arkansas)

Saucy Blueberry Lemon Muffins

These wonderfully tart creations melt in your mouth.

½ cup butter or margarine, softened
½ cup sugar
2 eggs
2 cups flour
3 teaspoons baking powder

¼ teaspoon salt (optional)
⅓ cup milk
1 cup blueberries, canned or frozen,
   thawed and drained
Rind of 1 lemon, grated finely

Preheat oven to 350°. Grease muffin cups. Cream butter, sugar, and eggs in a small bowl. In large bowl, combine flour, baking powder, and salt. Add creamed mixture alternately with milk, stirring only until mixed. Fold in blueberries and lemon zest. Fill muffin cups ⅔ full. Bake at 350° for 25-30 minutes.

SAUCE:
¼ cup fresh lemon juice
⅓ cup sugar

Combine lemon juice and sugar in small pan and bring to boiling. Spoon sauce evenly over top of baked muffins. Makes 12 muffins.

Nothin' but Muffins (Colorado)

★★★★★★★★★★★★ ★★★★★★★★★★★★

Six Weeks Muffins

Ready-to-bake, then easy-to-take for a terrific breakfast on the run.

1 (10-15-ounce) box raisin bran	**2 teaspoons salt**
3 cups sugar	**4 eggs, beaten**
5 cups flour	**1 cup vegetable oil**
5 teaspoons baking soda	**1 quart buttermilk**

Use a giant-sized mixing bowl to mix raisin bran, sugar, flour, baking soda, and salt. Add beaten eggs, oil, and buttermilk; mix well.

Store covered in refrigerator and use as desired. Keeps 6 weeks, and these are better all the time. Do not stir when putting mixture into greased muffin tins. Fill ⅔ full and bake at 375° for 18-20 minutes.

Family Favorites (Pennsylvania)

Tiny Pecan Muffins

Easy and delicious!

½ cup self-rising flour	**1 teaspoon vanilla extract**
1 cup light brown sugar	**1 cup chopped pecans**
½ cup melted butter or oleo	**2 eggs, beaten**

Mix all ingredients. Bake in greased miniature muffin tins in a 350° oven for 15 minutes. Do not bake longer than 15 minutes. Makes 3 dozen.

Shared Treasures (Louisiana II)

Peach French Toast

1 cup brown sugar	12-14 slices French bread
½ cup butter or margarine	(1 inch thick)
2 tablespoons water	5 large eggs
1 (29-ounce) can sliced peaches,	1½ cups milk
drained	3 teaspoons vanilla

Over medium-low heat, stir brown sugar and butter until butter melts. Add water and cook until sauce is thick and foamy, about 5 minutes. Pour into 9x13x2-inch baking dish. Let cool 10 minutes.

Place peaches on top of sauce. Cover with bread, trimming to fit in one layer. Whisk together eggs, milk, and vanilla. Pour over bread. Cover and refrigerate overnight. Bake at 350°, uncovered, 40 minutes or until set and golden. Cover with foil if browning too quickly. Serve with warmed reserved peach syrup, if desired. This is rich and yummy!

The Fifth Generation Cookbook (Ohio)

Waffled French Toast

The kids love these . . . everyone does, and any leftovers can be reheated in the toaster.

½ cup milk	½ teaspoon salt
4 eggs	2 tablespoons butter, melted
1 tablespoon sugar	8-10 slices bread

Preheat waffle iron. If the iron is well seasoned (in other words, had its share of waffles baked in it without being abused by soap!), there should be no need to oil it. In a shallow bowl, with a flat whisk, combine milk, eggs, sugar, and salt, then melted butter. Dip bread slices, one at a time, in egg mixture and drain. Bake in waffle iron 2-3 minutes, until brown. Serve with bacon or sausage and maple syrup or Strawberry Butter. Yields 8-10 slices.

STRAWBERRY BUTTER:
Just wonderful over pancakes, waffles, and French toast.

½ pound butter, softened	10 ounces frozen strawberries,
½ cup powdered sugar	thawed and drained

Combine all in a mixer or food processor until smooth and creamy. It's best served at room temperature, but can be stored in fridge for several weeks. Yields 2½ cups.

Hollyhocks & Radishes (Michigan)

Grandma BB's Pineapple Fritters

These are the greatest!

1 cup flour
1 teaspoon baking powder
¼ teaspoon salt
2 tablespoons sugar
¼ teaspoon cinnamon
¼ teaspoon nutmeg

1 egg
⅓ cup milk
1 tablespoon melted fat
1 tablespoon lemon juice
1 cup crushed or shredded
    pineapple, drained

Mix and sift all dry ingredients into a small bowl. Beat egg slightly and add milk and butter. Stir the liquid mixture into the dry ingredients, beating until you have a smooth batter. Add lemon juice and drained pineapple. Drop into hot deep fryer using a teaspoon. Fry until golden brown. Remove, pat excess oil off with paper towel, and then roll in sugar or powdered sugar while hot.

Home Cookin' Creations (Colorado)

Country Apple Biscuits

If you like something sweet at coffee time, try making this easy biscuit recipe. It has that taste-tempting look.

1½ cups chopped, peeled apples
1 (10-ounce) can Hungry Jack Flaky
  Biscuits
1 tablespoon oleo
⅓ cup firmly packed brown sugar

¼ teaspoon cinnamon
⅓ cup light corn syrup
1 large egg
½ cup pecan halves and pieces

GLAZE:
⅓ cup powdered sugar
1-2 teaspoons milk

¼ teaspoon vanilla

Generously grease bottom and sides of 9-inch round cake pan. Spread 1 cup chopped, peeled apples in bottom. Separate 1 can Hungry Jack Flaky biscuits into 10 biscuits, and cut each into 4 pieces. Arrange over apples, point-sides-up. Top with another ½ cup apples.

In small bowl, combine oleo, brown sugar, cinnamon, light corn syrup, and egg. Beat until sugar is partially dissolved. Stir in ½ cup pecan halves and pieces. Spoon over biscuit pieces. Bake in 350° oven for 35-45 minutes or until deep golden brown. Mix Glaze ingredients and drizzle over biscuits while warm. Store leftovers in refrigerator.

Sharing Our Best (Indiana)

★★★★★★★★★★★   ★★★★★★★★★★★

Baked Apple Pancake

Baked Apple Pancake is one of my guests' favorite breakfasts. Nothing could be simpler than putting all of the ingredients, except the apples and butter, in a blender. The combination of crisp apples and custard, sprinkled with brown sugar, not only tastes scrumptious, but will bring oh's and ah's from your guests as you bring this puffy creation from the oven to the table.

6 large eggs	¼ teaspoon cinnamon (more if
1½ cups milk	desired, up to 1 teaspoon)
1 cup flour	½ cup butter or margarine
3 tablespoons granulated sugar	2 large Granny Smith apples
1 teaspoon vanilla	3 tablespoons brown sugar
½ teaspoon salt	

Place eggs, milk, flour, granulated sugar, vanilla, salt, and cinnamon in blender. Set aside. Put butter or margarine in a 9x13-inch glass baking dish. Place in 425° oven to melt. (Don't let it burn.) Remove from oven when melted.

Peel apples, slice thinly, and arrange in bottom of dish over melted butter. Put in oven until butter sizzles. Remove. Blend ingredients in blender until smooth. Pour slowly over apples. Sprinkle with brown sugar.

Bake in 425° oven for 20 minutes. Test for doneness by inserting a knife in center. If it comes out clean, it is done. Cut in serving portions and serve immediately. Pass the maple syrup, if desired. Serves 10.

Have Breakfast with Us...Again (Wisconsin)

★ **Editor's Extra:** One half recipe fits nicely in pie plate. Also, this works with low-fat margarine, egg substitute and skim milk—tastes great!

Cinnamon Cheese Coffee Cake

1 tube of crescent rolls	1 egg yolk
½ teaspoon vanilla	1 (8-ounce) package cream cheese,
½ cup sugar	softened

TOPPING:

¼ cup sugar	¼ cup chopped nuts
½ teaspoon cinnamon	

Lay ½ of crescent rolls flat in 8x8-inch pan. Mix vanilla, ½ cup sugar, and egg yolk into cream cheese. Spoon this mixture over dough. Lay remaining ½ of crescent rolls on top. Mix topping and sprinkle over top. Bake at 350° for 30-35 minutes. Makes 8 slices.

The Indiana Bed & Breakfast Association Cookbook (Indiana)

★★★★★★★★★★★★ ★★★★★★★★★★★★

Pineapple Crunch Coffee Cake

2 cups flour
1½ cups sugar
1 teaspoon baking soda
½ teaspoon salt

¼ cup packed brown sugar
1 (1 pound, 4-ounce) can crushed
   pineapple, undrained
1 cup chopped walnuts

Combine flour, sugar, baking soda, salt, brown sugar, pineapple with juice, and nuts. Mix well. Pour into ungreased 9x13-inch pan. Bake at 350° for 35 minutes.

ICING:
⅔ cup sugar
¼ cup milk

½ cup margarine or butter

Combine the above in a small saucepan and boil 2 minutes. Pour over warm cake. Sprinkle with coconut, if desired. Serves 6.

Ship to Shore I (North Carolina)

Pull-Apart Coffee Cake

An amazing presentation! Perfect for overnight guests.

1 (16-ounce) package frozen bread
   rolls, still frozen
1¼ sticks butter
1 (3⅝-ounce) package vanilla
   pudding (dry, not instant)

4 teaspoons cinnamon
½ cup brown sugar, packed
½ cup nuts, chopped

Butter a tube pan (or a 9x13-inch pan) heavily. Place rolls in pan. Pull each roll apart. Melt butter. Pour over rolls. Combine and sprinkle over rolls, pudding, cinnamon, brown sugar, and nuts.

Let stand, uncovered, on cabinet top overnight. Bake at 375° for 20 minutes. When done, remove from oven and let set 10 minutes. Invert on plate. Yields 8 servings.

Variation: May use 1 cup brown sugar, 1 package butterscotch pudding (dry, not instant), 1 stick butter and ½ cup chopped nuts.

Calf Fries to Caviar (Texas)

★ **Editor's Extra:** One pound brown sugar equals 2¼ cups firmly packed. To soften hardened brown sugar, place box of sugar alongside a cup of water in microwave and heat about 2 minutes.

Blintz Soufflé

This is a wonderful brunch or morning bridge dish.

½ cup butter, softened
½ cup sugar
6 eggs
1½ cups sour cream
½ cup orange juice
1 cup flour

2 teaspoons baking powder
Blintz Filling
Sour cream (for topping)
Blueberry syrup or assorted jams
   (for topping)

Preheat oven to 350°. Butter a 9x13-inch dish and set aside. In a large bowl, mix butter, sugar, eggs, sour cream, orange juice, flour, and baking powder until well blended. Pour ½ batter into prepared dish. Place remaining ½ aside. Prepare Blintz Filling.

BLINTZ FILLING:

1 (8-ounce) package cream cheese,
   softened
1 pint small curd cottage cheese

2 egg yolks
1 tablespoon sugar
1 teaspoon vanilla extract

In a medium bowl or food processor fitted with metal blade, combine all ingredients. Mix until well blended. Drop filling by heaping spoonfuls over batter in dish. With a spatula or knife, spread filling evenly over batter; it will mix slightly with batter. Pour remaining batter over filling. Bake, uncovered, at 350° for 50-60 minutes or until puffed and golden. Serve immediately with sour cream and blueberry syrup or assorted jams. May be made a day ahead. Cover and refrigerate until ready to use. Before baking, bring to room temperature. Yields 8 servings.

Vintage Vicksburg (Mississippi)

★★★★★★★★★★★★   ★★★★★★★★★★★★

Down East Blueberry Crisp

4 cups fresh blueberries
2-4 tablespoons sugar
2 teaspoons lemon juice
¼ cup cold margarine
¼ cup packed brown sugar

⅓ cup all-purpose flour
¼ teaspoon cinnamon
Dash of salt (optional)
¾ cup old-fashioned rolled oats

Preheat oven to 375°. Place blueberries in a greased-with-margarine 8 or 9-inch baking dish. Sprinkle with sugar and lemon juice. In a medium bowl, combine margarine, brown sugar, flour, cinnamon, and salt; mix until crumbly. Stir in rolled oats and sprinkle evenly over blueberries. Bake in 375° oven for 35-40 minutes. Serve warm. Yields 6-8 servings.

A Taste of New England (New England)

★ **Editor's Extra:** I like this with whipped or sour cream, or even cottage cheese.

Maw Maw's Apricot Strudel

Impressive make-ahead breakfast treat!

¼ cup sugar
¾ cup ground nuts
¾ teaspoon cinnamon
2 sticks oleo
1 (8-ounce) package Philadelphia
  cream cheese

2 cups unsifted flour
1 (18-ounce) jar apricot preserves
¾ cup powdered sugar

Mix sugar, nuts, and cinnamon together and set aside. Soften oleo and cream cheese and mix together; add flour. Mix well. Divide dough in 4 portions. Wrap each in foil and refrigerate overnight. (It can be frozen.)

Next day, roll out one portion at a time thin, but not too thin, on a very lightly floured board. Be sure to flour your rolling pin. Spread a thin layer of apricot preserves very gently and lightly over dough. Sprinkle some of nuts and sugar mixture over this. Roll up like a jelly roll, being very careful not to tear dough. Bake on ungreased cookie sheet in a 325° oven for 45 minutes. The top of strudel should be lightly brown when done. Cut on diagonal while hot, 1-inch pieces. Sprinkle with powdered sugar. When cold, sprinkle again.

This can be stored in foil and frozen for 3 months. When thawed, warm, and sprinkle more sugar.

The Country Gourmet (Mississippi)

Eggs À La Buckingham

Fit for a queen.

2 tablespoons butter or margarine
4 teaspoons all-purpose flour
Salt and pepper
¾ cup milk
1 (2.3-ounce) package smoked
  sliced beef, snipped
4 eggs

1 tablespoon milk
1 tablespoon butter or margarine
2 English muffins, split and toasted
½ cup shredded sharp processed
  American cheese
Salt and pepper

Melt the 2 tablespoons butter or margarine; blend in flour and a dash each salt and pepper. Add ¾ cup milk. Cook and stir till bubbly; cook 1 minute more. Add beef; keep warm. Beat eggs with the 1 tablespoon milk and a dash each salt and pepper.

In skillet, melt 1 tablespoon butter. Add egg mixture. Cook over low heat just till set; lift and fold so uncooked part goes to bottom. Place muffins on baking sheet; spoon beef mixture over. Top with eggs. Bake in 350° oven 8 minutes. Sprinkle with cheese and bake 1 minute more. Makes 4 servings.

Shattuck Community Cookbook (Oklahoma)

★ **Editor's Extra:** Also good with smoked ham or turkey instead of beef.

Crustless Quiche

This is a favorite for our Y bridge luncheons.

1 cup Swiss cheese, grated
8-10 slices bacon, crisply cooked
  and crumbled
¼ cup onion, minced
4 eggs
13-14 ounces small curd cottage
  cheese

1 package frozen chopped spinach,
  cooked with 1 teaspoon salt,
  then drained
½ teaspoon salt
½ teaspoon pepper
1 teaspoon Worcestershire sauce
3 dashes Tabasco sauce

Sprinkle cheese, bacon, and onion in that order in a 10-inch greased pie plate. Beat remaining ingredients until well blended. Pour over bacon mixture. Bake at 350° for 35-40 minutes. Let stand 10-15 minutes before cutting.

Note: This recipe may be baked in greased miniature muffin tins for 42 individual servings; bake for approximately 20 minutes; regular muffin tins will yield 14 servings. Bake for approximately 25 minutes.

Cookin' Wise (Texas)

Tramp Eggs

Back during the Depression, those lean, gray years stretching from 1929 through the late 1930s, tramps came often to our house to ask for a meal. Mother never turned one away; whatever we had to eat, she shared with the shabby strangers who stopped at our kitchen door.

A favorite Sunday breakfast dish at our house was eggs baked in a casserole with rich milk, dabs of butter, and generous sprinkles of grated cheese. We were having this breakfast one Sunday morning when a hungry tramp appeared at the back door. As always, Mother fixed him a plate, including a generous serving of the eggs.

We thought he had eaten and gone (tramps usually put their empty plates on the back porch and left hurriedly after they'd eaten, possibly wishing to avoid any involvement with the wood pile near the back gate), when we heard him knock at the door again.

Mother went to see what he wanted. "Lady," he said as he handed her the empty plate. "Would you please give me the recipe for those eggs? They're the best I ever ate!"

So ever since then, our Sunday morning eggs have been called Tramp Eggs. The recipe follows.

1 egg per person	**Butter**
Salt	**Grated Cheddar cheese**
Milk	

Butter a shallow baking dish and break into it the number of eggs needed to serve the eaters. Sprinkle salt on the eggs and pour milk around them until the yellow tops are peeping half out. Dot with dabs of butter. Grate cheese over the top. Bake in a slow oven (300°) until cheese is bubbly and eggs are of desired doneness (15 minutes or so). Serve atop crisp toast or in a nest of grits.

Treasured Alabama Recipes (Alabama)

★ **Editor's Extra:** The baking dish you use should not be too big; be sure the eggs touch each other and the sides of the dish.

★★★★★★★★★★★★ ★★★★★★★★★★★★

Mexican Omelet

¼ cup diced yellow onion
3 large fresh mushrooms
1 teaspoon butter
3 eggs
¼ teaspoon pepper
Dash of salt

¼ teaspoon milk
Hot pepper sauce
¼ cup jalapeño-flavored processed
  American cheese, cubed
1 teaspoon red salsa (very hot)
2 strips crisp bacon, crumbled

Sauté onions and mushrooms together in the butter. Take out of the pan and reserve.

Beat eggs; add pepper, salt, milk and hot pepper sauce. Put into the same pan over medium heat. Sprinkle the cheese over egg mixture. Add onions and mushrooms and spread salsa over the top. Sprinkle the bacon on top and cook until moist and set, but not hard.

Serve as is or with tomato salsa and a warm flour tortilla. Serves 1.

New Mexico Cook Book (New Mexico)

Wake Up Casserole

2 cups seasoned croutons
1 cup shredded Cheddar cheese
1 (4-ounce) can mushroom pieces,
  drained
1½ pounds country-fresh sausage,
  browned and crumbled
½ cup chopped onion

6 eggs
2½ cups milk, divided
½ teaspoon salt
½ teaspoon pepper
½ teaspoon dry mustard
1 (10¾-ounce) can cream of
  mushroom soup

Place croutons in greased 9x13x2-inch pan. Top with cheese and mushrooms. Brown sausage and onion; drain and spread over cheese. Beat eggs with 2 cups of milk and seasonings; pour over sausage. Cover and refrigerate overnight. (May be frozen at this point.) Mix soup with ½ cup milk and spread on top. Bake at 325° for 1 hour. Serves 8.

The Indiana Bed & Breakfast Association Cookbook (Indiana)

Breakfast Pizza

1 pound bulk pork sausage
1 (8-ounce) package refrigerated
   crescent rolls
1 cup frozen loose-pack hash brown
   potatoes, thawed
1 cup shredded sharp Cheddar
   cheese
5 eggs, beaten

¼ cup milk
½ teaspoon salt
½ teaspoon pepper
2 tablespoons grated parmesan
   cheese
Pimiento (optional)
Fresh oregano (optional)

Cook sausage in medium skillet until brown; drain and set aside. Separate crescent dough into 8 triangles. Place with elongated points toward center of greased 12-inch pizza pan. Press bottom and sides to form a crust. Seal perforations. Spoon sausage over dough. Sprinkle with hash brown potatoes and Cheddar cheese. Combine eggs, milk, salt and pepper; pour over sausage mixture. Bake at 375° for 25 minutes. Sprinkle with parmesan cheese and bake an additional 5 minutes. Garnish with pimiento and fresh oregano, if desired. Yields 6-8 servings.

Cooks and Company (Alabama)

Grits Casserole

Great with jalapeño cheese instead of Cheddar, too!

1 cup grits
4½ cups salted water
1 stick butter
1 package garlic cheese (or 8 ounces
   sharp Cheddar and 1 teaspoon
   garlic powder, or jalapeño cheese)

2 beaten eggs
¾ cup milk
Buttered bread crumbs

Cook grits in water. When done, add butter, garlic cheese, eggs, and milk. Stir until melted. Pour into greased casserole and sprinkle buttered bread crumbs on top. Bake 45 minutes (or until center is done) in 350° oven. Serves 6.

Mountain Elegance (North Carolina)

★ **Editor's Extra:** To make delicious buttered bread crumbs, process 2 slices of bread in food processor, then add a pat of butter and whirl until uniform. For toasted crumbs, spread on cookie sheet and bake 3-4 minutes in 450° oven.

Orange Breakfast Treat

1 tablespoon butter
6 ounces orange marmalade
¼ cup chopped nuts
1 cup firmly packed brown sugar

½ teaspoon cinnamon
2 (10-ounce) cans Hungry Jack
   Buttermilk Biscuits
1 stick melted butter

Grease a tube pan with butter. Drop marmalade in by teaspoons evenly around bottom. Sprinkle with nuts.

Mix sugar and cinnamon together in a small bowl. Dip biscuits in melted butter, then in sugar mixture, one at a time. Stand them up close together around pan in two rows. Sprinkle any leftover sugar or butter over top. Bake at 350° for 30-40 minutes or until golden brown. Cool 5 minutes. Invert onto plate.

Jarrett House Potpourri (North Carolina)

★ **Editor's Extra:** Also good with apricot preserves in place of orange marmalade.

Fried Apples

Our Mom used to serve these with fried quail, biscuits, and gravy for breakfast when we were kids. They are also excellent served with pork.

¼ cup margarine
6 medium tart apples, unpeeled
  and sliced (Jonathans are best)

½ cup sugar
1 teaspoon cinnamon
¼ cup water (more if needed)

In a skillet, heat margarine; add apples, sugar, cinnamon, and water. Cover. Simmer for about 20 minutes or until apples are tender. (If apple mixture starts to thicken before apples are tender, add a little more water.)

Country Classics (Colorado)

Soups

The Golden Gate Bridge in San Francisco was completed in 1937, taking more than four years to build. It is considered to be one of the world's most spectacular bridges.

Guaranteed Good Gazpacho

A committee favorite—we learned to have this on hand all summer!

1 (59.2-ounce) bottle Bloody Mary
  mix
1 (12-ounce) can tomato juice
3 cucumbers, peeled
1 large onion
1 bell pepper
1 celery stalk

2 large tomatoes
4-6 tablespoons wine vinegar
4-6 tablespoons sugar
2 tablespoons lemon juice
2 tablespoons Worcestershire sauce
2-4 tablespoons olive or vegetable oil

In a large container, stir together Bloody Mary mix and tomato juice. Set aside. In food processor, blend cucumbers, onion, bell pepper, celery, and tomatoes. Add vegetable mixture to juice mixture and stir. Add vinegar, sugar, lemon juice, Worcestershire sauce, and oil. Stir well. Refrigerate before serving. Yields 16 servings.

Cordon Bluegrass (Kentucky)

Cold Peach Soup

It's good on a hot summer day!

3 cups sliced canned peaches
1 cup sour cream or vanilla yogurt

¼ teaspoon almond extract

Blend ingredients in blender. Chill before serving and garnish with a fresh strawberry and/or sprig of mint. I like to serve this soup as an appetizer with Mexican and other highly seasoned foods.

The Museum Cookbook (South Carolina)

French Onion Soup

5 medium-size onions, thinly sliced
2 tablespoons margarine
3 (10½-ounce) cans beef consommé
2 (10½-ounce) cans water
1 tablespoon Worcestershire sauce
½ teaspoon salt

⅛ teaspoon pepper
8 slices French bread, cut ¾ inch
  thick, toasted
3 thin slices mozzarella cheese the
  size of the bread
⅓ cup grated parmesan cheese

Separate onions into rings and cook in melted margarine until glossy. Add consommé, water, Worcestershire, salt, and pepper. Bring to boil, cover tightly, and cook over low heat 15 minutes.

Pour into 6-8 oven-worthy bowls; top with toasted bread and a slice of mozzarella; sprinkle with parmesan. Heat in a 400° oven for 15 minutes or until bubbly. Makes 6-8 servings.

What Is It? What Do I Do With It? (North Carolina)

Peanut Soup

A light soup that is quick to prepare.

1 packet dry onion soup mix
2 ribs celery, chopped, or
  4 teaspoons parsley flakes
2 tablespoons butter

1 quart chicken stock
½ tablespoon flour
½ cup creamy peanut butter
1 cup milk

Mix first 4 ingredients and heat to boiling, then add ½ tablespoon flour which has been mixed with cooled stock to the mixture. Pour this all through a strainer and then add the peanut butter and milk. Cook at low heat—do not boil—until warmed and blended. Serve garnished with additional crushed peanuts.

Note: I usually use low-fat milk and some powdered milk to thicken to my own liking. Regular milk will do fine, or cream for a very full-bodied soup.

The Smithfield Cookbook (Virginia)

Paul Bunyan's Split Pea Soup

Paul Bunyan sent one of his cooks to a nearby town to get a wagonful of split peas. On the journey home, the wagon broke and spilled the full load of peas into a lake. To make the best of the situation, Paul threw 300 hams into the lake and then built a big fire around it. Dozens of cooks paddled around in rowboats to keep things from scorching. After a few hours it was ready—a lake full of split pea soup! Everyone said it was the best soup they had ever eaten.

1 pound dried split peas	2 tablespoons butter or margarine
½ cup chopped celery	1 or 2 smoked ham hocks
½ cup chopped onion	(about ½ pound each)
½ cup chopped carrot	¼ teaspoon pepper
1 clove garlic, minced	1½ teaspoons salt

Cover peas with water and soak overnight. The next day, sauté celery, onion, carrot, and garlic in butter until tender. Drain beans and reserve liquid. Add enough water to soaking liquid to make 10 cups. Put in a pot and add the rest of the ingredients. Heat to boiling and then reduce to low heat. Cover and simmer 3 hours. Remove meat from ham hock and return meat to soup. Serves 8.

Winning Recipes from Minnesota with Love (Minnesota)

Luscious Lentil Soup

This is the only way my kids will eat lentils. In fact, they love it so much, I always double the recipe. This also freezes quite well.

2 tablespoons olive oil	1½ cups dried lentils, picked over
2 cups chopped raw onion	and rinsed
4 coarsely grated raw carrots	Salt and pepper to taste
1 teaspoon crumbled marjoram	6 ounces dry red wine
1 teaspoon crumbled thyme	⅓ cup chopped fresh parsley
1 (28-ounce) can tomatoes with juice,	4 ounces Cheddar cheese, grated
coarsely chopped	
7 cups broth (beef, chicken, or	
vegetable)	

Heat oil in large saucepan and sauté the onion, carrots, marjoram, and thyme, stirring the vegetables for about 5 minutes. Add tomatoes, broth, and lentils. Bring soup to a boil, reduce the heat, cover pan, and simmer for about 1 hour or until the lentils are tender. Add the salt, pepper, wine, and parsley and simmer the soup for a few minutes. Serve with cheese sprinkled on top. Serves 18.

Think Healthy (Virginia)

Taco Soup

1 pound lean ground beef
1 onion, chopped
1 envelope taco seasoning mix
1 (16-ounce) can pinto beans
1 (16-ounce) can kidney beans
1 (16-ounce) can golden hominy
1 (17-ounce) can cream-style corn
1 (14-ounce) can diced stewed
  tomatoes
1 (10-ounce) can diced tomatoes
  with chilies (optional)
1 envelope ranch-style dressing mix
Tortilla chips
1 cup (4 ounces) grated Cheddar or
  Monterey Jack cheese

Brown ground beef and chopped onion; drain. Add taco seasoning; mix thoroughly. Add, without draining, the cans of beans, hominy, corn, and tomatoes. Stir in dry ranch dressing mix. Simmer over low heat until bubbly. Serve over tortilla chips and top with grated cheese. Serves 4-6.

Coastal Cuisine (Texas II)

★ **Editor's Extra:** One of the most voted for recipes in the entire Best of the Best collection.

Taco Seasoning Mix

¼ cup dried minced onion flakes
4 teaspoons cornstarch
4 tablespoons chili powder
3 teaspoons cumin
1½ teaspoons oregano
3 teaspoons garlic powder
2 teaspoons instant beef bouillon
3 teaspoons cayenne pepper

Mix all together; store in an airtight container in refrigerator. Three tablespoons equals one commercial package.

Easy Recipes for 1, 2, or a Few (Colorado)

★★★★★★★★★★★ ★★★★★★★★★★★

Capitol Hill Bean Soup

1 pound dried navy beans	1 clove garlic, minced
1-pound (about) ham bone	½ cup mashed potatoes*
3 cups chopped onions	2 teaspoons salt
3 cups chopped celery	Pepper to taste
¼ cup chopped fresh parsley	

Sort and wash beans. Cover with water and soak overnight. (If you have forgotten to put beans on to soak, you can: cover beans with water and heat to a rolling boil; cover and let sit for an hour or so.) Drain and cover with water; add soup bone or chopped ham.

Bring to a boil and add onions, celery, parsley, and garlic. Cook until done. Add the mashed potatoes and seasonings; cook slowly for a while longer. Makes 12-15 servings.

Note: I usually use turkey ham cut in small cubes.

Asbury United Methodist Church Cook Book (Arkansas)

★ **Editor's Extra:** If you don't have leftover mashed potatoes on hand, microwave a small peeled, cubed potato in 2 tablespoons salted water 5 minutes on HIGH, covered. Mash.

★ ★ ★ ★ ★ ★ ★ ★ ★ ★ ★ ★ ★   ★ ★ ★ ★ ★ ★ ★ ★ ★ ★ ★ ★ ★

Pumpkin Bowl Stew

Served in its own shell, pumpkin stew is a favorite main course for Halloween or Thanksgiving.

1 medium pie pumpkin (pie
   pumpkins have thick, meaty sides)
1 cup sliced carrots
1 cup diced potatoes
1 cup sliced parsnips
1 cup chopped onion
1 cup chopped celery

1 (10½-ounce) can chicken broth
¼ teaspoon allspice
¼ teaspoon cinnamon
2 tablespoons chopped basil
3 tablespoons chopped Italian
   parsley
1 tablespoon chopped thyme

Clean pumpkin, remove seeds, and scrape the inside. Reserve the "hat." Put the ingredients (uncooked) into the pumpkin. Place the pumpkin on a cookie sheet. Bake in a preheated 300° oven for 3-4 hours. The pumpkin and root vegetables will combine to make their own thickening. Replace "hat."

Herbs in a Minnesota Kitchen (Minnesota)

Working Barn Stew

A filling, zesty family stew.

2 tablespoons olive oil
4 boneless, skinless chicken breast
   halves (about 1 pound), cut into
   1-inch pieces
1 cup chopped onion
½ medium green bell pepper,
   chopped
½ medium yellow pepper, chopped
1 teaspoon chopped garlic

2 (14½-ounce) cans stewed
   tomatoes
1 (15-ounce) can pinto beans,
   drained and rinsed
¾ cup medium picante sauce
1 tablespoon chili powder
1 tablespoon ground cumin
½ cup shredded Cheddar cheese
6 tablespoons sour cream

In large stockpot, heat olive oil over medium heat. Add chicken, onion, bell peppers, and garlic, and cook until chicken is no longer pink. Add tomatoes, beans, picante sauce, chili powder, and cumin. Reduce heat to low and simmer 25 minutes or up to 2 hours. Place in individual serving bowls and top with cheese and sour cream. Makes 6 servings.

Colorado Collage (Colorado)

★★★★★★★★★★★ ★★★★★★★★★★★

Chili

1¼ pounds ground beef	½ teaspoon garlic powder or
2 cups diced onion	3 garlic cloves, minced
1 (6-ounce) can tomato paste	1 small bay leaf
1 (14½-ounce) can whole tomatoes,	1 teaspoon oregano
with juice	¼ teaspoon cayenne pepper
2½ tablespoons chili powder	1 (15-ounce) can kidney beans
2½ teaspoons cumin	1½ cups grated Cheddar cheese
1½ teaspoons salt	¾ cup coarsely chopped onion
1¼ cups water or beef stock	6 tablespoons sour cream

To prepare the chili: Sauté the meat and the onions over medium heat until the meat loses its pink color. Add all of the remaining ingredients except the beans and toppings. Simmer, stirring occasionally, for 1 hour. Add the beans and simmer the mixture for 15 minutes longer. (The chili will hold, refrigerated, for 4 days at this point; the flavors will mellow and improve with time.)

For service: Heat the chili slowly to a simmer. Continue to simmer for 20 minutes, until thoroughly heated, stirring occasionally. Serve in heated crocks or bowls. Top each serving with grated Cheddar cheese, chopped onion, and sour cream. Serves 6.

The Great Chefs of Virginia Cookbook (Virginia)

Stormy Weather Chili

Easy, tomatoey, good!

2 medium onions, diced	1-2 (15-ounce) cans red kidney
1 cup diced celery	beans
2 tablespoons cooking oil	Salt and pepper to taste
1½ pounds ground beef	1 tablespoon sugar
4 cups canned tomatoes	1 bay leaf
1 (15½-ounce) can chili beans	2-3 teaspoons chili powder

Sauté onions and celery in cooking oil in large kettle. When golden, stir in ground beef and thoroughly brown. Stir in remaining ingredients; simmer for one hour. Remove bay leaf before serving.

Note: Using a pressure cooker will shorten cooking time. Cook for about 20 minutes at 10 pounds pressure. Put cooker under cold running water until pressure is down before trying to open lid.

Up a Country Lane Cookbook (Iowa)

★★★★★★★★★★★★   ★★★★★★★★★★★★

White Bean Chili

1 pound dried Great Northern
  white beans
2 pounds ground turkey
1 tablespoon olive oil
2 medium onions, chopped
4 cloves garlic, minced
2 (4-ounce) cans chopped mild
  green chilies
2 teaspoons ground cumin
1½ teaspoons dried oregano,
  crumbled

¼ teaspoon ground cloves
¼ teaspoon cayenne pepper
6 cups chicken stock or canned
  broth
3 cups grated Monterey Jack cheese,
  divided
Salt and pepper to taste
Sour cream to garnish
Salsa to garnish
Chopped fresh cilantro to garnish

Rinse beans and sort out any bad ones. Place beans in large heavy pot. Add enough cold water to cover by at least 3 inches and soak overnight. Cook turkey in a large heavy saucepan until cooked through; set aside. Drain beans.

Heat oil in same pot used for beans over medium-high heat. Add onions and sauté until translucent, about 10 minutes. Stir in garlic, then chilies, cumin, oregano, ground cloves, and cayenne pepper; sauté 2 minutes. Add beans and stock and bring to boil. Reduce heat and simmer until beans are very tender, stirring occasionally, for about 2 hours.

Add turkey and 1 cup grated cheese and stir until cheese melts. Season to taste with salt and pepper. Ladle chili into bowls. Serve with remaining cheese, sour cream, salsa, and cilantro. Yields 8 servings.

Holy Cow! (Illinois)

Cincinnati Chili

The first chili parlor opened its doors next to the Empress Burlesque (later named the Gaiety) in downtown Cincinnati in 1922, naming itself The Empress Chili Parlor. This establishment was owned by Greek Tom Kiradjieff who banked on the city sharing his taste for the unusual blend of spices. The rest is history. The original recipe which has always been mixed secretly at home, was never revealed. Yet chili restaurants sprang up all over town, including Skyline and Gold Star. Local chili aficionados developed preferences for their favorites. Al Heitz, a Camp Washington devotee, liked the old recipe best because it left his lips numb; old timers say that the chilies have indeed "cooled off" through the years. Inevitably, various chili recipes were published in homemade cookbooks. Recently, a packaged Cincinnati Chili Mix has appeared on supermarket shelves. Whether the chili is hot or not, Cincinnati prides itself on being a true chili capital.

2-3 pounds ground beef	2 teaspoons cinnamon
1 quart cold water	1 teaspoon allspice
1 (6-ounce) can tomato paste	2 cayenne peppers (more to taste)
2 large onions, chopped (about 1½ cups)	1½ tablespoons unsweetened cocoa
1½ tablespoons vinegar	Salt and pepper to taste
1 teaspoon Worcestershire sauce	1½ pounds cooked spaghetti
1 garlic clove, chopped fine	1 pound Cheddar cheese, grated
2 tablespoons chili powder	1 box oyster crackers
5 bay leaves	1 (16-ounce) can kidney beans
	1 onion, chopped fine (optional)

Crumble the raw ground beef into the water. Add all of the ingredients except the spaghetti, cheese, crackers, beans, and onions, and bring to a boil. Stir well, breaking all the meat up before it cooks. Cover and simmer 2 hours or more, stirring occasionally. Yields 8-10 servings.

Note: The proper way to serve this chili is over spaghetti on an oval dish. (There should be a piece of pepper for every serving for absolute authenticity.) For a "3-Way," top it off with a pile of grated cheese and a dish of crackers on the side. To make a "4-Way," add a spoonful of onions before the cheese is placed on top. For a "5-Way," add warmed beans in addition to onions and cheese.

Cincinnati Recipe Treasury (Ohio)

Cream of Corn Soup

2 strips bacon, finely chopped
2 tablespoons finely chopped onion
2 cups frozen or fresh corn
2 tablespoons butter
2 tablespoons flour
2 cups milk
1 teaspoon salt
½ teaspoon pepper (or to taste)
2 cups light cream

Fry diced bacon until crisp; put aside and sauté onion in drippings until soft. Put corn through chopper; add to bacon and onion. Add butter and then the flour; cook slowly for 3 minutes. Add milk, salt and pepper and cook till thickened, then add cream and heat till smooth. Serves 4.

The Best of Friends (Colorado)

Corn Soup

It is hard to believe this creamy soup is not full of heavy cream. You can garnish it with chopped green onions when serving.

1 onion, chopped
1 green bell pepper, seeded and
  chopped
½ teaspoon minced garlic
1 (16-ounce) bag frozen sweet corn
1 (8½-ounce) can cream-style corn
1 (10-ounce) can diced tomatoes and
  green chilies
1 (14½-ounce) can fat-free
  chicken broth
1 tablespoon Worcestershire sauce
Salt and pepper to taste
2 cups low-fat milk
⅓ cup all-purpose flour

In a pot coated with nonstick cooking spray, sauté the onion, green pepper, and garlic over medium-high heat until tender, about 5 minutes. Add the frozen corn, cream-style corn, diced tomatoes and green chilies, chicken broth, Worcestershire sauce, and salt and pepper. In a separate bowl, blend together the milk and flour. Gradually stir into the corn mixture. Cook for 15 minutes, until hot throughout. Makes 8 (1-cup) servings.

Cal 125; Fat .04g; Cal from Fat 2.9%; Sat Fat 0.1g; Sod 387 mg; Chol 1 mg.

Trim & Terrific American Favorites (Louisiana II)

Creamy Broccoli Soup

1 small onion, minced
4 tablespoons butter or margarine
5 tablespoons all-purpose flour
1 teaspoon salt
3 cups light cream
1-2 cups chicken broth
2 (10-ounce) packages frozen
  chopped broccoli, slightly thawed
½ teaspoon nutmeg

Sauté onion in butter until tender; stir in flour and salt. Gradually add cream, stirring constantly. Add broth according to desired thickness of soup. Add broccoli and nutmeg. Cook over low heat 25 minutes. Stir occasionally. Yields 6-8 servings.

Variation: ⅛ teaspoon mace may be substituted for nutmeg. Cauliflower can be used in lieu of broccoli.

Market to Market (North Carolina)

Vegetable Soup

This is noted pianist Van Cliburn's favorite, as prepared by his aunt, Mrs. Mattye Cliburn, of the Linwood Community.

2 pounds boneless stew meat
8 cups water
Salt and pepper
1 (6-ounce) can tomato paste
1 large onion, sliced thin, divided
1 soup bone
⅓ cup barley
1 (32-ounce) can tomatoes, undrained
2 (10-ounce) packages frozen mixed
  vegetables, or 2 (16-ounce) cans
  mixed vegetables
1 large potato, chopped
1 (16-ounce) can whole kernel corn
3 sprigs parsley, finely cut
¼ teaspoon rosemary
¼ teaspoon marjoram
¼ teaspoon thyme
½ bay leaf

Cut meat into small chunks. Place in large Dutch oven. Add water, salt, pepper, tomato paste, ½ onion, and soup bone. Simmer, covered, for 1½ hours, or until meat is tender. Remove bone; skim fat from top. Add barley; simmer for 45 minutes. Add rest of onion, tomatoes, vegetables, parsley, rosemary, marjoram, thyme, and bay leaf. Simmer until vegetables are tender. Remove bay leaf. Seasonings should be omitted or adjusted, according to taste. Makes 8-10 large servings.

Giant Houseparty Cookbook (Mississippi)

★ ★ ★ ★ ★ ★ ★ ★ ★ ★ ★   ★ ★ ★ ★ ★ ★ ★ ★ ★ ★ ★

Heidelberg Soup

Wonderful for a soup and salad luncheon.

5 medium potatoes, diced
3 medium onions, diced
5 cups water
1 (16-ounce) package frozen mixed
   vegetables

2 cans cream of celery soup or
   1 can each cream of celery and
   cream of mushroom soup
1 pound Velveeta cheese

Cook onions and potatoes in 5 cups of water until tender. Add frozen mixed vegetables; cook until hot. Add soups and Velveeta cheese. Stir until cheese melts.

A Tasting Tour Through Washington County (Kentucky)

Cream Soup Mix

1 cup powdered low-fat milk
¾ cup cornstarch
¼ cup instant chicken bouillon
   cubes

2 tablespoons dried onion flakes
1 teaspoon basil
1 teaspoon thyme
½ teaspoon pepper

Mix all ingredients together. Store in an airtight container until ready to use. For the equivalent of 1 can of cream soup, substitute ⅓ cup dry mix and 1¼ cups cold water. Cook in a saucepan until thick.

Dry mix yields the equivalent of 9 cups of canned soup.

Amount per serving: Calories 285; Grams of fat 1.0; Cholesterol 5mg; Sodium 905mg; % of fat 3%.

Eat To Your Heart's Content, Too! (Arkansas)

Potato Cheese Soup

3 medium potatoes
2 cups boiling water
3 cups milk
2 tablespoons butter or margarine
1 small onion (finely chopped)

2 tablespoons flour
1 teaspoon salt
¼ teaspoon cayenne
1 cup grated Cheddar cheese

Cook potatoes in boiling water. Drain almost all of the water out and mash the potatoes coarsely. Add milk and heat to a simmer. Melt butter, add onion, and simmer until onion is transparent. Add flour and seasonings. Combine with potato mixture and simmer, stirring every 5 minutes. Add cheese and beat until smooth. Serve hot, garnished with chives and crushed potato chips. Serves 4.

The Sandlapper Cookbook (South Carolina)

Baked Potato Soup

4 large baking potatoes
⅔ cup butter or margarine
⅔ cup all-purpose flour
6 cups milk (2%)
¾ teaspoon salt
¾ teaspoon pepper

4-8 green onions, divided
16 slices bacon, cooked and
   crumbled, divided
1½ cups shredded Cheddar cheese,
   divided
1½ cups sour cream

Wash potatoes and prick several times with fork. Bake at 400° for 1 hour or until done. Let cool. Peel and partially mash, leaving chunks. Melt butter in saucepan over low heat. Add flour, stirring until smooth. Cook 1 minute, stirring constantly.

Gradually add milk. Cook over medium heat, stirring constantly until mixture thickens and bubbles. Add potatoes, salt, pepper, 4 tablespoons green onions, ½ cup bacon, and 1 cup cheese. Cook until thoroughly heated; stir in sour cream; do not boil. Add extra milk, if needed, for desired thickness. Serve with remaining onions, bacon, and cheese, or you can put all in soup at one time. Makes 20 servings.

Per serving: Cal 348; Prot 12g; Fat 19g; Chol 34g.

Wadsworth-Rittman Hospital Cookbook (Ohio)

Sweet Potato Bisque

This unusual soup can legitimately boast a richness, not only in taste, but also in vitamin and mineral content.

LOW-FAT VERSION:

Butter Buds Mix equivalent to 8 tablespoons butter (1 packet)
¼ cup water
½ cup chopped onions
1 cup chopped celery
2 large sweet potatoes, peeled and diced

3 cups defatted chicken broth
⅛ teaspoon black pepper
Salt to taste (optional)
½ cup evaporated skim milk

Combine Butter Buds Mix and water and blend until smooth. Place into a nonstick Dutch oven or soup kettle with onions and celery. Sauté until tender. Add diced sweet potatoes and chicken broth. Cover and cook until potatoes are well done.

Remove from heat and cool slightly. Pour mixture into food processor or blender and purée. (This may have to be done in several batches due to quantity.) Pour mixture back into Dutch oven. Add pepper and salt, if desired. Stir in evaporated skim milk. Reheat and serve. Serves 6.

Per serving: Calories, 90; Fat, 0.3gr; Cholesterol, less than 1mg.

Note: Traditional recipe uses real butter and cream.

Convertible Cooking for a Healthy Heart (Pennsylvania)

★ **Editor's Extra:** I use leftover baked sweet potatoes and make this in 20 minutes! Soup-erb!

Oyster Stew

6 green onions (scallions), finely
  chopped
1 rib of celery, chopped fine
1 stick butter or margarine
2 tablespoons flour
2 or 3 dozen small oysters with
  liquid

1 quart milk, heated
Salt and pepper
Worcestershire sauce
Slices of toasted bread cut into
  croutons
2 sprigs parsley, minced

Sauté chopped vegetables in margarine and flour. Drain oysters and add liquid to vegetables. Add preheated milk, then oysters, and simmer until oysters are plump and edges begin to turn. Add salt, pepper, and Worcestershire sauce to taste. Serve with croutons. Sprinkle with parsley. Serves 4.

Louisiana's Original Creole Seafood Recipes (Louisiana)

She-Crab Soup

"She-crab" is much more of a delicacy than "he-crab," as the eggs add a special flavor to the soup. The street vendors make a point of calling "she-crab" loudly and of charging extra for them.

1 tablespoon butter
1 teaspoon flour
1 quart milk
2 cups white crabmeat and
  crab eggs
½ teaspoon salt

Few drops onion juice
⅛ teaspoon mace
⅛ teaspoon pepper
½ teaspoon Worcestershire
4 tablespoons dry sherry
¼ pint cream (whipped)

Melt butter in top of double boiler and blend with flour until smooth. Add the milk gradually, stirring constantly. To this, add crabmeat and eggs and all seasonings except sherry. Cook slowly over hot water for 20 minutes. To serve, place 1 tablespoon of warmed sherry in individual soup bowls, then add soup and top with whipped cream. Sprinkle with paprika or finely chopped parsley. Serves 4-6.

Secret: If unable to obtain "she-crabs," crumble yolks of hard-boiled eggs in bottom of soup plates.

Charleston Receipts (South Carolina)

Crab Bisque Thirty-Seventh

Elizabeth on 37th is one of Savannah's most popular restaurants, and its owner/chef, Elizabeth Terry, is one of the nation's most publicized cooks. She was one of Food and Wine's 25 "Hot New Chefs," and has been featured in Town and Country and Time, among other magazines. Elizabeth creates all the recipes herself, and does much of the actual cooking while her husband Michael is chief host, wine steward, and worrier. They make a great team. Here is one of the Savannah restaurant's specialties.

6 tablespoons butter
1 cup minced green onion
½ cup minced celery
1 tablespoon minced carrot
6 tablespoons flour
2½ cups milk
2½ cups chicken broth,
  preferably homemade

¼ teaspoon nutmeg
¼ teaspoon white pepper
⅛ teaspoon cayenne pepper
1 cup cream
¼ cup good sherry
1 pound claw crabmeat,
  picked over

Melt butter over low heat in saucepan. Mince green onion, celery, and carrot in food processor. Add to butter and cover. Sweat until tender, about 5 minutes. Whisk in flour and cook for 2 minutes to remove starchy taste. Whisk in milk and broth. Bring to a boil, whisking occasionally. Add seasonings, cream, sherry, and crab. Serve immediately. Serves 12.

Savannah Collection (Georgia)

Connecticut Coastline Seafood Chowder

You can't beat the powerful aroma of this chowder simmering on the stove on a chilly afternoon.

CHOWDER BASE:

¼ pound diced salt pork
2 large onions, peeled and chopped
2 leeks, cleaned and sliced
1 rib celery, sliced
1 cup water
2 cups Doxie clam juice or fish stock

3 cups peeled and diced potatoes
1 tablespoon chopped fresh parsley
½ teaspoon oregano
½ teaspoon thyme
1 bay leaf, broken in half
Freshly ground pepper

Cook the salt pork in a large soup kettle over medium heat until fat is rendered and pork is crisp. Add onions and leeks and sauté for 4 minutes. Add remaining chowder base ingredients to the pot, bring to the boil, reduce heat and simmer, covered, for about 15 minutes or until potatoes are tender. Cool base and chill overnight, if possible.

INGREDIENTS TO FINISH CHOWDER:

½ pound bay scallops
½ pound firm white fish, cubed
3 dozen quahogs (or any kind of
  clams), coarsely chopped

4 cups light cream
Few drops Tabasco
2 tablespoons unsalted butter

Return pot to stove and bring base to a simmer. Add seafood, including any clam liquor, and simmer for 3 minutes. Add remaining ingredients and cook over low heat until just heated through. Serve chowder immediately. Yields 8 servings.

Off the Hook (New England)

Mamaw's Shrimp Gumbo

A family favorite, an easy method . . . everybody loves it!

1 stick butter or margarine
1 pound frozen cut okra
⅔ cup vegetable oil
¾ cup flour
1 (12-ounce) bag frozen chopped
  onion
½ (10-ounce) bag frozen chopped
  bell pepper
2½ quarts water, divided

1 (28-ounce) can tomatoes, chopped
1 teaspoon chopped garlic
2 teaspoons salt
½ teaspoon ground bay leaves
½ teaspoon black pepper
1 teaspoon Tabasco
¼ teaspoon crushed red pepper
3-4 pounds raw shrimp, peeled

In big, heavy pot, melt butter; add okra and cook on medium heat till not ropy anymore—about 15-20 minutes—stirring often. In another big iron pot or skillet, heat and stir oil and flour slowly to make dark brown roux. Add vegetables which have thawed slightly (the frozen kind sizzle a bit more, but keep stirring, it works just fine). Add a cup of hot water slowly to the roux, stirring till smooth. Now combine the two mixtures in the bigger pot.

Add tomatoes, remaining water, garlic, and all seasonings, and bring to a boil. Add shrimp, bring back to a slight boil, lower heat and simmer about 30 minutes. Serve over fluffy rice with potato salad and buttered crackers and iced tea. Makes about 10-15 bowls, depending on size.

The Little Gumbo Book (Louisiana II)

★ **Gwen's Extra**: This was my mother-in-law's favorite gumbo. I often watched her make it and lovingly serve it to family and friends. She chopped fresh vegetables, of course, often from her own garden, which I heartily recommend. To save on time (and tears), I use the frozen, already chopped vegetables in this gumbo without sacrificing its family-favorite flavor. I know Carrie McKee (from Folsom, Louisiana) would be pleased and proud to know her recipe was being shared by those who will be sure to serve her delicious gumbo as she did . . . with a lot of love.

K's Cajun Seasoning

Quick to fix; eliminates search for numerous cans and jars of spices—they are all mixed here in one spicy blend for quick, tasty seasoning.

1 (26-ounce) box salt
3 tablespoons black pepper
2 tablespoons garlic powder
1 teaspoon onion powder
1 teaspoon nutmeg

2 tablespoons Accent (optional)
2 tablespoons dried parsley flakes
4 tablespoons cayenne pepper
2 tablespoons chili powder

Mix all in large bowl. Fill a shaker for daily use; store remainder in tightly covered container.

Quickie Tip (in Cajun dialect): Brang some o' dis K's Cajun Seasoning to your frans, cher; d'ell ahpreeciate dat a' planty!

Quickies for Singles (Louisiana)

Microwave Roux with Vegetables

Frozen chopped vegetables work just fine—they just sizzle a bit more and require a few more seconds cooking time. Grandmother would even be fooled by this one!

⅔ cup vegetable oil
⅔ cup flour
⅔ cup chopped onions
⅔ cup chopped celery
⅔ teaspoon minced garlic

⅔ cup chopped bell pepper
⅔ cup chopped green onions
 (optional)
⅔ cup hot water

Mix oil with flour in a 4-cup glass measuring bowl. Microwave uncovered on HIGH for 6 minutes. Stir and cook another 30-60 seconds on HIGH till the color of mahogany.

Now you can add your chopped vegetables, stir well, and "sauté" them on HIGH for another 5 minutes till soft but not brown.

Now, before stirring, pour oil off top. Add hot tap water, stirring until smooth. Beautiful! And it freezes for later use.

The Little Gumbo Book (Louisiana II)

Salads

★★★★ ★★★★

The siege of the Alamo was a 13-day moment in history that turned a ruined Spanish mission into a shrine. That defeat inspired others to "Remember the Alamo" and win Texas independence from Mexico.

Seafoam Salad

1 large can pears, drained, juice
  reserved
1 package lime gelatin
1 (8-ounce) package cream cheese,
  softened

½ pint whipping cream, whipped
1 small bottle maraschino cherries,
  drained

Heat 1 cup of pear juice. Pour over gelatin and stir until dissolved.
Mash drained pears with fork. Soften cream cheese with a little pear
juice. Add mashed pears and cheese to gelatin; cool. Fold in whipped
cream and cup of cherries. Mold as desired and chill until firm.

Cooking with H.E.L.P. (New England)

Cranberry Sour Cream Swirl Salad

*A festive salad for holiday meals, but good the year round. A real crowd
pleaser.*

2 (3-ounce) packages cherry or
  red raspberry gelatin
1½ cups boiling water
1 (15-ounce) can crushed pineapple

1 (16-ounce) can whole cranberry
  sauce (break apart with fork)
1 cup (½ pint) dairy sour cream

Dissolve gelatin in boiling water. Stir in undrained crushed pineapple
and cranberry sauce. Chill until partially set. Spoon into 8-inch square
dish. Spoon sour cream on top and stir to swirl. Chill until firm. Cut
into squares to serve.

Holiday Treats (Virginia)

Party Apple Salad

3 apples, diced
2 cups celery, diced
1 can crushed pineapple, drained
  (reserve juice)

1 cup chopped nuts
1 cup whipping cream, whipped

DRESSING:
Juice from pineapple
1 egg
3 tablespoons flour

3 tablespoons sugar
2 tablespoons lemon juice

Boil dressing ingredients until thickened. Pour over apples, celery,
pineapple, and nuts; mix well. Fold in whipped cream.

Centennial Cookbook (Iowa)

Cucumber Mousse

Good on crackers as appetizer or in lettuce cups for salad.

1 package lime-flavored gelatin
1 cup boiling water
1 teaspoon salt
2 tablespoons vinegar or lemon juice
1 cup sour cream
¼ cup mayonnaise

1½ cups finely cut, drained
  cucumber
3 tablespoons minced green onions
  and tops
1 tablespoon chopped green
  pepper

Dissolve gelatin in water. Add salt and lemon juice. Cool to room temperature and add sour cream and mayonnaise. Chill until syrupy and fold in cucumber, onions, and green pepper. Chill until firm in 8-inch ring mold. Needs no additional dressing.

Five Loaves and Two Fishes II (Illinois)

★ **Editor's Extra:** Pretty to thinly slice ¼ of an unpeeled cucumber and place on bottom of ring mold or cake pan. Pour mousse over. To add a little color, use red bell pepper in place of green.

Raspberry Pretzel Salad

2 cups pretzels, crushed
3 tablespoons sugar
¾ cup butter or margarine, melted
1 (8-ounce) package cream cheese,
  softened
½ cup confectioner's sugar
1½ cups Cool Whip

2 cups miniature marshmallows
2 (3-ounce) packages raspberry
  Jell-O
2 cups boiling water
2 (10-ounce) packages frozen
  raspberries

Crush pretzels; mix with sugar and butter. Press into 9x13-inch pan, and bake at 350° for 15 minutes. Set aside to cool. Cream softened cheese; add sugar and beat well. Fold in Cool Whip and marshmallows. Spread this mixture over cooked crust.

Dissolve Jell-O in water and stir in raspberries, breaking up as to thaw them. Chill until thick. Spread this over cream layer. Chill and put into the refrigerator until served.

Cooking with Daisy's Descendants (Illinois)

Cookie Monster Fruit Salad

1 cup buttermilk
1 (3-ounce) package instant vanilla
  pudding
1 (8-ounce) carton Cool Whip
1 small can mandarin oranges,
  drained

1 small can crushed pineapple,
  drained
14 chocolate striped cookies,
  crushed

Mix buttermilk and pudding together; fold in Cool Whip. Fold remaining ingredients into pudding mixture. Chill well before serving. Makes 8 servings.

St. Mary's Family Cookbook (Wisconsin)

Snicker Apple Salad

Sooo simple and sooo good!

1 (8-ounce) container Cool Whip
1 (8-ounce) container sour cream
6 apples, chopped

4 Snickers bars, chopped
  (can use more)

Mix together, refrigerate, and serve. Can be fixed ahead of time.

Fire Gals' Hot Pans Cookbook (Iowa)

Horseradish Salad

DISSOLVE:
1 package lemon Jell-O and
1 package lime Jell-O in
2 cups boiling water; cool and add

1 large can crushed pineapple,
  drained

BLEND:
1 (8-ounce) carton cottage cheese with

1 cup mayonnaise

ADD:
Jell-O and 1 can condensed
  sweetened milk
2 heaping tablespoons horseradish

3 tablespoons lemon juice
¼ teaspoon salt

Stir and pour into a large mold or individual molds. Serves about 16.

Lost Tree Cook Book (Florida)

Quick Jell-O Salad

1 (3½-ounce) box dry lime Jell-O   1 small carton cottage cheese
1 can crushed pineapple, drained   1 small container Cool Whip

Mix all ingredients together and chill. It's ready to be served.
Bethany Lutheran Church Celebrating 125 Years (Minnesota)

Great Lakes German Potato Salad

8 medium-sized potatoes, peeled   ¼ teaspoon pepper
¾ cup chopped onions   4 tablespoons sugar
8 slices bacon, cut in 1-inch pieces   1 cup water
2 tablespoons flour   ½ cup vinegar
1½ teaspoons salt

Dice potatoes and cook in lightly salted water until tender. Drain and
keep warm. While potatoes are cooking, fry bacon until crisp. Remove
bacon and discard all but 3 tablespoons of drippings. Add onions and
cook until tender, about 5 minutes. Mix together dry ingredients. Add
to onions and stir to blend. Add water and vinegar. Bring to a boil until
thickened. Pour over hot cooked potatoes. Add bacon and toss gently.
May be kept in oven at 200° or in crock pot on low setting. Serves
approximately 8 people.

How to Make a Steamship Float (Michigan)

Creamy Dijon Potato Salad

9 medium potatoes   2 tablespoons Dijon mustard
4 hard-cooked egg whites, chopped   2 teaspoons salt
⅔ cup finely chopped dill pickle   1 teaspoon paprika
½ cup finely chopped celery   1 teaspoon finely ground black
⅓ cup finely chopped onion   pepper
2 cups Hellmann's reduced-fat   1 teaspoon Lawry's seasoned salt
  mayonnaise

Boil potatoes until tender, then peel and cube (yields about 9 cups).
Combine potatoes with egg whites, dill pickle, celery, and onion.
Combine remaining ingredients and add to potato mixture, tossing gen-
tly. Refrigerate until served. Serves 14-16.

All About Bar-B-Q Kansas City Style (Great Plains)

Seafood Pasta Salad

Great as soon as it's made.

½ cup salad dressing
¼ cup zesty Italian dressing
2 tablespoons parmesan cheese
2 cups corkscrew noodles, cooked
  and drained
1½ cups chopped imitation
  crabmeat

1 cup broccoli florets, partially
  cooked
½ cup chopped green pepper
½ cup chopped tomato
¼ cup green onion slices

Combine dressings and cheese; mix well. Add remaining ingredients; mix lightly and chill.

Smyth County Extension Homemakers Cookbook (Virginia)

Pasta Salad Italiano

Colorful and delicious. Sure to impress your guests.

1 (8-ounce) bottle creamy Italian
  dressing
1 cup broccoli, cut into bite-sized
  pieces
½ cup cauliflower, cut into florets
½ cup fresh mushrooms, sliced
  (optional)
1 can water chestnuts, sliced

1 carrot, diced
¼ cup ripe olives, sliced
  (or green olives)
¾ cup cherry tomatoes, halved
4 ounces spaghetti noodles
¼ cup parmesan cheese
¼ cup real bacon bits

In medium-size bowl, pour dressing over vegetables. Cover and marinate in refrigerator at least 3 hours. Cook spaghetti, drain, and chill. Drain and reserve marinade from the vegetables. Combine marinade with noodles and cheese. Toss lightly. Place noodles in glass dish, adding vegetables. Sprinkle with more cheese and the bacon. Carry in cooler. Serves 8-10.

Note: If the spaghetti noodles are broken before cooking, it is easier to serve and eat.

Picnics on the Square (Wisconsin)

Bridesmaid's Luncheon Chicken Salad

One of the best chicken salads you will ever eat! Guaranteed to bring rave reviews!

1½ cups Hellmann's Mayonnaise
¾ cup Major Gray's Chutney
1 teaspoon curry powder
2 teaspoons grated lime peel
¼ cup fresh lime juice
½ teaspoon salt
4 cups cooked, small chunked
   white meat of chicken

2 (13¼-ounce) cans pineapple
   chunks, drained
2 cups diagonally sliced celery
1 cup thinly sliced green onions
   (tops and bottoms)
½ cup toasted whole or sliced
   blanched almonds

Into a really large mixing or salad bowl, combine mayonnaise, chutney, curry, lime peel and juice, and salt. (If there are fruit chucks in the chutney, slice them as thinly as possible.) Blend well and then gently fold in remaining ingredients. Chill 4-6 hours.

   Can be prepared the night before; just be sure to toss again before serving, and be sure to go all the way to the bottom of the container to mix in all accumulated juices when tossing for the final time. Serve on crisp, chilled salad greens. Yields 8-10 generous servings.

Too Good to be True III (Louisiana II)

79

★★★★★★★★★★★★★   ★★★★★★★★★★★★★

Chicken Salad Supreme

1 (2½ to 3-pound) cooked hen
1 cup seedless white grapes or
    seedless red grapes
1 (5-ounce) can sliced water
    chestnuts (optional)
1 cup diced celery

1 cup slivered almonds
1½ cups mayonnaise
1½ teaspoons curry powder
1 tablespoon lemon juice
1 tablespoon soy sauce
½ cup toasted slivered almonds

Remove chicken from bone and cut in bite-sized pieces. Mix chicken, grapes, chestnuts, celery, and the cup of slivered almonds. Then mix mayonnaise, curry powder, lemon juice, and soy sauce, and add to the chicken. Mix well. Serve on pineapple slices or crisp lettuce leaves. Top with mayonnaise and ½ cup toasted slivered almonds. This will serve 12-15.

The Mississippi Cookbook (Mississippi)

Shoe Peg Relish Salad

Tangy, tasty, soooo good!

1 (16-ounce) can French-style
    green beans
1 (17-ounce) can very young small
    sweet peas
1 (17-ounce) can shoe peg corn
1 onion, sliced into rings
1 green pepper, cut into thin strips

½ to 1 cup chopped celery
1 (2-ounce) jar pimientos, chopped
    (optional)
½ (8-ounce) can water chestnuts,
    sliced (optional)
Marinade

Drain canned vegetables thoroughly. Place all the ingredients except the marinade in a large bowl. Add hot marinade and mix well. Cover and chill overnight in the refrigerator. Drain before serving or serve with a slotted spoon. Will keep several days in the refrigerator.

MARINADE:
1 cup sugar
¾ cup vinegar
½ cup oil

1 teaspoon salt
1 teaspoon pepper

Blend the ingredients together well. Heat almost to boiling.

Favorite Fare II (Kentucky)

Broccoli Salad

DRESSING:

1 cup Hellmann's mayonnaise
½ cup sugar
2 tablespoons vinegar

1 teaspoon prepared mustard
1 teaspoon paprika

SALAD:

2 bunches broccoli florets
1 cup chopped purple onion
1 cup raisins
1 cup sliced fresh mushrooms

1 small can drained mandarin
 oranges
½ cup cashew pieces
8 slices fried bacon, crumbled

Mix dressing ingredients until smooth. Cover and refrigerate overnight. Just before serving, pour over remaining ingredients. Serves 8-12.

Heavenly Food II (Ohio)

The song "Yankee Doodle" had its origins in Norwalk, Connecticut. In 1756, a brigade of volunteers assembled at the home of Colonel Thomas Fitch where the young recruits set out to assist the British during the French and Indian War. Fitch's young sister stuck a feather into the hatband of each soldier as he pulled out on his plow horse. The British, amused by the appearance of the troops, wrote and sang the jingle in mockery. The rest is history. "Yankee Doodle" became the rallying song for the colonial troops during the Revolution and in 1978 became the official song of Connecticut.

Overnight Layer Salad

1 medium head lettuce, torn
4 ribs celery, chopped
1 bunch green onions, chopped
1 (10-ounce) box frozen peas, thawed
 but not cooked
3 hard-cooked eggs, chopped
6-8 slices bacon, fried crisp, crumbled

1½ cups sour cream
1½ cups mayonnaise or Miracle
 Whip
3 or 4 tablespoons sugar
½ teaspoon garlic salt
½ cup grated parmesan cheese

Place lettuce pieces in bottom of large glass or wooden bowl. Sprinkle the celery over lettuce, the green onions over celery, peas over the green onions, then eggs and half of the bacon. Make a dressing by combining the sour cream, mayonnaise, sugar, and garlic salt. Pour dressing over salad. Sprinkle parmesan cheese and remaining bacon over top. Chill overnight before serving. Serves 6-8.

Somethin's Cookin' at LG&E (Kentucky)

Summer Tomato Salad with Brie

5 medium garden fresh tomatoes,
 cut into chunks, save juice
½ pound Brie cheese, rind removed,
 torn into pieces
½ cup fresh basil, snipped into
 strips with scissors
3 large garlic cloves, minced

⅓ cup olive oil
½ teaspoon salt
½ pound fresh pasta (linguini,
 shells, etc.)
½ cup freshly grated parmesan
 cheese

Combine tomatoes and juice, Brie, basil, garlic, olive oil, and salt. Leave at room temperature at least 2 hours. Cook pasta as directed on package. Drain and immediately toss with tomato mixture. Brie should melt. Mix. Sprinkle with parmesan. Add more salt to taste. Serve at room temperature. Serves 6-8.

Note: Freeze Brie for 20 minutes to remove the rind easily.

Gourmet Our Way (Oklahoma)

Kentucky Ambrosia Salad

"Mother used to fix ambrosia for our family in Texas. And in my new home here in Kentucky, ambrosia is a favorite dish with dinner or afterwards as a dessert. It's yummy! The more you add, the more you can serve. The coconut makes it! Use a big clear glass salad bowl."—Phyllis George Brown—Former First Lady of Kentucky and Miss America 1971

1 cup mandarin oranges, drained
  (tangerines can be used, also)
1 cup pineapple tidbits, drained
3 bananas, sliced
1 cup sour cream

1 tablespoon mayonnaise
1 cup flaked coconut
1 cup miniature marshmallows
Maraschino cherries, if desired

Any combination of fresh fruit can be used. Combine fruits. Mix sour cream and mayonnaise. Fold in fruit. Add coconut and marshmallows. Garnish with cherries.

The Crowning Recipes of Kentucky (Kentucky)

Fantastic Fruit Salad With Banana Sauce

1½ cups watermelon balls
10 slices of cantaloupe
10 slices of honeydew

10 grapefruit sections
20 orange sections
1½ cups fresh strawberries

Mound watermelon balls in center of platter. Arrange remaining fruit around the center like rays of sun. Serve with Banana Sauce.

BANANA SAUCE:
2½ ripe bananas
2 tablespoons lemon juice
¼ cup brown sugar

¼ cup honey
1 cup heavy cream, whipped

Combine bananas, lemon juice, sugar, and honey in blender and blend till smooth. Fold in whipped cream. Serves: 6-8.

Juicy Miss Lucy Cookbook (Florida)

★★★★★★★★★★★★   ★★★★★★★★★★★★

Mild Tomato Aspic Salad

1 small package lemon Jell-O
¾ cup boiling water
1 cup tomato juice
1 teaspoon lemon juice
1 cup finely chopped celery

1 cup finely chopped green pepper
½ cup sliced stuffed olives
Mayonnaise and hard-cooked egg
 slices for garnish

Dissolve the Jell-O in the boiling water, add juices. Refrigerate until mixture begins to thicken, then add remaining ingredients. Pour into mold or pan. Chill until set. Garnish with egg slices and dabs of mayonnaise.

Variation: For luncheon salad, add 1½ cups cleaned, cooked small shrimp (or two 4½-ounce cans).

The American Gothic Cookbook (Iowa)

Orange-Almond Salad

The best!

DRESSING:
½ teaspoon salt
Dash of pepper
2 tablespoons sugar

2 tablespoons red wine vinegar
¼ cup oil
1 tablespoon parsley, chopped

Combine all ingredients in blender and then refrigerate. Shake well before using.

SALAD:
¼ cup sliced almonds
4 teaspoons sugar
¼ head iceberg lettuce
¼ head romaine
1 cup celery, chopped
2 green onions, thinly sliced

½ cup green olives
1 cup artichoke hearts
½ cup fresh mushrooms, sliced
1 can cocktail baby corn
1 (8-ounce) can mandarin oranges,
 drained

In small saucepan, cook almonds and sugar over low heat. Stir constantly until sugar is melted and almonds are coated, about 3 minutes. When sugar is liquid, pour onto waxed paper. Cool and break apart, as for brittle. This can be done one day ahead. Store at room temperature.

 Tear lettuce and romaine into bite-sized pieces. Place greens, celery, onions, green olives, artichoke hearts, mushrooms, and baby corn in large bowl. Pour dressing on about 5-10 minutes before serving. Arrange in serving bowl or individual salad dishes. Garnish with mandarin oranges and almonds.

Generation to Generation (Ohio)

Spinach and Strawberries with Poppy Seed Dressing

⅓ cup raspberry vinegar
1 teaspoon salt
½ cup sugar
1 teaspoon dry mustard
1½ tablespoons minced onion
1 cup vegetable oil

1½ tablespoons poppy seeds
1-2 pounds spinach, washed and torn
1 pint strawberries, sliced
½ cup pecan halves

Put vinegar, salt, sugar, mustard, and onion in blender. Blend slowly. Add oil. When thick, add poppy seeds. Just before serving, toss spinach, strawberries, and pecans with dressing.

Woman's National Farm and Garden Association—
Rochester Cookbook II (Michigan)

Caesar Salad

2 heads romaine lettuce, washed and dried
½ cup parmesan cheese

1 can anchovies
Croutons

DRESSING:
1 coddled egg (boiled 1½ minutes)
⅓ cup olive oil
¼ cup salad oil
Juice of 1 lemon

1 tablespoon Worcestershire sauce
2 garlic cloves, pressed
½ teaspoon mustard powder
Salt and pepper, to taste

In a large salad bowl, tear lettuce into bite-size pieces. Combine all ingredients for dressing, beat well and pour over salad. Sprinkle with parmesan cheese and toss. Add cut-up anchovies and croutons, and toss again lightly. Serve immediately. Serves 8-10.

C-U in the Kitchen (Illinois)

★★★★★★★★★★★★   ★★★★★★★★★★★★

Ranch Dressing

Cowboys were never known for their love of fresh greens. Some clever cookie invented this sensational dressing made with those cowboy favorites, buttermilk and mayonnaise (both used with a heavy hand in modern ranch cooking), and cowboys have been asking for seconds of salad ever since.

¾ cup mayonnaise
¼ cup buttermilk
⅓ cup minced celery with leaves
2 tablespoons chopped fresh parsley
1 tablespoon grated onion (1 small
  onion)

1 clove garlic, crushed through a
  press
¼ teaspoon dried thyme
¼ teaspoon celery seed
¼ teaspoon salt
⅛ teaspoon freshly ground pepper

In a medium bowl, combine all the ingredients. Cover and refrigerate until ready to use, up to 5 days. Makes about 1½ cups.

Variation: Cucumber Ranch Dressing: Peel a medium cucumber. Cut in half lengthwise and scoop out the seeds with the tip of a spoon. Grate on the large holes of a cheese grater. A handful at a time, squeeze out the excess liquid from the grated cucumber. Stir the grated cucumber into the prepared ranch dressing.

National Cowboy Hall of Fame Chuck Wagon Cookbook (Oklahoma)

Sensation Salad Dressing

Outstanding over mixed greens and fresh parsley.

6 tablespoons Romano cheese,
  grated
2 tablespoons bleu cheese,
  grated
2 cloves garlic, pressed

Juice of 1 lemon, more if desired
⅓ cup olive oil
⅔ cup vegetable oil
¼ teaspoon black pepper
½ teaspoon salt

Grate cheeses and mix together. Set aside. Combine remaining ingredients. For each individual serving of tossed green salad, sprinkle with 1 tablespoon of the mixed cheeses and 3 tablespoons dressing.

Hint: Freeze bleu cheese to grate.

'Tiger Bait' Recipes (Louisiana)

J&J's Basil Cream Dressing

Whenever possible, use fresh basil for this dressing. Dried basil works well, but is not nearly as pungent and aromatic.

1 clove garlic, minced
2 tablespoons chopped parsley
¼ cup white wine vinegar
2 tablespoons Dijon mustard
1 egg
⅔ cup vegetable oil

4-6 tablespoons fresh minced basil
　or 3-4 tablespoons dried
Dash of sugar
Salt and freshly ground pepper to
　taste

Place garlic, parsley, vinegar, mustard, and the egg into the bowl of a food processor. Mix well. With the processor running, add the vegetable oil in a slow, steady stream and process until smooth and thickened.

Stop the machine for a minute to add the basil, sugar, salt, and pepper. Process briefly until blended. Taste and correct the seasonings as needed. To serve, spoon over a mixed garden salad and enjoy! Makes 1 cup.

Recipes From a New England Inn (New England)

No-Yolk Mayonnaise

2 large egg whites
1 teaspoon Dijon mustard
⅛ teaspoon sugar
¼ teaspoon salt

¼ teaspoon pepper
¾ cup corn oil
1 tablespoon fresh lemon juice
1 teaspoon white wine vinegar

In blender, blend egg whites, mustard, sugar, salt, and pepper at slow speed for 1 minute. With motor running, add oil in a thin stream, then turn motor off. Add lemon juice and vinegar. Blend mixture until it is combined. Makes about 1 cup.

Cooking to Your Heart's Content (Arkansas)

★ **Editor's Extra:** Okay to use egg substitute in either of the above recipes. Works just fine.

★★★★★★★★★★★   ★★★★★★★★★★★

Butter Churn Croutons

Children love these—a good way to introduce them to salads is to include these.

6 slices stale bread   **Dashes of seasoned salt, garlic salt,**
4 tablespoons butter   **red pepper, and lemon pepper**

Cube bread. Melt butter in large skillet. Add seasonings, then add bread cubes all at once and stir to coat evenly. Spread on cookie sheet and bake 10 minutes in 325° oven, then turn it off and leave in the oven for several hours.

A Salad A Day (Mississippi)

Over 8,000 years old, The Natchez Trace was originally a Chicksaw Indian trail through Central Mississippi. It was extended, improved, and made a U.S. mail route by 1801. Its 500 inns and trading posts became deserted after steamboats came into use and it fell into disrepair. Today it is a national parkway, lush with unobstructed, natural scenic beauty, and extends from Natchez, Mississippi, to Nashville, Tennessee.

Vegetables

In the heart of North America lies one of the world's greatest rivers, the Mighty Mississippi. Shown here at Vicksburg, "The Big Muddy" is 2,350 miles long and includes tributaries from 32 states.

★★★★★★★★★★★★ ★★★★★★★★★★★★

Old Settler's Baked Beans

½ pound ground beef
¼ pound bacon, cut up
1 small onion, chopped
1 can red kidney beans
1 can pork and beans
1 can butter beans

½ cup brown sugar
½ cup white sugar
¼ cup catsup
½ teaspoon mustard (not dry)
2 tablespoons molasses

Brown beef, bacon, and onion. Mix all ingredients and put in casserole dish. Heat uncovered one hour or more, as desired, at 350°. Can be made ahead of time.

Renaissance Cuisine (Michigan)

Bean Chalupa

Great after a football game or day of Christmas shopping.

1 pound pinto beans
3 pounds pork roast
7 cups water
½ cup chopped onion
2 cloves garlic, minced
1 tablespoon salt
2 tablespoons chili powder

1 tablespoon cumin
1 teaspoon oregano
1 (4-ounce) can chopped green
    chilies
1 (2-ounce) jar pimientos, diced
Frito corn chips

TOPPINGS:
Shredded Cheddar cheese
Diced avocado
Sliced green onions

Diced tomatoes
Hot sauce

Place uncooked beans, roast, water, onion, garlic, seasonings, chilies, and pimientos in a heavy kettle. Cover and simmer on top of the range about 5 hours or until roast is fork-tender. Remove roast and break up with a fork. Return meat to the pot and continue to cook until mixture thickens, about ½ hour.

Place a handful of corn chips in a soup bowl or mug. Serve meat mixture over the chips. Garnish individually to taste. Serves 8-10.

Jubilee (Illinois)

On Mardi Gras Day in 1699, Pierre le Moyne, Sieur d'Iberville, founded a military outpost named Point Mardi Gras at the mouth of the Mississippi River. The state of Louisiana has been celebrating Mardi Gras ever since. The statewide party begins on January 6th, the Twelfth Night Feast of the Epiphany, and ends on "Fat Tuesday" (Mardi Gras Day), 46 days before Easter.

★ ★ ★ ★ ★ ★ ★ ★ ★ ★ ★ ★   ★ ★ ★ ★ ★ ★ ★ ★ ★ ★ ★ ★

Lundi Red Beans and Rice

When it's Monday in New Orleans, it's time for red beans and rice. So good, so good for you . . .

1 pound dry red beans	**2 cloves garlic, minced**
8 cups water	**2 bay leaves**
1 meaty ham bone or ham hocks	**Few shakes Tabasco sauce**
2 onions, chopped	**Salt and pepper to taste**

Place all in a big heavy pot. When it comes to a boil, lower heat and let it simmer, stirring occasionally, for at least 3 hours, but longer is fine. When they are soft enough, mash some of the beans against the side of the pot—makes for a wonderfully creamy sauce to serve over hot fluffy rice. Serves 6-8.

The Little New Orleans Cookbook (Louisiana II)

★ **Gwen's Extra:** Soaking the beans overnight cuts cooking time in half. The seasoning meat varies; my Aunt Tiel wouldn't dream of making red beans without pickled pork, Ma Mère insisted on ham hocks, and my daddy liked hot sausage in his. But the real New Orleans secret is the ham bone marrow. Crack the bone to release that wonderful full-bodied flavor and creamy texture. A tradition that is still alive and well today, red beans and rice has always been cooked on Monday with the bone left over from Sunday's ham. Before washing machines, that fit in quite well with the all-day chore of Monday washing. (Lundi is French for Monday; Mardi is Tuesday—bet you knew that.)

Sweet and Tangy Beans

Not every good bean recipe starts with dried beans. In this one, canned pintos get dressed up with barbecue sauce, apples, and raisins. They make a perfect pairing with baked ham.

3 strips bacon
1 medium apple, peeled, cored, and
   cut into ½-inch pieces
1 medium onion, finely chopped
1 cup golden raisins

1 cup prepared barbecue sauce
¾ cup packed light brown sugar
3 (16-ounce) cans pinto beans,
   drained

Preheat oven to 350°. Rub the inside of a 2-quart round flameproof casserole with one of the bacon strips to lightly grease, and place the bacon strip in the bottom of the casserole. Cut the remaining 2 bacon strips into 1-inch pieces.

In a large bowl, stir the apple, onion, raisins, barbecue sauce, and sugar until well combined. Stir in the beans. Transfer to the prepared casserole. Top with the bacon pieces.

Cover and bake 30 minutes. Uncover and continue baking until bubbling throughout and the bacon is browned, about 30 more minutes. Serve the beans hot. Makes 4-6 servings.

National Cowboy Hall of Fame Chuck Wagon Cookbook (Oklahoma)

Barbecued Green Beans

A real crowd-pleaser. Kids love 'em!

6 slices bacon, diced
1 onion, chopped
4 (1-pound) cans cut green beans,
   drained (fresh do not work well)

1 cup firmly packed brown sugar
1 cup catsup

Preheat oven to 250°. Cook bacon and onion together in medium-size skillet over medium heat until bacon is crisp. Remove with slotted spoon and place in ungreased 2-quart baking dish. Add green beans.

Mix brown sugar and catsup in medium-size bowl. Fold into green beans. Bake, covered, at 250° for 3 hours. Serves 6-8.

Winners (Indiana)

★★★★★★★★★★★   ★★★★★★★★★★★

Pennsylvania Dutch Green Beans

3 strips bacon, cooked and crumbled
1 small onion, sliced
1 can water chestnuts, sliced
1 (1-pound) can cut green beans
2 teaspoons cornstarch

¼ teaspoon salt
¼ teaspoon dry mustard
1 tablespoon brown sugar
1 tablespoon vinegar

Brown onion and water chestnuts slightly in hot bacon fat. Drain beans, saving ½ cup liquid. Mix liquid with remaining ingredients and add to onion in skillet. Cook, stirring until mixture boils. Add beans and heat thoroughly. Serve garnished with crumbled bacon. Four servings.

Bountiful Harvest Cookbook (Pennsylvania)

Swiss String Beans

3 (10-ounce) packages frozen French-
   style string beans
3 tablespoons butter or margarine
4 tablespoons onion, chopped
2 tablespoons all-purpose flour
2 teaspoons sugar

1 teaspoon salt
1 pint sour cream (16 ounces)
6 ounces Swiss cheese, grated
1 small package slivered almonds
   (optional)

Cook string beans according to package directions. Drain. Make a cream sauce by melting butter over low heat and adding onion, flour, sugar, salt, and sour cream. In a 2½-quart casserole, layer beans, sauce, cheese, and almonds. Repeat layers. Bake at 350° for 25 minutes. Serves 8-10.

Stir Crazy! (South Carolina)

Hominy Cheese Casserole

2 cans yellow or white
  hominy
1 can mushroom soup

½ - 1 can Ro-tel tomatoes
1 cup grated Cheddar cheese
1 cup crushed corn chips

Mix all ingredients except corn chips. Put in 2-quart casserole dish and cover with corn chips. Bake for 35 minutes at 350°.

Mrs. Noah's Survival Guide (New Mexico)

Easy Corn on the Cob

For cooking small batches of corn on the cob, no method is easier than microwaving, and it allows the corn to retain its flavor and crispness. Plan on 2-3 minutes for each ear of corn—less time if corn is very tender, a little more if it's not as fresh. As Iowans will tell you, it's important to get the corn from the field to the table as quickly as possible. Also, buy corn still in the husks, because the husks help retain flavor and freshness.

2 large ears of corn, husks and
  silks removed

1 teaspoon water

Place the corn in a microwave-safe dish. Add water and cover with waxed paper or plastic film. Pierce the paper several times and microwave on HIGH for 5-6 minutes. Let stand in microwave for 1 minute to complete cooking. Remove waxed paper or plastic wrap carefully to prevent being scalded by the steam.

Variation: Many corn lovers believe that microwaving corn in the husks brings out more of the natural corn flavor. Just remove any outer husks that are wilted or soiled and follow the above instructions. The silks will pull away easily after cooking. Serves 2. Contains 0 grams of fat per serving.

New Tastes of Iowa (Iowa)

★★★★★★★★★★★ ★★★★★★★★★★★★

Tennessee Fried Corn

Cream-style fresh roastin' ears, not really fried, but so called by most middle Tennesseans.

2 cups (6-8 ears) fresh corn
5 tablespoons butter and bacon
  drippings, mixed
1 teaspoon sugar

Salt and pepper to taste
½ to ¾ cup water for each cup
  of corn

Select corn with full, round, milky kernels. Remove shucks and silks. Cut tips of kernels from ears of corn; scrape with edge of knife to remove all of milky portion remaining on cob. Heat fat in skillet. Add corn, seasonings, and water, stirring constantly for about 2 minutes to heat through. Lower heat and cook, stirring frequently, until corn is thickened and color almost transparent (about 15-20 minutes). Serves 4-6.

The Nashville Cookbook (Tennessee)

Crusty Corn Casserole

½ cup margarine, divided
1¼ cups fine cracker crumbs
¼ cup green pepper, chopped
¼ cup onion, finely chopped
1 tablespoon butter or margarine
2 tablespoons flour

1 cup milk
1 large can cream-style corn
½ teaspoon salt
½ teaspoon sugar
2 eggs or 4 yolks, beaten

Mix 7 tablespoons margarine and crumbs and press into deep-dish pie plate. Cook green pepper and onion in 1 tablespoon butter; add flour and cook until bubbly; blend in milk and cook until thickened. Stir some of the hot mixture into eggs, add to remaining hot mixture, stirring constantly. Add corn, salt, and sugar and mix thoroughly. Pour in pie shell and bake at 400° for 30 or 35 minutes or until set.

Into the Second Century (Mississippi)

Once known as the "Great American Desert," Nebraska has developed into a rich agricultural resource that helps feed the nation and the entire world. Nebraska's gold is its corn, hence the nickname "The Cornhusker State."

★★★★★★★★★★★★ ★★★★★★★★★★★★

Gourmet Potatoes

6 medium potatoes
2 cups shredded Cheddar cheese
¼ cup butter
1½ cups sour cream
Paprika

⅓ cup green onion, finely chopped
1 teaspoon salt
¼ teaspoon pepper
2 tablespoons butter

Cook potatoes in skins and cool. Peel and shred coarsely. In a saucepan over low heat, combine cheese and the ¼ cup butter; stir occasionally until almost melted. Remove from heat and blend in sour cream, onion, and seasonings. Fold in potatoes. Turn into a greased 2-quart casserole. Dot with 2 tablespoons butter and sprinkle with paprika. Bake uncovered in 350° oven for 30 minutes or until heated through. Serves 8.

Thank Heaven for Home Made Cooks (Oklahoma)

Ruth's Smashed Potato Bites

A perfect treat for unexpected guests because you can make them in advance, freeze them, and pop them in the oven when friends drop by.

1½ pounds potatoes, preferably red
2 slices bacon
1 small onion (¼ cup finely chopped)

1 cup crushed barbecue potato chips
¼ cup grated parmesan cheese
1 egg, beaten

Peel potatoes and cut in half. Boil until tender when pierced with a fork (about 20 minutes); drain. Preheat oven to 400°. Cook bacon in microwave until crisp; crumble into fine pieces. Finely chop onion. Mash potatoes with bacon and onion. Form into 1-inch balls. Combine cheese and chips. Roll balls in egg and then in cheese/chip mixture. Bake on cookie sheet 8-10 minutes, or until hot throughout. Makes 24-30.

Note: If you are in a hurry, use instant dry potato flakes to make the mashed potatoes. Try other potato chip flavors for variety.

Hall's Potato Harvest Cookbook (Great Plains)

★★★★★★★★★★★   ★★★★★★★★★★★

Potatoes Appleyard

7 good-sized potatoes
¼ pound butter
¼ pound mild Cheddar cheese,
  crumbled
1 large onion, minced

½ teaspoon pepper
1 teaspoon paprika
Salt to taste
½ cup milk
½ cup cream

Peel potatoes. Slice thin. Melt 2 tablespoons butter in a large iron frying pan. Put a layer of potatoes into pan. Dot with butter, sprinkle with cheese, onion, and seasonings. Repeat until you have 4 layers. Put extra butter on top layer. Now pour milk and cream into pan. The liquid should come up to the top layer but not cover it. It is somewhat difficult to give precise amounts of ingredients because size of potatoes and pans vary. If you're in doubt, be generous.

Bake all in a preheated 450° oven for 10 minutes. Reduce heat to 350° and bake 35-40 minutes longer. The potatoes should absorb all the liquid and be brown on top and a glazed brown underneath. Cut into pie-shaped wedges on a hot platter. If the pan is thoroughly buttered to begin with, the wedges will come out with no trouble. Serves 6.

Mrs. Appleyard's Family Kitchen (New England)

Creamy Grilled Potatoes

5 medium potatoes, peeled and
  thinly sliced
1 medium onion, sliced
6 tablespoons butter or margarine
½ cup Cheddar cheese, shredded

2 tablespoons parsley, minced
2 tablespoons Worcestershire sauce
Salt and pepper to taste
⅓ cup chicken broth
2 tablespoons bacon bits

Place sliced potatoes and onion on 18x22-inch piece of heavy-duty foil. Dot with butter. Sprinkle with cheese, parsley, Worcestershire sauce, salt and pepper. Fold up foil around potatoes; add chicken broth. Sprinkle with bacon bits. Seal edges tightly. Grill packet on covered grill over medium-hot briquets about 35 minutes or until potatoes are tender. Serves 6.

The Never Ending Season (Missouri)

Cattlemen's Club Twice-Baked Potatoes

5 large potatoes, scrubbed and
  baked
⅓ cup half-and-half
1 cup sour cream
3 tablespoons green onions or chives,
  minced
4 strips bacon, fried and crumbled
1 cup Cheddar cheese, grated

1½ to 2 teaspoons salt
½ teaspoon pepper
¼ teaspoon garlic salt
1 egg, beaten
⅓ cup butter
½ cup mushrooms, sliced and
  sautéed in butter

Bake potatoes for 1 hour at 350° until tender in center. Cut in half lengthwise. Scoop out potato carefully so as not to tear skins. Mash potatoes with mixer, add half-and-half and continue to beat until smooth. Add all other ingredients and mix well. Mixture should be somewhat softer than regular mashed potatoes to prevent drying out when baking again. Fill skin shells with mashed potato mixture and arrange on cookie sheet. Top each with extra grated cheese. Bake at 350° for 20 minutes. Great with steaks! Serves 8-10.

Kitchen Keepsakes (Colorado)

Delicious Company Potatoes

1 (2-pound) bag frozen hash browns
  (in cubes)
½ cup melted butter
1 can cream of chicken soup,
  undiluted

½ cup onion, finely chopped
10 ounces Cheddar cheese, grated
16 ounces sour cream

Combine all ingredients together. Spread evenly in 9x13-inch pan. Bake for 45 minutes in 350° oven. This dish works well for barbecue or brunch.

Variation: For topping combine ¼ cup melted butter and 2 cups crushed cornflakes. Spread over potato mixture. Yields at least 12 servings.

Florida Flavors (Florida)

★★★★★★★★★★★   ★★★★★★★★★★★★

Crusty New Potatoes

Wonderfully tender inside, and brown and crusty outside. Serve elegantly with chicken breasts or steak.

8 small new potatoes, preferably red
1/4 cup butter

1/2 teaspoon Lawry's or other seasoning salt
1 cup crushed cornflakes – *PANKO*

Preheat oven to 400°. Boil unpeeled potatoes (in salted water, if desired) until tender when pierced with a fork (about 20 minutes); drain and peel. Melt butter and add seasoning salt. Roll each potato in seasoned butter, then in crushed cornflakes; place in glass baking dish. Repeat with each potato. Bake potatoes 25 minutes. Serves 4.

Hall's Potato Harvest Cookbook (Great Plains)

Pennsylvania-Dutch Potato Pancakes

2 medium-size potatoes (about 12 ounces), peeled
1 tablespoon lemon juice
1/4 cup butter or margarine, melted
2 tablespoons all-purpose flour
1/4 cup finely chopped onion
1 tablespoon thinly sliced scallions

1 large egg, beaten
1/2 teaspoon salt
1/4 teaspoon black pepper
1/4 teaspoon baking powder
1 tablespoon vegetable oil
1 tablespoon butter or oleo

Using coarse side of grater, grate potatoes into large bowl. Toss with lemon juice to coat well. Let stand 5 minutes; drain well. Add melted butter, flour, onion, scallions, egg, salt, pepper, and baking powder to potatoes. Stir to mix well.

In 8-inch skillet over medium-high heat, heat 1 tablespoon each oil and butter. Working in batches of 3-4 pancakes, add potato mix in heaping tablespoons to skillet. Using tines of fork, flatten each portion into very thin round pancakes, about 2 1/2 inches each. Cook 3-4 minutes on each side until golden brown. Drain on paper towels. Makes 16 pancakes.

Birthright Sampler (Pennsylvania)

Devonshire Potato and Mushroom Pie

Delicious.

3 cups cooked mashed potatoes
  (seasoned to taste)
1½ cups sliced fresh mushrooms
¼ cup chopped onion
2 tablespoons butter

1 teaspoon lemon juice
¼ teaspoon salt
Dash black pepper
½ cup dairy sour cream

Place a layer of half the mashed potatoes in a buttered 9-inch pie pan. Sauté mushrooms and onion in butter. Add lemon juice, salt and pepper. Mix well. Spoon over potato layer. Spread sour cream over mushrooms and onion layer. Top with remaining half of mashed potatoes. Bake at 350° for 45 minutes or until browned. If desired, paprika may be sprinkled on top for additional color. Serves 6.

Ferndale Friends Cook Book (Michigan)

Baked Sweet Potatoes and Apricots

Anyone with a "sweet tooth" will love this dish!

6 fresh medium sweet potatoes or
  2 large cans of sweet potatoes,
  drained
1 (17-ounce) can apricot halves in
  light syrup, cut into thirds
1½ tablespoons brown sugar

1 tablespoon cornstarch
¼ teaspoon salt
½ teaspoon cinnamon
⅓ cup golden raisins
¼ cup dry sherry
1 teaspoon grated orange peel

Cook fresh sweet potatoes in boiling water until tender, 30-35 minutes. Peel and halve potatoes lengthwise. Place in 9x13x2-inch baking dish.

Drain apricots, reserving syrup; add water to syrup, if necessary, to equal 1 cup of liquid and set aside. Arrange apricots over potatoes.

In saucepan, combine brown sugar, cornstarch, salt, and cinnamon. Stir in apricot syrup and raisins. Cook and stir over high heat until mixture comes to a boil. Stir in sherry and orange peel. Pour mixture over potatoes and fruit.

Bake, uncovered, in 350° oven, basting occasionally for 20 minutes or until well glazed. Serves 6.

Light Kitchen Choreography (Ohio)

Crunch-Topped Sweet Potato Casserole

2 (16-ounce) cans sweet potatoes,
  undrained
¼ cup melted butter
1 cup sugar

½ teaspoon salt
2 eggs, well beaten
½ cup milk
½ teaspoon vanilla

In a saucepan, heat undrained potatoes to the boiling point. Drain. Mash potatoes with butter. Add next 5 ingredients and blend well. Turn into a 9-inch square glass baking dish.

TOPPING:
1 cup firmly packed brown sugar
¼ cup butter
⅓ cup flour

2 teaspoons cinnamon
1 cup chopped nuts

In a saucepan, combine brown sugar, butter, flour, and cinnamon. Heat gently over medium heat. Remove from stove and stir in nuts. Spread over sweet potatoes. Bake at 350° for 40 minutes. Can be made ahead. Serves 10-12.

Nutbread and Nostalgia (Indiana)

Harvard Beets

1 tablespoon cornstarch
⅓ cup sugar
¼ cup water
¼ cup vinegar

½ teaspoon salt
2 cups diced boiled beets (or canned)
2 tablespoons melted butter

Mix cornstarch and sugar; add the water, vinegar, and salt, and bring to a boil, stirring until thick and smooth. Add beets and cook over slow fire 15 minutes. When ready to serve, add butter and bring to a boil. Serves 4.

Good Maine Food (New England)

Copper Penny Carrots

Easy to make and attractive to serve.

1 pound carrots, sliced and cooked
1 onion, chopped
1 green pepper, diced
1 can tomato soup, undiluted
¼ cup salad oil
¼ cup vinegar

¾ cup sugar
1 teaspoon Worcestershire sauce
1 teaspoon prepared mustard
Dash hot pepper sauce
Salt and pepper to taste

Prepare vegetables. In separate bowl, mix soup, oil, vinegar, sugar, and seasonings. Pour over vegetables and let stand in refrigerator overnight. Serve cold as a salad or as a hot vegetable.

Heart of the Home Recipes (Great Plains)

Carrots and Celery Au Beurre Tarragon

2 tablespoons corn oil
⅔ stick butter
6 medium carrots, cut in 2-inch
  lengths

3 medium ribs celery, split and cut
  in 2-inch lengths
2 teaspoons tarragon

Heat oil on medium heat in a large skillet or fry pan that can be covered. Add butter and melt. Place carrots in pot and cover. Cook on low heat for 15 minutes. Turn carrots during cooking to cook evenly. Add celery and tarragon and cook for 20 minutes. Gently turn carrots and celery during last 20 minutes of cooking, two times, to cook evenly. Serves 6-8.

Paul Naquin's French Collection II (Louisiana)

★★★★★★★★★★★★   ★★★★★★★★★★★★

Honey-Glazed Pineapple Carrots

3 cups cut, peeled carrots
½ cup water
½ cup brown sugar
2 tablespoons butter

1 tablespoon honey
⅓ cup crushed pineapple
Chopped chives or parsley for
   garnish

Cut the carrots into 2-inch strips. In a microwave-safe dish, combine the carrots and water. Microwave covered on HIGH for 4-6 minutes, until carrots are tender.

Add brown sugar, butter, honey, and pineapple. Mix well and microwave covered for an additional 2 minutes. Sprinkle with chopped chives or parsley as garnish. Makes 6 servings.

Recipes from Minnesota with Love (Minnesota)

Spinach Madeleine

Also delicious as a dip!

2 (10-ounce) packages frozen
   chopped spinach
4 tablespoons butter
2 tablespoons flour
2 tablespoons chopped onion
½ cup evaporated milk
½ cup vegetable liquor

½ teaspoon black pepper
¾ teaspoon celery salt
¾ teaspoon garlic salt
Salt to taste
1 (6-ounce) roll jalapeño cheese
1 teaspoon Worcestershire
Red pepper to taste

Cook spinach according to directions on package. Drain and reserve liquor. Melt butter in saucepan over low heat. Add flour, stirring until blended and smooth, but not brown. Add onion and cook until soft, but not brown. Add liquids slowly, stirring constantly to avoid lumps. Cook until smooth and thick; continue stirring. Add seasonings and cheese which has been cut into small pieces. Stir until melted. Combine with cooked spinach.

This may be served immediately or put into a casserole and topped with buttered bread crumbs. The flavor is improved if the latter is done and kept in refrigerator overnight. This may also be frozen. Serves 5-6.

To use as a dip, heat in a saucepan and put in chafing dish; serves 20.

Southern Secrets (Tennessee)

Spinach Casserole

This usually appeals even to "spinach-haters."

2 packages frozen chopped spinach
1 (8-ounce) package cream cheese
1 stick butter, divided in half

Salt and pepper (cayenne) to taste
1 cup Pepperidge Farm Herb
   Stuffing

Cook spinach according to directions on package. Drain and add softened cream cheese and ½ stick butter. Mix well and season in casserole; cover with herb stuffing to form a top crust. Pour on the remaining butter, melted. Bake in moderate (350°) oven 20-30 minutes, until thoroughly hot. Serves 6.

Old Mobile Recipes (Alabama)

Spinach Pie Superb

1 (10-ounce) package frozen chopped
   spinach
1 (3-ounce) package cream cheese,
   softened
1 cup shredded sharp Cheddar cheese
5 eggs, slightly beaten
½ teaspoon salt

¼ cup chopped green onion or
   1 tablespoon dehydrated onion
¼ cup chopped parsley or 1½
   teaspoons dehydrated parsley
1 (9-inch) pie shell, unbaked
1 tomato, thinly sliced
¼ cup grated parmesan cheese

Cook spinach according to directions on package. Drain well and squeeze to remove excess water; set aside. Combine cream cheese, Cheddar cheese, eggs, salt, onion, and parsley. Beat lightly with a fork. Stir in spinach and pour into pie shell. Arrange tomato slices on top and sprinkle with parmesan cheese. Bake at 450° for 35 minutes or until set.

Windsor Academy Cookbook (Georgia)

 The world's largest gold depository is at Fort Knox Military Reservation in Kentucky.

Spinach Stuffed Tomatoes

3 strips bacon
¼ cup chopped onion
½ pound fresh spinach, snipped
½ cup sour cream

4 medium tomatoes
Salt
½ cup shredded mozzarella
  cheese

Cook bacon until crisp; drain, reserving 2 tablespoons drippings. Crumble bacon and set aside. Cook onion in reserved drippings until tender; stir in spinach. Cook, covered, until tender, 3 to 5 minutes. Remove from heat; stir in sour cream and bacon. Cut tops from tomatoes; remove centers, leaving shells. Drain on paper towels. Salt shells, then fill with spinach mixture. Place in an 8x8-inch baking pan and bake for 20 to 25 minutes at 375°. Top with shredded cheese and bake for 2 to 3 minutes more, until cheese is melted.

Note: This is an elegant accompaniment, especially good with a beef entrée. Yields 4 servings.

Out of this World (Tennessee)

Spinach Soufflé

This soufflé is so easy to prepare. For spinach lovers who prefer a low cholesterol spinach soufflé, use egg beaters and low cholesterol cheese. I have prepared this recipe both ways. Believe me, you can't tell the difference.

20 ounces frozen chopped spinach
  (2 boxes)
2 pounds small curd creamed
  cottage cheese
¼ pound sharp Cheddar cheese,
  grated

¼ pound Swiss cheese, grated
6 eggs, beaten
6-7 tablespoons flour
¼ pound butter, melted
4 scallions, chopped and sauteed

Allow spinach to stand at room temperature to defrost completely (do not soak in water). Squeeze very dry and combine with remaining ingredients, mixing well. Pour into greased 9x13-inch baking dish. Bake in preheated 350° oven for one hour or until brown. Serve with a crisp tossed salad and crusty bread. Makes 6 servings.

Opaa! Greek Cooking Detroit Style (Michigan)

★ **Editor's Extra:** This is easy to halve and bake in a smaller baking dish to serve 3-4. It will take less time to bake, about 40 minutes.

★★★★★★★★★★★   ★★★★★★★★★★★

Broccoli Swiss Bake

Nice colors!

1½ cups summer squash
  (½-inch pieces)
3 cups fresh broccoli, cut
½ cup butter or margarine
1 egg, beaten
½ cup shredded Swiss cheese

¼ cup milk
¼ teaspoon dry mustard
1 teaspoon salt
Pepper and cayenne to taste
½ cup parmesan cheese
2 tablespoons toasted sesame seeds

Steam squash and broccoli so they are crisp-tender. Layer in casserole.
Melt butter and mix with egg, Swiss cheese, milk, and seasonings. Pour
over broccoli and squash. Top with parmesan cheese and sesame seeds.
Bake 20 minutes at 350°. Serve immediately.

With Hands & Heart Cookbook (Missouri)

Broccoli Soufflé Restaurateur

Very elegant.

¼ cup butter
¼ cup flour
½ cup whipping cream, scalded
½ cup rich chicken broth
3 egg yolks
1 teaspoon grated onion
1 teaspoon chopped parsley

1 teaspoon Worcestershire sauce
1 teaspoon finely chopped chives
Salt, pepper, nutmeg
1½ cups cooked chopped broccoli
⅓ cup grated Cheddar cheese
4 egg whites, stiffly beaten

Melt butter; stir in flour. Gradually stir in scalded cream mixed with
chicken broth. Cook, stirring constantly, until mixture thickens.
Remove from heat. Beat egg yolks with onion, parsley, Worcestershire
sauce, and chives. Add salt, pepper, and nutmeg to taste. Stir a little hot
mixture into the egg yolks; combine with remainder. Add broccoli and
cheese. Fold in egg whites. Turn into 2-quart buttered soufflé dish.
Bake at 400° for 25 minutes. Makes 6 servings.

Soupçon II (Illinois)

Of more than 2,000 land engagements of the American Civil War, the Battle of
Gettysburg ranks supreme. Although the battle did not end the Civil War, it is
considered the turning point of the war. At Gettysburg, Pennsylvania, on July 1, 2, and 3,
1863, more men actually fought and died than in any other battle before or since on North
American soil.

★★★★★★★★★★★   ★★★★★★★★★★★

Onion Pie

CRUST:

1 cup saltine cracker crumbs   ¼ cup butter, melted

Mix together and press into a 9-inch pie pan. You may use regular pie crust if you prefer.

FILLING:

3 cups diced onions   1 teaspoon salt
¼ cup butter   ¼ teaspoon cayenne pepper
½ pound Swiss cheese, finely grated   3 eggs, beaten well
1 tablespoon flour   1 cup scalded milk

Sauté onions in butter slowly, stirring constantly until golden. Remove from fire; drain (if there is excess liquid) and put into pie shell. Combine cheese, flour, salt, and cayenne; stir in eggs and milk. Pour over onions and bake in a 350° oven for 40 minutes. Cut into small wedges and serve. Yields 8 or more servings.

May be used as a main dish if hungry men are not to be fed.

The Gulf Gourmet (Mississippi)

★★★★★★★★★★★   ★★★★★★★★★★★

Broccoli-Onion Deluxe

1 pound fresh broccoli or 2 (10-ounce)
   packages frozen broccoli
2 cups frozen small whole onions or
   2 medium onions, quartered
4 tablespoons butter
2 tablespoons all-purpose flour
1 cup milk

¼ teaspoon salt
Dash of pepper
1 (3-ounce) package cream cheese
2 ounces sharp Cheddar cheese,
   shredded (½ cup)
1 cup soft bread crumbs

Cook broccoli; drain. Cook onions; drain. In saucepan, melt 2 table-spoons butter; blend in flour, salt, and dash of pepper. Add milk; cook and stir until thick and bubbly. Reduce heat; blend in cream cheese until smooth.

   Place vegetables in a 1½-quart casserole. Pour sauce over and mix lightly. Top with cheese. Melt 2 tablespoons butter, toss with crumbs. Bake casserole about 30 minutes at 350°, then sprinkle crumbs around edge and continue baking uncovered until heated (about 20 minutes more). Serves 6.

Knollwood's Cooking (North Carolina)

★ **Editor's Extra:** Cook frozen broccoli per package instructions. Steam fresh broccoli and onions in small amount of water about 5 minutes, till al dente (crisp tender). I like to sauté the onions in a skillet with a tad of butter or spray.

Vegetables in Wisconsin Beer Batter

1⅓ cups flour
2 tablespoons parmesan cheese
1 tablespoon parsley
1 teaspoon salt
Dash garlic
1 (12-ounce) can Wisconsin beer, at
  room temperature and flat

2 eggs, separated
Green peppers, cauliflower, onion,
  artichoke hearts, zucchini, or
  broccoli, cut into bite-sized pieces
Oil for deep-frying

In a large bowl, combine flour, cheese, parsley, salt, and garlic. Stir in beer and egg yolks. Beat egg whites until stiff and fold into beer mixture. Dip vegetable pieces into batter. Heat oil to 375° and fry a few pieces of batter-dipped vegetables at a time in oil until golden. Drain on paper toweling. Serve immediately.

License to Cook Wisconsin Style (Wisconsin)

Crowd-Pleasing Casserole

2-3 cups yellow squash, sliced
  and cooked
1 onion, chopped (Vidalia preferred)
2 carrots, grated
1 egg, slightly beaten
½ stick butter, sliced
½ cup mayonnaise
1 tablespoon sugar

1 cup sharp Cheddar cheese,
  grated and divided
1 to 1½ cups Ritz crackers,
  crumbled and divided
Dash cayenne pepper
Salt and pepper
Oregano

Put well-drained, hot squash in large mixing bowl. Add onion, carrots, egg, butter, mayonnaise, sugar, half of cheese, and half of cracker crumbs. Season with cayenne pepper, salt, pepper, and oregano. Mix all ingredients well. Put into buttered 1½-quart casserole and top with remaining cheese and crumbs. Bake at 350° for 20 minutes.

Island Events Cookbook (South Carolina)

Holiday Squash

1 butternut squash (approximately
  2½ to 3 pounds)
¼ cup butter or margarine, melted
1 cup raisins
2 apples, finely chopped

¼ cup brown sugar
½ teaspoon grated nutmeg
½ teaspoon salt
½ cup piñon nuts

Cut squash in half. Scoop out seeds and add a small amount of water directly into each cavity. Wrap the squash halves with plastic wrap and cook in microwave until soft enough to scoop the squash out of the shell. Mash and mix the squash with the other ingredients. Spread out evenly in a lightly greased Pyrex square baking dish. Bake in a 325° oven for about 20 minutes. Serves 4-6.

Christmas in New Mexico Cook Book (New Mexico)

Pan-Roasted Vegetables

⅓ cup butter
½ teaspoon thyme leaves
¼ teaspoon salt
¼ teaspoon pepper

3 cups cauliflower flowerets
2 cups broccoli flowerets
2 cups carrots, cut into small strips
2 small onions, quartered

Preheat oven to 400°. Melt butter in 9x13-inch baking pan, in oven (5-6 minutes). Stir in thyme, salt, and pepper. Add remaining ingredients; toss to coat. Cover with foil, bake for 22-27 minutes or until vegetables are crisply tender.

Blissfield Preschool Cookbook (Michigan)

Zucchini Deluxe

6 large zucchini
1 cup fresh bread crumbs
¼ cup chopped onion
1 tomato, chopped
½ teaspoon salt

¼ teaspoon pepper
2 tablespoons margarine, melted
½ pound Cheddar cheese, grated
¼ cup milk

Wash and trim ends of zucchini. Cook, covered, in boiling salted water for 5-8 minutes. Drain. Cut in half lengthwise. Scoop out center of each. Chop up and combine with bread crumbs, onion, tomato, seasonings, and margarine. Toss lightly. Fill shells and place in dish. Heat cheese and milk in saucepan over low heat, stirring until sauce is smooth. Pour sauce over stuffed zucchini. Bake in 350° oven for 25-30 minutes. Serves 6-12.

In Good Taste (North Carolina)

Calabacitas

The Spanish settlers of Chimayó, following the example of the Pueblos, grew a good deal of squash, one of the few vegetables that flourished in the area. During the harvest season they feasted on this mélange of zucchini and yellow crookneck squash mixed with green chile and corn, drying the remainder of the summer squash crop for use during the winter months.

4 tablespoons oil, preferably
 corn or canola
4-6 medium zucchini, or a mix
 of zucchini and other summer
 squash, to yield approximately 5
 cups when sliced into bite-size
 chunks
1 medium white onion,
 chopped
2 cups corn, fresh or frozen

½ cup chopped, roasted green
 chile, preferably New Mexico
 green or Anaheim, fresh or
 frozen
3 tablespoons water, or more as
 needed
½ teaspoon salt (or to taste)
Grated mild Cheddar cheese,
 (optional) for garnish

In a large skillet, heat the oil, and add the squash and the onion. Sauté the vegetables over medium heat until they begin to wilt. Add the corn, green chile, water, and salt. Cook, covered, over low heat until tender, about 15-20 minutes. Another tablespoon or two of water can be added if the vegetables become dry. Remove from the heat and mix in the cheese, if desired. Serve immediately. Makes 6-8 side-dish or 4 main-dish servings.

The Rancho de Chimayó Cookbook (New Mexico)

Eggplant-Zucchini Parmigiana

1 medium eggplant, peeled, cut into
  ¼-inch slices (approximately 12)
1 tablespoon mayonnaise or
  sandwich spread
¼ cup Italian bread crumbs
1 cup low-fat cottage cheese
1 egg, slightly beaten

¼ teaspoon garlic salt
1 (8-ounce) can tomato sauce
2 tablespoons parmesan
1 cup grated mozzarella
2 small zucchini, cut in ⅛ -inch
  slices

Put peeled eggplant slices on cookie sheet. Spread with mayonnaise and crumbs. Bake in preheated 475° oven for 10 minutes.

Remove and turn oven to 375°. Mix cottage cheese, egg, and garlic salt. Layer in greased casserole all of eggplant, half of cottage cheese mixture, half of tomato sauce, half of parmesan, and mozzarella cheese. Top with zucchini and then layer the last half of the remaining ingredients. Bake uncovered at 375° for 30 minutes. Let stand for 5 minutes before cutting. Serves 6-8 .

Cookin' in the Spa (Arkansas)

Stuffed Baked Eggplant or Mirlitons

A Cajun specialty . . . c'est bon!

3 large mirlitons or medium-size
  eggplants
½ cup chopped onions
¼ cup bell pepper
¼ cup celery
1 tablespoon pimento

½ cup butter
1 cup cooked chopped shrimp
1 cup white crabmeat
Salt, pepper, garlic powder
½ cup bread crumbs
¼ cup chopped green onions

Cut eggplants in half and steam until tender. Cool, scoop out, and keep shells intact. Brown vegetables in melted butter. Add shrimp, crabmeat, and pulp of eggplant. Season well. Stir together and cook 10 minutes. Add bread crumbs and green onions. Add more melted butter, if too dry. Stuff shells of eggplant and place in baking dish. Sprinkle top with more bread crumbs. Bake at 350° until hot (about 15-20 minutes).

The Best of South Louisiana Cooking (Louisiana)

Sherried Hot Fruit

Enjoy!!!

1 (16-ounce) can pears
1 (16-ounce) can dark pitted cherries
1 (16-ounce) can pineapple chunks
4 bananas, sliced (more if desired)
1 (16-ounce) can peaches
½ cup (1 stick) butter, divided
½ cup brown sugar, divided

1 (2½-ounce) package slivered
  almonds, divided
½ (16-ounce) package macaroons,
  crumbled
¼ cup sherry or juice from canned
  fruit

Drain fruit and cut into bite-sized pieces. In a 3-quart casserole dish, layer fruit, dotting each layer with butter, a sprinkle of brown sugar, and almonds. Top with macaroons. Sprinkle with sherry or fruit juice. Bake at 350° for 20 minutes. Serves 10-12.

Recipes of Note for Entertaining (Minnesota)

Ye Olde Coffee Shop's Pineapple Delight

2 (14-ounce) cans chunk pineapple
6 tablespoons flour
1 cup sugar

2 cups grated sharp Cheddar cheese
Ritz crackers
1 stick margarine

Drain the pineapple. Stir together the flour and sugar, then stir in the pineapple chunks and grated cheese. Put mixture into a casserole and crumble Ritz crackers over the top. Melt the margarine and drizzle it over the crumbs. Bake at 375° for 25-30 minutes. This hot fruit makes a perfect accompaniment to baked ham or other baked meat. Serves 8.

Georgia's Historic Restaurants and their Recipes (Georgia)

Spiced Peaches

4 cups sugar
2 cups cider vinegar
1 cup water
1 tablespoon whole allspice

1 tablespoon whole cloves
4 (3-inch) sticks cinnamon
4 pounds (16 medium) peaches

Mix sugar, vinegar, and water in 5-quart pan. Tie allspice and cloves in cheesecloth. Put this and cinnamon into mixture. Cover and boil 5 minutes. Peel peaches; drop into boiling syrup a few at a time. Simmer until tender, about 5 minutes. Pack peaches in sterile jars. Cover with syrup. Seal. Yields 2 quarts.

A Taste of Georgia (Georgia)

Beet Jelly

This is different and delicious, also very colorful. Fun to have everyone guess what the ingredients are. Everyone wants this recipe!

4 cups strained beet juice*
½ cup fresh lemon juice
1 package Sure-Jell

6 cups sugar
1 small package raspberry Jell-O

Mix beet juice, lemon juice, and Sure-Jell in medium saucepan. Bring to a full boil. Add sugar and gelatin and boil hard for 10 minutes. Ladle into prepared jelly glasses and cover with ⅛ inch melted paraffin.

*Note: To make beet juice, scrub fresh beets and cover with boiling water. Boil until beets are tender. Remove beets and use the water they have been cooked in. Save beets to eat later. (You can have your beets and eat them, too!)

Mystic Mountain Memories (Colorado)

Pasta, Rice, Etc.

The spectacular Niagara Falls is 182 feet high with approximately 700,000 gallons of water flowing over it per second.

★★★★★★★★★★★★ ★★★★★★★★★★★★★

Spaghetti Pie

6 ounces spaghetti
2 tablespoons oleo
1/3 cup grated parmesan cheese
2 eggs, well beaten
1 cup cottage cheese
1 pound ground beef or bulk pork
  sausage
1/2 cup chopped onion

1/4 cup green peppers, chopped
1 (8-ounce) can tomatoes, cut up
6 ounces tomato paste
1 teaspoon sugar
1 teaspoon dried oregano, crushed
1/2 teaspoon garlic salt
1/2 cup shredded mozzarella cheese

Cook spaghetti according to directions and drain. (Should have about 3 cups cooked spaghetti.) Stir in oleo until melted. Stir in parmesan cheese and eggs. Form spaghetti mixture into a "crust" in a buttered 10-inch pie plate. Spread cottage cheese over the bottom of spaghetti crust.

In a skillet cook meat, onion, and green pepper until cooked. Drain off fat. Stir in undrained tomatoes, tomato paste, sugar, oregano, and garlic salt. Heat through. Add meat mixture over cottage cheese in "crust." Bake uncovered at 350° for 20 minutes. Add mozzarella cheese on top and bake for 5 minutes longer. Serves 6.

Amish Country Cookbook III (Indiana)

★ **Editor's Extra:** Both of these dishes are make-again favorites. Good to freeze, and great to take and bake elsewhere.

Supreme Beef Casserole

1 pound ground chuck
1 teaspoon shortening
1 (16-ounce) can tomatoes
1 (8-ounce) can tomato sauce
1 teaspoon salt
2 teaspoons sugar

2 garlic buds, crushed (or garlic salt)
1 (5-ounce) package egg noodles
1 (8-ounce) container sour cream
1 (3-ounce) package cream cheese
6 green onions, chopped
1 cup grated cheese

Brown beef in shortening and drain. Break up tomatoes and add to beef with tomato sauce, salt, sugar, and garlic. Simmer 20-25 minutes. Cook noodles and drain. Mix with sour cream, cream cheese, and chopped onions. Grease a 3-quart casserole. Put a small amount of meat sauce, layer of noodles, and grated cheese. Repeat and top with meat sauce. Bake at 350° for 35 minutes. May be frozen and reheated to serve. Serves 6-8.

Madison County Cookery (Mississippi)

Football Casserole

Keep one of these in the freezer for after the game.

1 pound ground beef
2 tablespoons shortening
1 medium onion, chopped
2 cups canned tomatoes
1 tablespoon catsup
1 tablespoon steak sauce
¼ cup chopped pepper (optional)

2 tablespoons chopped parsley
1 (5-ounce) package elbow macaroni
Salt and pepper to taste
1 can cream of mushroom (or
   chicken) soup
1 cup grated cheese

Brown beef in shortening. Add onion, tomatoes, catsup, steak sauce, green pepper, and parsley. Simmer 30 minutes. Cook macaroni according to directions on package. Drain. Combine macaroni and ground beef mixture in casserole. Season to taste. Gently spoon mushroom soup into mixture. Mix lightly. Sprinkle with grated cheese. Bake at 350° or until bubbling and brown.

When Dinnerbells Ring (Alabama)

Fettuccine Primavera

A modern updated recipe—wonderful with shrimp scampi.

1 cup broccoli florets
1 cup zucchini squash, sliced
½ cup chopped green pepper
½ cup chopped onion
½ teaspoon dried basil leaves
¾ cup margarine (1½ sticks)
2 fresh tomatoes, peeled and cut
   into wedges

½ cup mushrooms, sliced
1 teaspoon salt
1 (12-ounce) package fettuccine
   noodles
Parmesan cheese, grated

In skillet, over medium-high heat, sauté broccoli, zucchini, green pepper, onion, and basil in margarine until tender. Stir in tomatoes, mushrooms, and salt, and simmer 5-10 minutes. In the meantime, cook fettuccine as directed on label; drain. Toss vegetable mixture with hot fettuccine. Sprinkle with parmesan cheese. Serves 5.

Lasting Impressions (Georgia)

★★★★★★★★★★★★   ★★★★★★★★★★★★

Spaghetti Carbonara

1 (8-ounce) package spaghetti
½ stick butter
1 cup chopped ham or bacon
⅓ cup sliced onion
⅓ cup chopped green pepper

½ sliced mushrooms
Salt and pepper to taste
1 egg, beaten
½ cup half-and-half
½ cup parmesan cheese

Boil spaghetti in large pot of salted water. Drain. Melt butter and sauté ham, onion, green pepper, and mushrooms until tender. Add drained spaghetti. Salt and pepper to taste. Add egg beaten with cream. Toss in parmesan cheese and stir until heated through. Remove from heat and serve. Serves 4.

Magic (Alabama)

Fettuccine with Zucchini-Basil Sauce

1 zucchini, cut into ¼-inch slices
2 tablespoons olive oil
1 small onion, peeled and finely
    diced
2 medium cloves garlic, peeled
    and minced
¾ cup whipping cream
¾ cup slivered fresh basil (or
    ½ cup pesto)

2 tablespoons minced parsley
½ teaspoon salt
¼ teaspoon freshly ground
    pepper
8 ounces fettuccine noodles,
    cooked according to package
    directions
½ cup freshly grated
    parmesan cheese

Stack the zucchini slices, a few at a time, and cut into ¼-inch sticks. Set aside. Heat the olive oil in a heavy frying pan over medium-low heat; add the onion and garlic and sauté slowly for 5 minutes. Add the zucchini sticks; turn the heat up to medium and continue to sauté for 5 minutes. Add the whipping cream, basil, parsley, salt and pepper; turn the heat up to medium-high and slowly boil for 1-2 minutes. The sauce will have thickened at this point. Remove from heat. Drain the fettuccine through a colander and put back into the hot pan. Pour the sauce over the fettuccine; add the parmesan cheese and stir to coat the noodles. Serve the fettuccine immediately on warm plates. Serves 4.

A Fork in the Road (New Mexico)

★★★★★★★★★★★★ ★★★★★★★★★★★★★

Low Country Fettuccini

4 ounces fettuccini
1 tablespoon diced pimentos
¼ pound small bay scallops
¼ pound small shrimp, peeled
¼ pound crabmeat
½ teaspoon salt
½ teaspoon pepper

⅓ stick butter
Sherry or white wine to taste
   (optional)
Garlic-Dill Cream Sauce (see below)
½ cup frozen baby green peas
Fresh parsley to garnish

Cook the fettuccini according to directions on the box about the same time as starting the sauce. Start the seafood about 5 minutes before the sauce and fettuccini are done. The peas are best when lightly cooked. They may be placed in a wire mesh strainer or colander in the boiling fettuccini water the last minute or two.

Sauté the pimentos, scallops, shrimp, and crabmeat with the salt, pepper, and butter in skillet until almost done (2-3 minutes). Stir in sherry or wine and cook until just done (about a minute more). Stir in the cream sauce and the peas, and ladle over individual plates of fettuccini. Serve immediately. Serves 2-3.

GARLIC-DILL CREAM SAUCE:

⅓ stick butter
1 tablespoon self-rising flour
1 cup half-and-half

½ teaspoon sugar
½ teaspoon dill weed, dried
½ teaspoon garlic powder

Melt butter in top section of double boiler. Add flour and stir well. Cook 2 minutes, stirring often. Slowly stir in the half-and-half and add the sugar, dill, and garlic powder. Stir almost constantly as the sauce gradually thickens.

Southeastern Wildlife Cookbook (South Carolina)

★★★★★★★★★★★★   ★★★★★★★★★★★★

Seafood Supreme with Pasta

1 pound shrimp, cut up
½ cup butter, melted
2 cloves garlic, minced
½ teaspoon thyme
¼ teaspoon oregano
¾ teaspoon salt

½ teaspoon paprika
¼ teaspoon ground red pepper
⅛ teaspoon black pepper
1 pint whipping cream
¾ pound angel hair pasta or thin
   spaghetti

Marinate shrimp overnight in all of the above ingredients except whipping cream and pasta. Cook pasta. Get skillet hot and cook shrimp until barely pink; add cream and remove from stove. Pour over hot pasta. Pass parmesan cheese and freshly ground black pepper.

Hopewell's Hoosier Harvest II (Indiana)

Gourmet Chicken Spaghetti

3 pounds chicken
8 ounces thin spaghetti
8 tablespoons butter, divided
4 tablespoons flour
1 cup cream
1 cup chicken broth
1 cup mayonnaise
1 cup sour cream

1 cup parmesan cheese
⅛ cup lemon juice
⅓ cup white wine
½ teaspoon garlic powder
½ teaspoon cayenne
1 teaspoon dry mustard
1 teaspoon salt
8 ounces fresh mushrooms, sliced

Boil and bone chicken. Break spaghetti into thirds and boil in chicken stock. Make basic white sauce. Melt 4 tablespoons butter; add flour and cook until bubbly. Add cream and chicken broth, stirring and cooking until thickened. Add mayonnaise, sour cream, parmesan, lemon juice, wine, and seasonings. Sauté mushrooms in remaining butter. Place mushrooms, chicken, and spaghetti in flat 3-quart casserole. Add sauce and mix well. Sprinkle paprika and additional parmesan on top. Bake at 350° for 30-40 minutes. May be made ahead of time and frozen. Serves 8-10.

Lagniappe (Texas)

Pesto Chicken with Bow Tie Pasta

2 whole chicken breasts, boned,
  skinned
2 tablespoons olive oil
Garlic powder, salt, and pepper to
  taste

12 ounces uncooked bow tie pasta
8 ounces prepared pesto
½ cup grated parmesan cheese
½ cup grated Romano cheese

Rinse chicken and pat dry. Rub with olive oil; sprinkle with garlic pow-der, salt, and pepper. Place in baking dish. Bake at 350° for 20 minutes or until tender. Cut into bite-sized pieces. Cook pasta using package directions; drain. Toss with chicken, pesto, and cheeses in bowl. Yields 6 servings.

Approximately Per Serving: Cal 620; Prot 49g; Carbo 47g; Fiber 2g; T Fat 31g; 45% Calories from Fat; Chol 66mg; Sod 596mg.

Rhode Island Cooks (New England)

Lasagna Pie

1 (13-ounce) container small curd
  cottage cheese or ricotta
½ cup parmesan cheese
1 pound extra-lean ground beef
1 medium onion, chopped
1 green pepper, chopped
1 teaspoon dried oregano
½ teaspoon dried basil

1 (6-ounce) can tomato paste
1½ cups shredded mozzarella
  cheese, divided
Salt and pepper to taste
1 cup milk
⅔ cup packaged biscuit mix
2 eggs

Preheat oven to 400°. Lightly grease a 10-inch pie pan. Place the cot-tage cheese in a layer on the bottom, then top with parmesan cheese. Brown beef over low heat and add onion and green pepper, cooking until the onion is translucent. Add oregano, basil, tomato paste, ¾ cup of mozzarella, salt and pepper to taste. Spoon over the cheese layers in pie pan.

Beat milk, biscuit mix, and eggs until smooth (1 minute or so with hand beater). Pour into pie pan. Bake for about 30 minutes or until gold-en brown. Knife inserted halfway between center and edge will come out clean. Sprinkle with remaining mozzarella. Let stand for 5-10 min-utes before serving.

The Other Side of the House (Virginia)

★★★★★★★★★★★★   ★★★★★★★★★★★★

Vegetarian Lasagna

Superb!

8 ounces lasagna noodles
1 pound fresh (or frozen leaf) spinach
2 cups sliced fresh mushrooms
1 cup grated carrots
½ cup chopped onion
1 tablespoon cooking oil
1 (15-ounce) can tomato sauce
1 (6-ounce) can tomato paste

½ cup chopped ripe olives
1½ teaspoons oregano
2 cups (16 ounces) cream-style cottage cheese
16 ounces Monterey Jack cheese, sliced
Grated parmesan

Cook lasagna noodles in boiling unsalted water for 8-10 minutes, or until tender; drain. Rinse spinach; cook covered (no extra water) for 5 minutes, turning.

In saucepan cook sliced mushrooms, carrots, and onions in hot oil till tender, but not brown. Stir in tomato sauce, tomato paste, olives, and oregano. In greased 9x13x2-inch baking dish, layer half each of the noodles, cottage cheese, spinach, Jack cheese, and sauce mixture; repeat layers, reserving several cheese slices for top. Bake at 375° for 30 minutes. Let stand 10 minutes before serving. Pass the parmesan.

A Taste of Toronto–Ohio, That Is (Ohio)

Mexican Lasagna

2 pounds lean ground pork (beef may be substituted)
1 (16-ounce) can refried beans
2 teaspoons dried oregano
1 teaspoon cumin
1 teaspoon garlic powder
1 (8-ounce) package lasagna noodles, uncooked

2½ cups salsa
2½ cups water
1 (16-ounce) container sour cream
2 cups Monterey Jack cheese
½ cup chopped green onions
1 (2.2-ounce) can sliced black olives

Mix uncooked ground pork, beans, and seasonings. Line bottom of 9x13x2-inch pan with uncooked lasagna noodles, spread half of meat mixture over noodles, make another layer of noodles and spread remaining meat mixture; if you have noodles left over, layer them on top.

Mix salsa and water; pour over casserole and cover tightly. Bake at 350° for 1½ hours. Cover with sour cream and shredded cheese. Top with green onions and olives. Bake for 5 more minutes to melt cheese. Yields 12-14 servings.

Canyon Echoes (Texas II)

Linguini Pesto

1½ pounds linguini
2 eggs, beaten
3 tablespoons butter
¾ cup heavy cream
2 cups grated parmesan
1 tablespoon salt
2 cups sliced mushrooms

Cook linguini according to package. Rinse in very hot water and drain well. Combine linguini with eggs, butter, cream, cheese, salt, and mushrooms.

PESTO SAUCE:
½ cup butter
½ cup chopped fresh parsley
4 tablespoons basil
¼ teaspoon pepper
¾ cup olive oil
¾ cup sliced water chestnuts
2½ cloves garlic, crushed
½ teaspoon salt

Combine all ingredients and mix thoroughly. Toss with linguini and serve at once. Serves 8.

The Best of the Bushel (Virginia)

Cowboy Casserole

1½ pounds ground beef
4 tablespoons oil
2 stalks celery, cut into thin strips
1 slice green bell pepper
¾ cup chopped onion
1 cup uncooked rice
1 (28-ounce) can chopped tomatoes
2 teaspoons salt
2 teaspoons chili powder
½ teaspoon pepper
1 teaspoon Worcestershire sauce
Tabasco sauce to taste
1 cup chopped large black olives
8 ounces Monterey Jack cheese, sliced

Brown ground beef in 2 tablespoons oil in skillet; drain. Remove ground beef to 2-quart casserole. Add remaining 2 tablespoons oil, celery, green pepper, onion, and rice to skillet. Cook until rice is browned. Add undrained tomatoes, salt, chili powder, pepper, Worcestershire sauce, Tabasco sauce, and half the olives; mix well. Bring to a boil. Pour over ground beef. Bake, covered, at 325° for 1 hour. Layer remaining olives and cheese over baked layers. Broil for 5 minutes or until cheese is bubbly. Yields 8 servings.

Approx. Per Serving: Cal 487; Prot 26g; Carbo 26g; Fiber 3g; T Fat 33g; 59% Calories from Fat; Chol 82mg; Sod 1078mg.

Gatherings (Texas II)

★★★★★★★★★★★★   ★★★★★★★★★★★★

Chicken Broccoli Quiche

3 cups grated Cheddar cheese
1½ cups cooked chicken, diced
⅔ cup chopped onion
1 package frozen chopped broccoli,
   thawed and drained

1⅓ cups milk
3 eggs
¼ teaspoon pepper
¾ cup Bisquick

Mix 2 cups of the cheese, chicken, onion, and broccoli in 10-inch deep greased pie plate. Beat remaining ingredients except cheese with hand mixer until smooth. Pour over mixture in pie plate. Bake at 350° for 20-30 minutes or until knife inserted comes out clean. Top with remaining cup of cheese. Bake until melted, 1-2 minutes. Cool 5 minutes. Serves 6-8.

M.D. Anderson Volunteers Cooking for Fun (Texas II)

Yellow Shrimp Risotto

2 tablespoons butter
½ cup thinly sliced celery
1 cup sliced fresh mushrooms
½ cup sliced green onions with tops
1 clove garlic, pressed
½ cup white wine
1 tablespoon soy sauce

1 teaspoon salt
1 teaspoon white pepper
1 pound fresh shrimp, shelled,
   cleaned, and cut in half
1 pint sour cream
1 cup yellow rice

Melt butter in large skillet or wok. Add celery, mushrooms, onions, and garlic and sauté lightly. Add wine, soy sauce, salt, and pepper, and bring just to a boil. Add shrimp and stir until they all turn pink. Turn heat down and add sour cream. Cover and simmer 10 minutes. Serve over rice cooked according to package directions. Serves 4.

Please Don't Feed the Alligators (South Carolina)

Easy Rice Casserole

1 cup Uncle Ben's long grain rice
1 medium can sliced mushrooms
  (do not drain)

1 can French onion soup
1 can sliced water chestnuts, drained
⅔ stick butter

Mix all ingredients. Top with extra butter pats and bake uncovered for 1 hour at 350°.

Palate Pleasers (Tennessee)

Wild Rice Chicken Casserole

May be made ahead, frozen, thawed, and baked. Easy—tossed salad and hot bread—yum!

1 (6-ounce) package wild rice mix
1 (10¾-ounce) can condensed
  cream of chicken soup
4 cups cooked chicken, cubed
1 cup chopped celery
¼ cup chopped onions
1 (5-ounce) can water chestnuts,
  sliced

1 (4-ounce) can mushrooms,
  drained
3 tablespoons soy sauce
1 cup chicken broth
Topping

Cook rice according to package directions. Blend in soup and next 6 ingredients; mix gently. Add broth and mix. Spread in a 9x13x2-inch dish. Sprinkle with topping; bake at 350° for 1 hour.

TOPPING:
1½ cups seasoned stuffing mix   ½ cup butter or margarine, melted

Toss together and sprinkle on top of casserole. Serves 8.

Connecticut Cooks III (New England)

The eagle was chosen June 20, 1782, as the emblem of our country, because of its long life, great strength and majestic looks, and also because it was then believed to exist on this continent only. Its image is on the Great Seal of the United States, and on the backs of our gold coins, the silver dollar, the half dollar and the quarter. Americans watch them with pride as they soar majestically over the tops of lofty mountains and above the valleys, representing our country's boundless spirit of freedom.

Wild Rice

Great for before-hockey game party or after-ski party! May be made day before and refrigerated.

1 cup uncooked wild rice
2½ cups water
1½ teaspoons salt
4 tablespoons butter
5 tablespoons flour
1 cup chicken broth

1½ cups evaporated milk
2 cups cooked chicken, diced
¾ cup mushrooms, diced
¼ cup pimento, diced
½ cup green pepper, sliced
½ cup almonds, sliced

Cook rice with water and one teaspoon salt. Combine butter, flour, and chicken broth. Simmer over low heat until butter melts. Add milk, one teaspoon salt, chicken, mushrooms, pimiento, and green pepper. Mix. Add rice. Place in buttered casserole dish. Cover with almonds. Bate at 350, uncovered, 30-40 minutes. Makes a large casserole.

A Thyme For All Seasons (Minnesota)

Sausage and Rice Casserole

1 pound hot sausage, browned
  and drained
1 cup chopped celery
1 cup chopped onion
1 cup chopped bell pepper

1 cup rice, uncooked
1 (14½-ounce) can chicken broth,
  combined with water to yield
  2 cups liquid
Salt and pepper to taste

Combine all ingredients in a 2-quart casserole. Cover and bake at 325° for 1 hour. Serves 6. Two cups raw shrimp may be substituted for sausage.

Stir Crazy! (South Carolina)

According to legend, rice was introduced to America around 1694 when a ship bound for England was forced to stop in Charleston, South Carolina, for repairs. The ship's captain bartered for the costly repairs with a small portion of his cargo of rice. This inexpensive portion of a rather unexciting cargo was the beginning of the rice fields which were to line the swampy riverbanks from Charleston to Savannah, Georgia.

★★★★★★★★★★★★ ★★★★★★★★★★★★

Turkey Jambalaya

2 tablespoons salad oil
1 cup chopped green pepper
1 cup chopped onion
1 clove garlic, minced
2 teaspoons salt
Pepper to taste
2 teaspoons (or more)
  Worcestershire

¼ teaspoon thyme or marjoram,
  or both
3 cups water
1½ cups uncooked rice
1 to 2 cups cubed cooked turkey or
  chicken
1 to 2 cups cubed cooked ham
1 small can mushrooms

Heat oil and cook green pepper, onion, and garlic until tender. Stir in seasonings and water and simmer for 10 minutes. Mix in rice, turkey, and ham. Cook, covered, over low heat for 25 minutes or until rice is done. Add mushrooms with a little of their liquid. Cook about 5 minutes longer. Serves 6.

River Road Recipes I (Louisiana)

Chicken and Sausage Jambalaya

1 small fryer
1 rib celery with leaves
1 onion, halved
1 clove garlic
2 cups converted long grain rice
1 pound smoked sausage, sliced into
  ½-inch pieces
1 pound ham, cubed
½ stick butter
1 cup chopped yellow onion

¾ cup chopped green pepper
¼ cup chopped fresh parsley
2 cloves garlic, minced
1 (6-ounce) can tomato paste
1 large bay leaf
¼ teaspoon thyme
2 teaspoons salt
½ teaspoon pepper
¼ teaspoon Tabasco

In a large pot, cover chicken with water; add celery, onion, garlic; boil until tender, about 1 hour. Reserve stock. Remove meat from bones. In 5 cups stock, cook rice until all liquid is absorbed, about 25 minutes.

In a Dutch oven, fry sausage and ham until lightly browned, about 3-5 minutes. Remove meat. Add butter to pan and sauté onion, pepper, and parsley until tender, about 3 minutes. Add chicken, sausage, and ham; stir in garlic, tomato paste, bay leaf, thyme, salt, pepper, and Tabasco. Add rice and mix thoroughly. Cook over low heat 15 minutes, stirring frequently. Remove bay leaf and serve. Serves 8-10.

Jambalaya (Louisiana)

Chicago-Style Pizza

Chicago is famous for its wonderful, thick, gooey, deep-dish pizzas. The special method was developed by Uno's Pizzeria in the 1950s.

CRUST:

1 package dry yeast
1¼ cups warm water
1 tablespoon sugar
1½ teaspoons salt

¼ cup oil, divided
3 cups flour
2 tablespoons cornmeal

Dissolve yeast in water. Add sugar, salt, and 2 tablespoons oil. Stir in flour to make a soft dough. Turn out onto well-floured board. Knead about 3 minutes. Put in greased bowl; cover and let rise in warm place until doubled in bulk, about 1½ hours.

SAUCE AND TOPPING:

1 (28-ounce) can Italian pear
  tomatoes, well drained and
  chopped
1 tablespoon oregano
1 teaspoon sugar

1 pound mozzarella or Scamorza
  cheese, thinly sliced
1 pound mild Italian sausage,
  broken up, cooked, and drained
½ cup grated parmesan cheese

Combine tomatoes, oregano, and sugar. Set aside.

Brush a 14-inch deep-dish pizza pan with 2 tablespoons oil; sprinkle with cornmeal. Punch dough down; press in bottom of pan. Let rise about 30 minutes. Arrange cheese over dough. Place sausage over cheese. Spread with tomato sauce. Sprinkle with parmesan cheese. Place pizza in a 500° oven. Immediately reduce heat to 450° and bake 20-25 minutes or until cheese is melted and crust is golden. Makes 4 (2-slice) servings.

Soupçon II (Illinois)

Poultry

Launching of the Space Shuttle Discovery at Kennedy Space Center, near Cape Canaveral, Florida. This is where America got its start in space flight, and the site of many historic launches, including Mercury, Gemini and Apollo.

Country Fried Chicken

1½ cups all-purpose flour
1½ teaspoons salt
½ teaspoon pepper
1 (2-3 pound) broiler-fryer chicken,
  cut up

1 cup buttermilk
4 tablespoons lard
4 tablespoons butter

Put flour into flat dish or plate and mix in salt and pepper with fingers. Dip each piece of chicken in buttermilk and then dredge in flour mixture and set aside. Put lard and butter in heavy skillet and place on hot burner; heat until near smoking point, then quickly put in pieces of chicken and carefully brown on both sides, then reduce heat and cover with tight lid. Fry for about 20 minutes or until tender. Yields 4-6 servings.

More Than Moonshine: Appalachian Recipes and Recollections
(Kentucky)

Chicken and Dumplings

1 (3 to 4-pound) hen, cooked and
  deboned
2 cups flour
1 teaspoon salt
½ cup shortening

½ to 1 cup ice water
2 cups chicken broth
2 cups milk
½ cup butter
Salt and pepper to taste

Blend flour, salt, and shortening until mixture resembles corn meal. Slowly add cold water until it makes a dough. Roll dough thinly on a floured board and cut into strips. In a Dutch oven, add equal amounts of broth and milk. Add butter, salt and pepper. Bring to a slow boil, lower heat, and simmer. Add one strip of dough at a time to this liquid. Do not stir. Push down with a spoon. Cook for 15 minutes, then add meat carefully. Serves 8.

Hospitality (Texas)

Stir-Fry Chicken

2 whole boneless chicken breasts
3 tablespoons cornstarch
4 tablespoons soy sauce
1 stalk fresh broccoli
2 tablespoons peanut oil
1 small onion, thinly sliced,
  separated into rings

¼ pound mushrooms, sliced
2 cups fresh bean sprouts
1 (8-ounce) can water chestnuts,
  drained, sliced
1 cup chicken broth

Cut chicken into thin slices. In small bowl, combine cornstarch and soy sauce; stir in chicken; stir to coat; marinate 15 minutes. Cut off broccoli flowerets; thinly pare stalks; slice inner stalk into thin slices.

Heat oil in wok or deep skillet over high heat. Add chicken; stir-fry until browned; remove; set aside. Add broccoli and onion; stir-fry 2 minutes; add mushrooms, bean sprouts, water chestnuts, and chicken. Stir in broth; cover and cook gently 5 minutes or until vegetables are crisptender. Serve over hot rice.

Celebration (Arkansas)

Sweet 'n' Sour Sauce

½ cup pineapple juice
2 tablespoons lemon juice
1 tablespoon vinegar
2 tablespoons brown sugar
1 tablespoon soy sauce

1 tablespoon cornstarch
¼ teaspoon powdered ginger
¼ green pepper, chopped
1 (9-ounce) can pineapple tidbits,
  undrained

Combine all ingredients except undrained pineapple tidbits and green pepper in a blender. Blend until mixed. Pour mixture into saucepan and add peppers and pineapple. Cook over moderate heat until thick and clear. Serve over roast lean pork or poultry. Serves 6.

Amount per serving: Calories 74; Grams of fat .02; Cholesterol 0mg; Sodium 151mg; % of fat less than 1%

Eat To Your Heart's Content, Too! (Arkansas)

★ **Editor's Extra:** Buy a large can of pineapple so you'll have enough pineapple juice—serve the extra pineapple with your stir fry.

Chicken with Almonds and Water Chestnuts

2 tablespoons oil
1 pound raw chicken, boned
  and sliced
¼ cup split almonds
¼ teaspoon pepper
1 tablespoon water

½ cup fresh or canned sliced
  mushrooms
½ cup sliced water chestnuts
2 tablespoons soy sauce
1 tablespoon cornstarch
2 tablespoons water

In a wok, heat oil and add chicken, almonds, and pepper; stir-fry until the chicken is browned. Add one tablespoon water, mushrooms, water chestnuts, and soy sauce. Stir-fry. Cover, lower heat and simmer 4 minutes. Combine cornstarch and 2 tablespoons water. Add to chicken mixture. Cook and stir until sauce thickens. Serves 4. Can be served with rice or chow mein noodles.

Kitchen Keepsakes (Minnesota)

Chicken Florentine with Mushroom Sauce

½ cup minced onion
1 tablespoon margarine
2 (10-ounce) packages frozen
  chopped spinach, thawed and
  drained

1 cup (4 ounces) shredded Swiss
  cheese
½ teaspoon ground nutmeg
4 skinless, boneless chicken breast
  halves, pounded flat

Sauté onion in margarine. Remove from heat and add spinach, cheese, and nutmeg. Spoon spinach mixture into 4 mounds in lightly greased 9x13x2-inch baking dish. Place chicken piece over each mound. Bake at 350° for 20-30 minutes or until chicken is done.

MUSHROOM SAUCE:

2 cups sliced fresh mushrooms
1 tablespoon margarine
2 teaspoons lemon juice
1 cup chicken broth

1 cup milk
½ cup dry white wine
White pepper to taste

Sauté mushrooms in margarine until liquid evaporates. Add lemon juice, broth, milk, wine, and white pepper to mushrooms. Bring to a boil and cook until liquid is reduced by ⅔ and sauce is slightly thickened. Spoon ¼ of sauce over each serving. Serves 4.

Per Serving: Cal 540; Prot 47.6g; Carb 19.2g; Fat 29.5g; Chol 124mg; Sod 578 mg.

Changing Thymes (Texas II)

★★★★★★★★★★★★ ★★★★★★★★★★★★

Garden Chicken Pie

4 tablespoons butter
½ cup onions, finely chopped
6 tablespoons flour
2 teaspoons instant chicken bouillon
½ teaspoon salt
¼ teaspoon pepper
1½ cups half-and-half
½ cup water

4 cups cooked chicken, chopped
1 cup carrots, thinly sliced
1 (9-ounce) package frozen peas, thawed
1 (4-ounce) jar sliced mushrooms, drained
1 stick butter, melted
10 sheets phyllo pastry*

Preheat oven to 375°. Melt butter in a saucepan. Add onions and sauté until wilted. Blend in flour, chicken bouillon, salt, pepper, half-and-half, and water. Cook, stirring, until slightly thickened. Add chicken, carrots, peas, and mushrooms. Stir to combine. Remove from heat.

Brush baking dish lightly with melted butter. Layer 5 sheets of phyllo in baking dish, brushing each sheet with butter. Keep phyllo sheets that you are not working with under a damp cloth to keep from drying out. Spread chicken filling over pastry sheets. Layer remaining 5 sheets of phyllo over chicken, brushing each sheet with butter. Bake pie for 25-35 minutes or until golden. Serve. Makes 10-12 servings.

*If phyllo sheets are 14x18 inches, only use 5 sheets and cut each sheet in half.

Stirring Performances (North Carolina)

Texas Strudel

Plan to do this for a summer party. It can be done a day before and baked when ready for your guests.

6 green onions, finely chopped
2 tablespoons butter
4 cups chicken breast, cooked, cubed
½ teaspoon salt
¼ teaspoon pepper
2 tablespoons fresh parsley, chopped
2 teaspoons ground comino
1 teaspoon garlic, minced
2 eggs
1½ cups Monterey Jack cheese,
  shredded

2 cups chopped green chilies
½ cup black olives, halved
½ cup golden raisins
½ cup almonds, chopped
20 sheets filo pastry
½ cup butter, melted
Garnish: Sour cream and black
  olives; or fresh sprig of oregano or
  cilantro

Preheat oven to 400°. Sauté onions in butter until tender. In a bowl, combine the sautéed onions, chicken, salt, pepper, parsley, comino, and garlic. Stir in the eggs, cheese, chilies, olives, raisins, and almonds.

In a 9x13-inch baking dish, brush butter on the sides and the bottom. Cut filo pastry sheets in half widthwise. Begin by laying one piece of filo pastry flat in the dish. Brush melted butter onto the sheet. Repeat this process until 10 more layers have been buttered. Spoon the filling over the layers and spread evenly. Lay a sheet of filo pastry over the filling and brush with melted butter. Repeat this process until 10 more layers have been buttered, including the top layer. Cut into desired serving sizes before baking.

Bake for 35 minutes, or until the crust is golden brown. Garnish with a dollop of sour cream and a black olive, or with a fresh sprig of oregano or cilantro. Serves 8-10.

The Peach Tree Family Cookbook (Texas II)

★★★★★★★★★★★★   ★★★★★★★★★★★★

Chicken Stoltzfus® and Pastry Squares

Named for our friends Elam and Hannah Stoltzfus, this has become one of the trademarks of Groff's Farm Restaurant. It is like the pastry shells filled with chicken that were served to wedding guests at our family banquets, but are served like the Amish serve their "wedding chicken."

1 (5-pound) roasting chicken,
  cleaned, giblets removed
1½ quarts water
2 teaspoons salt
⅓ teaspoon pepper
Pinch of saffron
12 tablespoons butter

12 tablespoons flour
1 cup light cream or ½ cup each
  milk and evaporated milk
¼ cup finely chopped fresh or
  ⅛ cup dried parsley
Parsley for garnish
Pastry Squares

Put the chicken in a 6-quart kettle. Add the water, salt, pepper, and saffron and bring to a boil. Reduce the heat to medium and simmer, partially covered, for 1 hour. Remove the chicken and cool enough to debone. Strain the stock. Continue cooking to reduce the stock to 4 cups. Remove the skin and bones from the pieces. Melt the butter in the pot in which the chicken was cooked and mix in the flour. Cook over medium-low heat until golden and bubbling. Add the cups of chicken stock and cream, stirring constantly. Cook over medium-high heat until the sauce comes to a boil. Simmer until thickened and smooth. Reduce heat and add chicken pieces and chopped parsley. Serve hot over Pastry Squares.

PASTRY SQUARES:
These may be made beforehand. Store in an airtight container.

½ cup lard or vegetable shortening
½ cup butter
2 cups all-purpose flour

1 teaspoon salt
About ½ cup ice water

Cut the lard and butter into the flour and salt with a pastry blender, or mix by hand, until it forms crumbs. Sprinkle ice water over the crumbs with one hand while tossing them lightly with the other hand. Use only enough water to hold the dough together. Press the dough into a ball and put on a lightly floured surface. Divide into 2 or 3 parts. Roll each part ⅛ inch thick to fit an ungreased cookie sheet. On the cookie sheets, cut the dough into 1-inch squares with a pastry wheel or sharp knife. Bake in a preheated 350° oven for 12-15 minutes until lightly browned. Arrange pastry squares on a heated platter. Spoon the chicken on top. Garnish with fresh parsley.

Betty Groff's Up-Home Down-Home Cookbook (Pennsylvania)

Chicken Puffs

Easy to double, and can be made in advance.

2 cups cooked, cubed chicken
½ teaspoon salt
⅛ teaspoon pepper
3 ounces cream cheese, softened
2 tablespoons milk
1 tablespoon minced onion
1 tablespoon pimiento

1 (8-ounce) can Pillsbury Crescent
 Dinner Rolls
1 tablespoon butter, melted
¾ cup parmesan cheese or crushed
 seasoned croutons
½ (10¾-ounce) can cream of
 chicken or cream of celery soup

Blend first 7 ingredients. Separate rolls into 4 rectangles and seal perforations. Spoon ½ cup chicken mixture into center of each rectangle. Pull up corners and seal. Brush tops with melted butter. Dip in croutons or sprinkle with parmesan cheese. Bake at 350° on ungreased cookie sheet 20-25 minutes, or until golden brown. Heat soup, undiluted or thinned with a little milk, and spoon over top of each puff. Serves 4.

Note: You may substitute crabmeat, shrimp, tuna, or your favorite ground beef mixture for the chicken. You may also substitute a cream sauce for the soup.

Well Seasoned (Tennessee)

Hawaiian Chicken

1 (3-pound) broiler-fryer, cut up
1 teaspoon salt
1 cup flour
2 cups cooking oil

1 cup crushed pineapple
1 cup Kraft barbecue sauce
1 tablespoon cornstarch
½ teaspoon ground ginger

Wash and drain chicken, salt, and let stand about 1 hour. Put flour in plastic bag, drop in chicken pieces, 2 or 3 pieces at a time, shake well; continue until all chicken is floured. Heat cooking oil in heavy 10-inch frying pan. When oil is hot, add the chicken and brown lightly on both sides; cook only long enough to brown. Place browned chicken in a 8x12x2-inch casserole. Mix pineapple, barbecue sauce, cornstarch, and ginger. Spoon over browned chicken, cover tightly with foil, and bake at 350° for 1 hour. Remove foil and return to oven for 10 minutes. Serves 6.

Strictly For Boys (South Carolina)

Creamy Baked Chicken Breasts

8 chicken breast halves
8 slices Swiss cheese
1 can cream of chicken soup

1 cup herb seasoned croutons,
  crushed
¼ cup melted butter

Arrange chicken in a lightly greased baking dish. Top with cheese slices. Spread soup evenly over all and top with crushed croutons. Drizzle with melted butter. Bake uncovered 45-50 minutes in a 350° oven. Use the extra sauce to top your baked potatoes.

Heavenly Delights (Great Plains)

Golfer's Chicken

1 envelope Lipton's Dry Onion
  Soup Mix
1 (8-ounce) bottle red Russian
  dressing

1 (8-ounce) jar apricot jam
4 chicken quarters

Combine dry soup, Russian dressing, and jam. Mix well until there are no lumps. Wash chicken and pat dry. Slightly overlap in flat Pyrex dish. Spoon and spread 1 tablespoon (or more!) of sauce on each piece. Bake at 225° for 4-5 hours or however long your game takes. Be careful to place well below heating element if using an electric oven.

    This can be done in 1 hour at 375° if not playing golf. Sauce keeps in refrigerator for months. Yields 4 servings.

For Crying Out Loud...Let's Eat (Indiana)

★ **Editor's Extra:** Try this with peach preserves or orange marmalade. Also try substituting French or Thousand Island dressing. Great served with yellow rice.

★★★★★★★★★★★★   ★★★★★★★★★★★★★

Ozark Chicken Casserole

2 cups cooked diced chicken
1 cup cooked rice
1 tablespoon lemon juice
1 cup chopped celery
1 medium onion, chopped
½ cup mayonnaise

3 hard-boiled eggs, chopped
1 can cream of chicken soup
Salt and pepper to taste
½ stick butter, melted
2 cups Pepperidge Farm Herb-
  Seasoned Stuffing Mix

Combine chicken, rice, juice, celery, onion, mayonnaise, eggs, soup, and seasoning thoroughly and place in greased casserole. Mix butter and stuffing and sprinkle on top. Bake at 350° for about 30 minutes.

Talk About Good (Missouri)

Baked Chicken Breasts
(Microwave)

6 chicken breast halves, skinned
  and boned
1 cup dairy sour cream
2 tablespoons lemon juice
2 teaspoons Worcestershire sauce

½ teaspoon celery salt
1 teaspoon paprika
¼ teaspoon garlic powder
1½ teaspoons salt
¼ teaspoon red pepper

Rinse and dry 6 chicken breast halves with paper towels. In a 2-quart dish, combine sour cream, lemon juice, Worcestershire sauce, celery salt, paprika, garlic powder, salt and pepper. Add chicken to sour cream mixture, coating each piece well. Let stand, covered, in refrigerator overnight, or at least 8 hours.

1 cup seasoned bread crumbs   ¼ cup margarine

Carefully remove coated chicken from sour cream mixture. Roll in crumbs, coating evenly. Arrange single layer in an 8-inch square shallow baking dish. Micromelt margarine in a 1-cup measure on HIGH 1 minute and drizzle over chicken. Microwave on HIGH 10 minutes or until chicken is tender. Serves 4-6.

Tout de Suite à la Microwave II (Louisiana)

★ **Editor's Extra:** A superb dish even if you don't let it marinate a long time.

★★★★★★★★★★★  ★★★★★★★★★★★

Honey Pecan Chicken

HONEY CREAM SAUCE:

2 tablespoons butter
1 tablespoon minced shallots
1 cup fresh orange juice
¼ cup bourbon

1 cup whipping cream
2 tablespoons honey
1 tablespoon cider vinegar
Salt and pepper to taste

Heat butter in medium saucepan; add shallots and cook over low heat 3-4 minutes or until tender, but not brown. Add orange juice and bourbon, increase heat, and continue cooking until liquid is reduced to ½ cup. Add cream and reduce until slightly thickened. Add honey and vinegar and season with salt and pepper.

PECAN CHICKEN:

¼ cup all-purpose flour
1 teaspoon minced fresh thyme
¼ cup finely chopped pecans
Salt and pepper to taste

6 boneless, skinless chicken breast
  halves
Olive oil for sautéing

Mix flour, thyme, pecans, salt, and pepper. Dredge chicken breasts in flour mixture. Heat a small amount of oil in a large sauté pan; add chicken and sauté until golden brown. Pour sauce onto each plate and place chicken breast in center. Serve additional sauce separately. Serves 6.
Recipe by Chef Clyde R. Nelson, The Home Ranch, Clark, Colorado.

Cooking with Colorado's Greatest Chefs (Colorado)

★ **Editor's Extra:** If chicken breasts are thick and large, cover pan after sautéing for 10 minutes, then remove lid and sauté another 5 minutes or so.

Chicken in a Package

1 large chicken breast, halved,
  skinned, and boned
Salt and pepper to taste
Spicy mustard
2 small potatoes, thinly sliced

2 small onions, thinly sliced
2 carrots, cut into julienne strips
4-5 mushrooms, sliced
2 tablespoons butter
Paprika

Preheat oven to 350°. Sprinkle the chicken with salt and pepper. Spread each breast half lightly with mustard; set aside.

On a large square of heavy-duty foil, alternate slices from one potato and one onion so that they overlap slightly. Repeat with the remaining onion and potato on another square of foil. Sprinkle half of the carrot strips over one, the rest over the other. Divide the mushrooms between the pieces of foil. Cut the butter into bits and sprinkle over the vegetables. Lay a chicken breast half on each pile of vegetables. Sprinkle both liberally with paprika.

Seal the foil and lay the packets on a cookie sheet. Bake for 25-30 minutes, or until the chicken is done and vegetables are tender. Serve at once. Makes 2 servings.

Love Yourself Cookbook (North Carolina)

Route 66 Diner Philly Chicken

One of the specials at the Route 66 Diner in Tulsa is the Philly Chicken.

½ cup celery, chopped
½ cup onion, chopped
¼ medium green pepper, chopped
3 tablespoons vegetable oil
½ teaspoon tarragon
¼ teaspoon lemon pepper
2 cloves garlic, minced
1 pint heavy cream

1 (8-ounce) package cream cheese,
  softened
¾ cup milk
1 chicken, cooked, skinned, and
  deboned (approximately 3 cups
  diced)
¼ cup parmesan cheese
Wild rice or pasta

In a large saucepan, sauté the celery, onion, and pepper in vegetable oil. Add the tarragon, lemon pepper, and garlic. Cook until vegetables are tender. Add cream, cream cheese, milk, and chicken and heat to simmer, but do not boil. Sprinkle with parmesan cheese and serve over wild rice or pasta. Makes 6-8 servings.

The Route 66 Cookbook (Oklahoma)

King Ranch Chicken Casserole

The King Ranch may be the most famous spread in America, and this just might be the best-loved recipe in Texas; it was sent in with only slight variations by good cooks all over the state. How the dish earned its name, its only connection to the illustrious ranch, nobody knows.

1 (10¾-ounce) can cream of
   chicken soup
1 (10¾-ounce) can cream of
   mushroom soup
2 cups chicken broth
1 (10-ounce) can Ro-tel Tomatoes
   and Green Chilies

12 tortillas, cut in pieces
1 (3 to 4-pound) chicken, cooked and
   cut into bite-sized pieces
1 large onion, chopped
2 cups grated American cheese

Combine soups, chicken broth, and tomatoes and set aside. Oil a 3-quart casserole. Layer half of tortilla pieces, half of chicken, half of onion, and half of cheese in the casserole. Pour half of chicken broth mixture over layers. Repeat layers of tortillas, chicken and onion, then pour remaining chicken broth over top with remaining cheese. Bake at 350° for 45-60 minutes. This can be frozen and reheated and will still taste great. Serves 8.

Tastes & Tales from Texas...with Love (Texas)

 With over 823,000 acres, the King Ranch is the largest in the US and covers all or part of four Texas counties.

Party Chicken Pineapple Cakes

Elegant for a bridal luncheon. Pretty and delicious!

FILLING:

2 whole chicken breasts, cooked
  and cubed
2 stalks celery, chopped fine

2 hard-boiled eggs, chopped
Mayonnaise
Salt and pepper to taste

Mix chicken, celery and hard-boiled eggs; add enough mayonnaise to moisten, and salt and pepper to taste.

SANDWICH:

6 ounces cream cheese
2 tablespoons pineapple juice
20-24 slices white bread

Butter
10-14 pineapple slices (reserve
  juice)

Mix cream cheese with enough pineapple juice to make a smooth consistency.

To assemble cake: Cut two slices of bread, using pineapple can. Butter both pieces on one side. Layer in this order: One slice of bread, buttered side up, one slice pineapple, one scoop of chicken filling, and topped with a slice of bread with buttered side down. Frost top and side of sandwich with cream cheese mixture. Makes 10-12.

To make the night before: Place sandwiches on a tray, cover with plastic wrap and a damp tea towel, refrigerate, and frost the next day.

Angels and Friends Favorite Recipes II (Ohio)

★ **Editor's Extra:** Place a pineapple tidbit or two with mint leaves on top of each one . . . beautiful!

★★★★★★★★★★★ ★★★★★★★★★★★

Hot Chicken Salad

4 cups cooked, cut-up chicken
2 tablespoons lemon juice
¾ cup mayonnaise
1 teaspoon salt
2 cups chopped celery
4 hard-cooked eggs, sliced

¾ cup cream of chicken soup
1 teaspoon minced onion
1 tablespoon chopped pimento
1 cup shredded cheese
½ cup toasted slivered almonds
1 (3-ounce) can chow mein noodles

Combine all ingredients except cheese, almonds, and noodles in a large mixing bowl. Pour into a 9x13x2-inch pan. Top with cheese, almonds, and noodles. Refrigerate, covered, overnight. Bake at 350° for 30-35 minutes or until lightly browned and bubbly. Yields 8 large servings.

T.W. and Anna Elliott Family Receipts (Iowa)

Cheesy Chicken
(Microwave) - Bake 350° - 40 min.

¼ cup butter or margarine
¾ cup cornflake crumbs
⅓ cup grated parmesan cheese
2 tablespoons chopped chives

2 tablespoons chopped parsley
1 broiler-fryer chicken, 3 pounds,
    cut in serving pieces

Place butter in an 8-inch square microproof baking dish. Cook on MEDIUM power for 1½ minutes, or until butter is melted. Combine cornflake crumbs, cheese, chives, and parsley in a shallow dish. Dip pieces of chicken in butter and roll in crumb mixture. Place chicken pieces in an 8-inch square microproof baking dish, skin-side-up, with thickest pieces of chicken toward outside of dish. Cover with waxed paper and cook on HIGH for 15-17 minutes, or until chicken is tender. Let stand, covered, about 15 minutes before serving. Yields 4 servings.

Note: Arrange coated chicken with the most attractive side up. Rotate the dish AND the crumb-coated chicken during the microcooking, but do not turn chicken over; this helps keep the crumbs crisp.

Kitchen Sampler (Alabama)

★ **Editor's Extra:** This is such an easy recipe and a favorite with everybody. Do note that microcooking time is for 3 pounds of chicken. If you use less chicken, and/or boneless, skinless breasts, cut the cooking time, checking often as you rotate. Also just fine to bake in 350° oven about 40 minutes.

Parmesan Chicken

1 cup crushed herb-seasoned
  stuffing mix
⅔ cup grated Parmesan cheese
¼ cup chopped, fresh parsley

¾ cup butter
1 large clove garlic, crushed
1 (3-pound) frying chicken, cut up

Preheat oven to 375°. Mix crumbs, cheese, and parsley together in small bowl. Melt butter in small skillet. Add garlic while butter is melting, so flavors can blend. Dip chicken in butter. Roll in crumbs. Place in baking dish. Sprinkle remaining crumbs and butter over chicken. Bake at 375° for 45 minutes, or until chicken is done. May be refrigerated several hours before baking. Makes 4 servings.

Elsah Landing Heartland Cooking (Illinois)

Simply Southwest

This recipe takes less than 15 minutes to get to the table, is very low in fat, and tastes fantastic!

1 (14¼-ounce) can chicken broth
2¼ cups quick-cooking brown rice
2 teaspoons sunflower oil
1 medium onion, chopped
2 garlic cloves, minced
2 cups diced cooked turkey breast

2 cups (2 small) thinly sliced
  zucchini
1 medium red bell pepper, chopped
  (use the seeds)
1 teaspoon ground cumin
½ cup picante sauce

Bring broth to boil; add rice. Cover and simmer on lowest heat 8-10 minutes. While it simmers, sauté onion and garlic in the oil. Add remaining ingredients to the onion/garlic mixture, and cook for just a few minutes—just until the vegetables are tender-crisp. Serve the turkey mixture on top of the rice. Makes 4 large servings.

Note: This dish can be made extra hot and spicy by the kind of picante sauce you use. Green bell pepper can be substituted for red, but the red pepper makes this a beautiful dish, plus it ups the beta carotene a tremendous amount. Also, you can use leftover cooked chicken or turkey. I like to bake a small turkey just to have meat available for dishes like this.

Variation: Try thin carrot slices and bite-sized pieces of cauliflower. Be creative. Enjoy!

Per serving: Cal 345; Fat 7g; Sod 545mg; Fiber 4.5g.

15 Minute Storage Meals (Oklahoma)

★★★★★★★★★★★   ★★★★★★★★★★★★

Sour Cream Chicken Enchiladas

4 chicken breasts
1 onion, chopped
1 tablespoon margarine
1 (4-ounce) can chopped green
   chilies
2 (4-ounce) cans sliced mushrooms,
   drained
1¼ cups shredded Cheddar cheese
½ teaspoon garlic powder
½ teaspoon chili powder

1 cup sour cream
12 flour tortillas
¼ cup flour
¼ cup melted butter
1 cup shredded Monterey Jack
   cheese
1½ cups sour cream
Chili powder to taste
1½ cups shredded Monterey Jack
   cheese

Rinse chicken and pat dry. Cook in water to cover in saucepan until tender. Drain, reserving 1½ cups broth. Cool and chop chicken.

Sauté onion in margarine in skillet. Add chicken, green chilies, mushrooms, Cheddar cheese, garlic powder, ½ teaspoon chili powder, and 1 cup sour cream; mix well. Microwave tortillas on HIGH for 1 minute or until softened. Spoon chicken mixture onto tortillas. Roll to enclose filling. Place seam-side-down in greased 9x13-inch baking dish.

Blend flour into butter in saucepan. Stir in reserved broth. Cook until thickened and bubbly, stirring constantly. Stir in 1 cup Monterey Jack cheese, 1½ cups sour cream, and additional chili powder to taste. Pour over enchiladas. Bake at 350° for 30 minutes. Sprinkle with remaining 1½ cups Monterey Jack cheese. Bake just until cheese melts. Yields 6 servings.

Approx per serving: cal 1001; prot 44g; carbo 76g; fiber 5g; t fat 61g; chol 164 mg; sod 1168.

Texas Cookin' Lone Star Style (Texas II)

In ancient Anasazi legend that dates back to 200 AD, Kokopeli the flute player was the symbol of happiness and joy. A fertility god and a traveling prankster, he was credited for good health, pregnancies, plentiful crops, and the bringing of spring.

★★★★★★★★★★★   ★★★★★★★★★★★

Southwest Orange-Chile Chicken with Black Beans

2 tablespoons olive oil
1 whole chicken (3 to 4 pounds), skinned and cut into serving pieces
1 large purple onion, halved and thinly sliced
4 garlic cloves, minced
1½ cups freshly squeezed orange juice
¾ cup chicken stock
3 tablespoons hot chile sauce
1¾ cups cooked black beans with 2 tablespoons liquid
1 red bell pepper, cut into strips
1 tablespoon dark rum
Salt and pepper to taste
Chopped fresh cilantro

Heat oil in a large skillet over medium heat. Brown chicken on all sides in oil; remove to a plate lined with paper towels. Sauté onion in pan drippings until limp and slightly browned, about 8 minutes. Add garlic, and sauté one minute. Return chicken to skillet, and add orange juice, stock, and chile sauce. Cover and simmer over low heat 30 minutes. Add black beans and liquid and bell pepper strips. Simmer, uncovered, 30 minutes. Add rum, salt and pepper; simmer 15 minutes. Sprinkle with cilantro, and serve immediately. Makes 4-6 servings.

Savoring the Southwest Again (New Mexico)

Chicken Breasts Eden Isle

This is a recipe I devised when I was first preparing menus for the Inn. We wanted to stress Arkansas products where possible. It has stayed on the menu more than 20 years because of its popularity, and we still get requests for the recipe.

6 chicken breasts, halved, boned
  and skinned
Pepper to taste
6 slices bacon

1 package dried beef
2 cans cream of chicken soup
1½ cups sour cream
1 (8-ounce) package cream cheese

Pepper, do not salt chicken breasts. Wrap one slice bacon around each breast. Place layer of dried beef in bottom of baking dish. Place bacon-wrapped breasts in dish. Mix together chicken soup, sour cream, and cream cheese in mixer or food processor. Cover chicken breasts with mixture, and cover baking dish tightly with foil. Place in 325° oven for 2 hours. When tender, remove foil and let brown well. Serve on a bed of rice. Serves 6.

Feasts of Eden (Arkansas)

Microwave Chicken Kiev

Pat Swinney's micro-quick recipe for the working girl. Very impressive dish for those unexpected guests.

4 whole chicken breasts
1 cup cheese crackers, crushed
1½ tablespoons taco seasoning
  mix, dry
5 tablespoons butter, divided
3 tablespoons soft Cheddar cheese

2 teaspoons instant minced onion
1 teaspoon monosodium glutamate
  (optional)
2 tablespoons chopped green chilies
1 teaspoon salt

Skin, bone, and halve chicken breasts; pound flat. Set aside. Combine crackers and taco seasoning; set aside. Mix together 3 tablespoons butter, cheese, onion, MSG, green chilies, and salt. Divide butter mixture into 8 balls. Roll chicken breasts around each butter-cheese ball. Tuck in ends and fasten with a toothpick. Dip each chicken piece in remaining melted butter and roll in cheese-cracker/taco seasoning mix. Lay in casserole and cover with waxed paper. Microwave on HIGH for 10-12 minutes.

More Calf Fries to Caviar (Texas II)

Monterey Chicken

4 chicken breasts, skinned, boned, and halved
Salt and pepper
½ cup flour
½ cup butter, divided
½ cup chopped onion
1 clove garlic, minced
8 ounces mushrooms, chopped
2 tablespoons flour

1 teaspoon salt
½ teaspoon white pepper
½ cup chicken stock
½ cup white wine
1 avocado, mashed
1½ cups grated Monterey Jack cheese, divided
¼ cup chopped green chilies, (optional)

Place chicken between 2 sheets of waxed paper and pound until about ¼ to ½ inch thick. Sprinkle with salt, pepper, and flour. Quickly sauté in ¼ cup butter until golden. Remove to plate and add remaining ¼ cup butter to pan and sauté onion, garlic, and mushrooms slowly until cooked but now browned. Stir in flour, salt, pepper, chicken stock, and wine. Cook until thickened, about 5 minutes. Stir in mashed avocados and ½ cup cheese. Arrange chicken breasts in glass baking dish. Top with sauce, remaining cheese, and green chilies, if desired. Bake at 350° for 10 minutes. Serves 8.

Lone Star Legacy II (Texas II)

Monterey Chicken Rolls

3 whole medium-size chicken
  breasts, skinned, halved, and boned
Salt and pepper
1½ ounces Monterey Jack
  cheese cut into pieces to match
  length of chicken

3 tablespoons all-purpose
  flour
2-3 beaten eggs
6 tablespoons fine dry bread
  crumbs

Place each piece of chicken between 2 pieces of clear plastic wrap. Working from center to edges, pound lightly with meat mallet, forming rectangles about ⅛-inch thick. Remove plastic wrap. Sprinkle each side with salt and pepper. Place one piece of cheese onto each piece of chicken, fold in sides; roll up jelly-roll style. Skewer closed with wooden picks. Roll chicken in flour, then dip in beaten eggs. Roll in fine dry bread crumbs to coat evenly.

Place chicken rolls, seam-side down, in a shallow baking dish. Bake, uncovered in 350° oven for 30 minutes.

SAUCE:
6 tablespoons dry white wine
3 tablespoons softened
  margarine
3 teaspoons snipped parsley

½ teaspoon dried oregano,
  crushed or dried marjoram,
  crushed

In a small saucepan, combine the white wine, margarine, parsley, and oregano (or marjoram). Cook and stir over low heat until margarine is melted. Pour the sauce over chicken rolls; continue baking about 10 minutes or until tender. Remove the wooden picks before serving. Makes about 6 servings.

Cooking with Kiwanis (New Mexico)

Like many New Mexico churches, San Miguel Mission in Socorro has massive adobe walls, large carved vigas, and supporting corbel arches. Given extensive restorations during the 1970s, it was originally built in 1598 by Franciscan priests, making it one of the earliest established churches in the US.

Rip's Barbecued Chicken (Texas Style)

1 (5-ounce) bottle Worcestershire
  sauce
5 ounces water
5 ounces vinegar
2 tablespoons margarine
2-3 slices uncooked bacon, chopped
½ teaspoon salt
½ teaspoon black pepper

½ teaspoon celery salt
½ tablespoon prepared mustard
Grated rind of ½ lemon
1-2 dashes Tabasco sauce
1-2 cloves garlic, crushed
3-4 chickens, about 1½ pounds
  each

Combine all ingredients except chicken, and simmer for 30 minutes. In the meantime, split chickens in half and season with salt and pepper. Place chickens on hot grill, skin-side-down, and brown on both sides, turning occasionally (takes about 15 minutes). Baste first with oily part of sauce that has floated to top. Continue basting and turning over gentle coals until done. Chickens will be tender and a deep, rich brown (takes about 45 minutes). Serves 6-8.

M.D. Anderson Volunteers Cooking for Fun (Texas II)

Barbecued Chicken

1 frying-size chicken, quartered

1 onion, sliced

Place chicken in roasting pan with slice of onion on top of each piece.

SAUCE:
¾ cup catsup
4 tablespoons Worcestershire sauce
2 teaspoons prepared mustard
¾ cup vinegar
2 bay leaves

½ cup water
1 tablespoon sugar
¼ teaspoon salt
Tabasco

Combine ingredients for sauce, pour over chicken, and cook at 350° for 2 hours. Baste frequently.

Queen Anne's Table (North Carolina)

★★★★★★★★★★★ ★★★★★★★★★★★

Beer-in-the-Rear Chicken

Don't cook just one—there won't be enough to go around!

Buy a whole frying-size chicken. This will work equally well on the BBQ pit or in the kitchen oven. You can prepare the chicken to suit individual tastes. You are limited only by your imagination. Some suggestions are to rub the chicken with olive oil and sprinkle some rosemary and thyme, or sprinkle with onion flakes and garlic flakes (inside and out). Place slice of onion, apple, or celery in cavity of the chicken.

After preparing chicken, open a can of light beer (removing tab and opening one or two additional holes) and insert can of beer upright into cavity of the chicken; place upright in shallow pan in oven at 325° for 2 hours, or until done.

If BBQing, place chicken upright on grill (after placing beer in cavity). Baste with sauce about 30 minutes before done.

Variation: Slit the skins and put seeded quarters of jalapeño between the skin and the meat. Then rub dry Hidden Valley Dressing Mix all over the chicken for seasoning, and set chicken on a can of beer in the pit.

The Authorized Texas Ranger Cookbook (Texas II)

Turkey à La King

5 tablespoons butter, divided
3 tablespoons flour
½ cup chicken broth
1 cup cream (or half-and-half)
¼ pound mushrooms, sliced
1 green pepper, cut in strips
3 cups diced, cooked turkey or
  chicken
1 (4-ounce) jar pimento
Salt and pepper
Paprika
1 (10-ounce) package frozen pastry
  shells (puff pastry), baked

In large saucepan over low heat, melt 2 tablespoons of the butter; stir in flour. Remove from heat and stir in broth and cream, stirring constantly until smooth. Put back on heat and cook on medium, stirring until thick. Set aside.

In 10-inch skillet, sauté mushrooms and green pepper in remaining butter. Cook until pepper is wilted and mushroom liquid evaporated. Stir into above sauce with turkey and pimento and season with salt, pepper, and paprika. Heat through. Serve on baked pastry shells.

To Tayla with TLC (Great Plains)

★★★★★★★★★★★★ ★★★★★★★★★★★★

Great New Way to Bake the Turkey

Takes courage, but it works!

1 (14-18-pound) turkey

Salt and pepper inside and out. Place in roaster or turkey pan with 6 cups of water. Tightly cover with lid or heavy-duty foil.

Bake the bird in a 500° preheated oven for 1 hour.* Turn off oven and DO NOT OPEN THE DOOR FOR 12 HOURS. It does work, and your turkey will be moist and tender. You will have lots of good juice for the dressing and gravy. Plus, your oven will be free for other baking if you do as I do and let him do his thing all night.

*For a 20-22-pound turkey, cook 1 hour and 15 minutes.

Collectibles II (Texas)

Ozarks Smoked Turkey

1 onion, minced
½ cup butter
3 tablespoons light brown sugar
1 (0.4-ounce) package Italian salad
  dressing mix

1 clove garlic, minced
1 teaspoon salt
Freshly ground pepper to taste
¾ cup tarragon vinegar
1 (20-pound) turkey

Combine all ingredients except turkey in a small saucepan. Simmer 3-4 minutes. (Stuff turkey, if desired, and truss as usual.) Brush generously with herb sauce. Cook in smoker according to manufacturer's directions. One hour before cooking is finished, add damp hickory chips to smoker and baste turkey every 20 minutes with the herb sauce. Serves 16-18.

Sassafras! The Ozarks Cookbook (Missouri)

In 1621, the Pilgrims, who came over on the Mayflower the year before, invited 91 Indians who had helped them survive their first year in America to a feast which lasted three days; Americans have celebrated Thanksgiving ever since. Exclusively an American holiday, it is celebrated the fourth Thursday in November.

Sharing food together seems to have many benefits. Recently a survey from a top national scholarship organization found that the winners had only one common bond: A strikingly high number of the successful students came from families that ate dinner together.

Grilled Duck Breasts

You've never tasted better!

8 tablespoons butter	6 duck breasts, removed from bone
1 tablespoon Worcestershire sauce	and skinned
1 garlic clove, finely minced	Salt, freshly ground black pepper,
¾ cup thinly sliced fresh	and cayenne pepper
mushrooms	6 strips of bacon

Melt the butter in a saucepan and add the Worcestershire sauce, garlic, and mushrooms; cook until mushrooms become slightly soft. Remove from heat. Light a fire in the barbecue pit and allow the coals to get glowing red hot. While you're waiting, rub the duck breasts well with salt, black pepper, and cayenne. Carefully wrap each breast with a strip of bacon, securing it with toothpicks. Let them stand at room temperature. (You might want to take this time to fix a green salad with a creamy spicy dressing and some wild rice cooked with a handful of chopped roasted pecans.)

When the coals are ready, grill the breasts quickly, 3-4 minutes on each side if you like them juicy and with a little red in the meat, longer if you prefer your meat well done. Baste with the butter sauce. To serve, place the breasts on toasted slices of bread, and pour the remaining butter and mushroom sauce over each breast. Serves 2.

Who's Your Mama, Are You Catholic, and Can You Make a Roux?
(Louisiana II)

★★★★★★★★★★★★   ★★★★★★★★★★★★

Doves Alfred

Mike Hughes, co-owner of the Broken Arrow Ranch in Ingram, says, "I don't know who Alfred is, but Hap Perry and his father, John, guaranteed that Doves Alfred is the best dove recipe known!"

12-16 doves, split down the back
¼ cup Burgundy wine
5 ounces currant jelly
¼ cup barbecue sauce
¼ cup orange juice
1 teaspoon orange rind, finely grated

1 stick butter
1 teaspoon arrowroot (cornstarch)
Watercress and orange slices for
** garnish**

In broiler pan, place doves, breasts down. In pan over medium heat, combine well next 6 ingredients; add arrowroot. Pour over birds; broil on top rack in oven for 10 minutes or until birds are brown; baste several times. Turn over birds; brush well with sauce; broil 10 minutes more or until crisp and brown; baste often. Remove to hot platter; spoon sauce over doves; garnish. Serves 6-8.

Great Flavors of Texas (Texas II)

Seafood

The Continental Divide runs through Rocky Mountain National Park.
Every drop of water to the west of the Divide flows toward the Pacific Ocean;
every drop to the east flows toward the Gulf of Mexico and Atlantic Ocean.

Beer Batter Fish

1 pound fish fillets
Mix, divided
⅓ cup lemon juice

⅔ cup beer
1 cup vegetable oil

MIX:
1½ cups unsifted flour
2¼ teaspoons baking powder

¾ teaspoon baking soda
1½ teaspoons salt

Place fish on paper towels; pat dry. Coat fish with ½ cup Mix. In large bowl, combine remaining mixture, lemon juice, and beer (this will foam). Stir until consistency of pancake batter. In large skillet, heat oil over medium heat. Dip fish into batter; fry until golden brown on both sides. Drain on paper towels.

Dr. Martin Luther Church 100th Anniversary Cookbook (Wisconsin)

Catfish Sesame

Crispy and flavorful.

3 pounds fresh or frozen catfish
  fillets or steaks
3 cups water
¼ cup vinegar
1 cup fine dry bread crumbs
3 tablespoons sesame seeds
2 tablespoons Greek seasoning

⅛ teaspoon white pepper
1 teaspoon salt
¼ cup all-purpose flour
1 egg, beaten
2 tablespoons milk
Vegetable oil
Lemon wedges

Place catfish in a bowl and cover with water and vinegar. Prepare more solution, using same proportions, if needed. Soak for an hour or more.

Place bread crumbs on wax paper and mix in sesame seeds, Greek seasoning, pepper, salt, and flour.

Mix egg and milk in a shallow dish. Drain and dry catfish. Dip in egg mixture and coat with bread crumb mixture.

Fry in 1-inch-deep hot oil (360°) 4-5 minutes to the side. Drain on paper towels and keep hot in a 200° oven. Garnish with lemon wedges. Makes 8 servings.

Hint: If preferred, bake fish on an oiled cookie sheet 15-20 minutes at 375° only until fish flakes easily with a fork.

Home for the Holidays (Arkansas)

Elegant Baked Fish

Everyone loves fish cooked this way.

1½ cups Hellmann's mayonnaise
1 tablespoon creole mustard
1 tablespoon lemon juice
1 tablespoon Tabasco
1 tablespoon Worcestershire sauce

2 teaspoons garlic powder
¾ teaspoon curry powder
8 fish fillets
Ritz crackers

Mix first 7 ingredients well and spread over fish fillets. Sprinkle with crumbled Ritz crackers and bake at 400° for about 20 minutes, uncovered. Fish is done when it flakes easily with a fork.

Of Magnolia and Mesquite (Texas)

Farm-Raised Catfish Williamsburg

1 teaspoon salt, divided
8 (4-ounce) catfish fillets or
    equivalent
1 (2-ounce) bottle Tabasco

1 teaspoon pepper
2 cups cornmeal mix
4 cups oil or more if needed

Lightly salt fish on both sides; liberally sprinkle and rub fish with Tabasco. Refrigerate for 1 hour. Combine pepper, cornmeal mix, and remaining salt. Dredge fish in cornmeal mixture; drop into oil heated to 375°. Cook until golden brown, about 5 minutes; drain well.

CAUTION: Do not overload oil with fish. Temperature of oil during cooking should not drop below 360°. Four cups of oil will cook about 2 fillets at a time. Serves 4.

Taste of the South (Mississippi)

Smothered Fish

Minnesota claims more lakes than any other state. Estimates range between 14,000 and 15,000, depending on how large a lake must be to "qualify." With all of the lakes in Minnesota, there are lots of fishermen and, hopefully, lots of fish to catch and prepare. Try this recipe if you're fishing for compliments.

3 pounds walleye, cod, trout, or
  whitefish (fillets or whole)
Salt and pepper
⅓ cup dry sherry
½ pound fresh mushrooms, sliced

6 tablespoons butter, divided
½ cup grated parmesan cheese
1 cup sour cream
Paprika

Place fish in a shallow baking dish. Season with salt and pepper. Sprinkle sherry over fish. Sauté mushrooms in 2 tablespoons butter; spread over fish. Combine 4 tablespoons melted butter, parmesan cheese, and sour cream. Spoon sour cream mixture on top of fish. Sprinkle with paprika. Bake at 350° for 30-40 minutes, or until fish flakes easily when pricked with fork. Serves 4-6.

Winning Recipes from Minnesota with Love (Minnesota)

Grilled Fresh Tuna

4 (¼-pound) tuna steaks
1 tablespoon honey
⅓ cup soy sauce
1 teaspoon fresh grated lemon peel

¼ cup fresh lemon juice
1 tablespoon Dijon mustard
½ cup salad oil
Lemon wedges (optional)

Place tuna in shallow dish or zip-closure plastic bag. Combine honey, soy sauce, lemon peel, lemon juice, mustard, and salad oil in a small bowl. Whisk to blend. Pour marinade over fish and turn to coat well. Cover tightly. Marinate in refrigerator 1-3 hours or longer, if desired.

  Preheat barbecue grill to medium-hot. Arrange tuna steaks on hot grill. Cook tuna over moderate heat about 4-6 minutes per side, basting occasionally until fish reaches desired doneness. Garnish with lemon wedges, if desired. Serves 4.

Back Home Again (Indiana)

★★★★★★★★★★★ ★★★★★★★★★★★★

Salmon with Cilantro Sauce

Moist, flavorful and easy.

1 (12-ounce) salmon fillet, cut
  into 4 equal-size portions
¼ cup lime juice
3 tablespoons chopped fresh
  cilantro

1 tablespoon olive oil
½ teaspoon ground cumin
¼ teaspoon salt
⅛ teaspoon pepper
3-6 drops Tabasco sauce

Preheat oven to 500°. Prepare 4 (12x12-inch) squares of aluminum foil, sprayed with nonstick spray. Place a piece of salmon on each foil square. Combine remaining ingredients; drizzle evenly over fish. Tightly seal foil into packets. Place baking sheet in oven 2 minutes to preheat. Put packets on hot baking sheet. Bake 8 minutes, or until fish is opaque and flakes easily with a fork. Makes 4 servings.

Palates (Colorado)

Salmon Steaks with Soy Marinade

2 tablespoons orange juice
¼ cup soy sauce
1 clove garlic, pressed

1 tablespoon butter (optional)
4 salmon steaks

Combine the orange juice, soy sauce, garlic, and butter, if desired, over medium-high heat in a small saucepan. Cook until the mixture becomes thick enough to coat the back of a spoon.

Wash and pat dry the salmon steaks. With a spoon, rub the soy marinade on both sides of the fish. Refrigerate 1-2 hours before preparing.

Preheat oven to 450° and bake for 10-15 minutes, until the fish flakes when tested with a fork.

Note: The salmon steaks may also be broiled, grilled, or microwaved. Serves 4.

Bouquet Garni (Missouri)

Snapper with Sour Cream

3-4 pounds fresh snapper, cut into
  fillets
1½ teaspoons salt

2 tablespoons margarine, melted,
  or oil

Cut a pocket in each fillet in order to stuff. Sprinkle fish inside and out with salt. Stuff fish loosely with Sour Cream Stuffing. Close opening with skewers or wooden picks. Place fish on a greased baking pan. Brush with margarine or oil. Bake at 350° for 40-60 minutes or until fish flakes easily. Baste while cooking. Serves 6.

SOUR CREAM STUFFING:

¾ cup celery, chopped
½ cup onion, chopped
¼ cup margarine, melted
4 cups dry bread crumbs
½ cup sour cream

¼ cup lemon, peeled and diced
2 tablespoons lemon rind
1 teaspoon paprika
1 teaspoon salt

Sauté celery and onion in margarine. Combine all ingredients and mix thoroughly.

Sugar Beach (Florida)

Baked Boston Scrod

Scrod, a young cod, is strictly a New England dish, and abundantly available. It is firm, tender, and moist—a delightful fish.

4 pieces scrod fillet (6-8 ounces each)
Salt and pepper to taste
2 tablespoons lemon juice

1½ cups white wine
½ cup butter, melted, divided
1 cup dried bread crumbs

Preheat the oven to 350°. Butter a baking pan large enough to hold the scrod in a single layer. Place the scrod in the prepared baking pan, and add the salt, pepper, lemon juice, and wine. Drizzle ¼ cup of the melted butter over the fish. Bake at 350° for approximately 20 minutes, or until the fish flakes but is still moist. Remove the pan from the oven and preheat the broiler. Scatter the bread crumbs over the fish, and drizzle with the remaining ¼ cup butter. Brown under the broiler for 2-5 minutes only, until lightly browned, and serve. Serves 4.

The Red Lion Inn Cookbook (New England)

★ **Editor's Extra:** This recipe is wonderfully simple and delicious with other kinds of fish, too. Try orange roughy or tilapia or even catfish fillets.

Easy Flounder Fillets

2 pounds flounder (or other fish)
  fillets, skinned (fresh or frozen)
2 tablespoons grated onion
1½ teaspoons salt
⅛ teaspoon pepper

2 large tomatoes, peeled, cut into
  small pieces
¼ cup melted butter or margarine
1 cup shredded Swiss cheese

Thaw fillets, if frozen. Place fillets in a single layer on a well-greased 6x10-inch bake-and-serve platter. Sprinkle fish with onion, salt, and pepper. Cover fillets with tomatoes. Pour butter over tomatoes. Broil about 4 inches from source of heat for 10-12 minutes or until fish flakes easily when tested with a fork. Remove from heat; sprinkle with cheese. Broil 2-3 minutes longer or until cheese melts. Yields 6 servings.

Southern Seafood Classics (Georgia)

Baked Flounder with Shrimp Sauce

A must for seafood lovers.

8 flounder fillets (bass, trout, or pompano may be substituted)

Place each fillet on a piece of aluminum foil and spread each with Shrimp Sauce. Bake at 350° for 45 minutes. Serve directly from foil.

SHRIMP SAUCE:

1 cup butter or margarine
3 tablespoons flour
1¾ cups milk
4 tablespoons chopped green pepper
1 tablespoon chopped pimento
½ cup chopped onion
1 teaspoon Worcestershire sauce
Dash red pepper

¾ teaspoon salt
½ garlic clove, minced
2 beaten egg yolks
¾ cup heavy cream
1½ cups chopped mushrooms
2½ pounds chopped, cooked
  shrimp

Using double boiler, make a thick sauce by melting butter and adding flour and then milk. Then add green pepper, pimento, onion, Worcestershire sauce, red pepper, salt, and minced garlic. Mix egg yolks and cream. Add to sauce. Then stir in mushrooms and shrimp. Yields 8 servings.

Flaunting Our Finest (Tennessee)

Broiled Stuffed Flounder

1 medium onion, minced
8 tablespoons butter, divided
2 stalks celery, chopped fine
1 cup shrimp, cleaned and peeled
1 small can mushrooms
½ pound crabmeat
1 small bay leaf
1 tablespoon Worcestershire
½ cup cream
Bread crumbs
Salt and pepper
3 ounces white wine, plus ½ ounce for basting
2 (2 to 2½-pound) flounders
2 tablespoons oil
Juice of ½ lemon

Sauté the finely chopped onion in 6 tablespoons butter until soft; add celery and sauté 2 or 3 minutes longer. Add shrimp and mushrooms (with their liquid) and sauté until the shrimp are pink; then add crabmeat, bay leaf, Worcestershire, cream, and enough bread crumbs to hold the dressing together. Season to taste. Add the wine and stuff the fish. Close the slits with the aid of small skewers and lace up.

Heat 2 tablespoons oil along with 2 tablespoons butter in broiler pan and place the fish in the pan. Broil the fish slowly under a low flame, basting with the butter/oil mixture as the fish begins to brown. Add a little more wine to the broiler pan to increase basting liquid and keep the fish moist. It is not necessary to turn the fish. Keep the flame low and when the top of the fish is golden brown or slightly darker, the fish will be cooked through. Spoon the remaining sauce from the pan over the fish. Sprinkle with lemon juice. Serves 4.

St. Philomena School 125th Anniversary Cookbook (Louisiana II)

★★★★★★★★★★★   ★★★★★★★★★★★★

New Orleans Patties

2 tablespoons bacon fat or oleo
1 pod garlic, minced
2 stalks celery, chopped
3 green onions and tops, chopped
    fine
2 tablespoons flour
3 dozen oysters

2 tablespoons oyster liquid
Dash of Accent (optional)
Dash of cayenne pepper
Salt and pepper to taste
2 tablespoons parsley, chopped
Patty shells

Melt fat in pan. Add garlic, celery, and onions; cook until soft. Blend in flour, oysters, oyster liquid, Accent, cayenne, salt and pepper. Cook on low heat, stirring constantly until oysters make more liquid. Simmer for 20 minutes. Add uncooked parsley and cool. Fill prepared patty shells and bake in 300° oven until heated, about 15 minutes.

Note: This recipe fills 5-6 large patty shells. It is also delicious served in bite-sized shells as an appetizer.

A Cook's Tour of Shreveport (Louisiana II)

Simply Scrumptious Virginia Bay Scallops in Wine Sauce

¾ cup bread crumbs
¼ cup parmesan cheese
4 tablespoons butter
2 tablespoons margarine
2 stalks celery, leaves removed, sliced
1½ medium onions, chopped

6 tablespoons flour
1 cup milk
½ cup white wine
4 ounces medium-sharp Cheddar,
    sliced
1 pound Virginia bay scallops

Preheat oven to 350°. Prepare topping by combining bread crumbs and parmesan cheese in a small bowl. Melt butter and margarine in a medium (2-quart) saucepan. Sauté celery and onions in melted butter and margarine. Blend in flour to make a paste; cook 1 full minute over medium heat. Gradually add milk, stirring after each addition. Stir wine into sauce. Add cheese and let it melt into sauce, stirring frequently. Fold in scallops. Pour into a greased 2-quart casserole dish. Sprinkle on topping. Bake for 20-30 minutes until bubbly. Serve over noodles or rice. Yields 5 servings.

The Great Taste of Virginia Seafood Cookbook (Virginia)

Crawfish Étouffée

Along about June, M'sieu "Le Mud Bug" was just about ready to bid us goodbye for the season, fold his claws, and silently swim away. But before he left, we would gracefully move into summer with the euphoric feeling of having polished off a bowl or two of wonderful Creole Crawfish Étouffée. First, we had to get our "crawfish picking" hands on about 10 pounds of live crawfish.

Mamete, my mother, used to say that June crawfish were the hardest to peel and the most delicious to eat. It seemed that, about this time of year, the shells got much thicker, making them more difficult to crack, but the crawfish were more mature and more full-flavored. The more formidable the obstacle, the greater the reward.

To make this delicious étouffée, first you need 10 pounds of crawfish to boil. (If you don't want to start from scratch, you can begin with 1 pound of crawfish tails.) Wash the live crawfish well a couple of times, then leave them for about 15 minutes in salted water to "purge." Even before you start this, though, have the courtbouillon in which the crawfish will boil cooking on the stove. (Put about 3 gallons of water in a pot and add to this 1 chopped onion, a few ribs of celery, 4 bay leaves, 1 chopped lemon, 1 teaspoon black pepper, ½ teaspoon cayenne or Tabasco, and ½ cup salt.) Let this boil while you clean the crawfish.

When the crawfish are ready, dump them into the pot. Bring to a boil again and cook for no longer than 10 minutes before you remove the crawfish. Cool the crawfish and peel. Set aside 1 cup of the courtbouillon for later. (If you decide to buy the crawfish tails from your friendly seafood dealer, ask him for about 1 pint of the water in which he made his crawfish "boils.")

To assemble the étouffée, first you need the crawfish, and also:

¼ pound butter	¼ teaspoon ground cloves
2 tablespoons flour	¼ teaspoon chili powder
2 onions, chopped	1 tablespoon lemon juice
2 ribs celery, chopped	½ cup crawfish water
3 toes garlic, minced	½ cup water
1 bell pepper, chopped	Salt and pepper to taste
1 tablespoon tomato paste	½ cup chopped green onions
¼ teaspoon thyme	2 tablespoons minced parsley
½ teaspoon basil	

First, melt the butter in a large heavy skillet. Stir in flour and lightly brown. Add onions, celery, garlic, and bell pepper and sauté over low heat for about 20 minutes, or until the vegetables are very soft. Add the crawfish tails, tomato paste, thyme, basil, cloves, chili powder, lemon

continued

★★★★★★★★★★★ ★★★★★★★★★★★

continued

juice, crawfish water, and water. Mix well and cook for about 15 minutes. Add salt and pepper to taste. Cover and let simmer for another 10 minutes. Add the green onions and parsley.

Remove from heat and let stand for about 10 minutes, covered, to allow the seasonings to blend. All you need now is some rice to serve it over and a hunk of crisp French bread.

La Bouche Creole (Louisiana)

Crawfish Étouffée à la Arceneaux
(Microwave)

½ cup margarine
1½ cups onion, finely chopped
¾ cup green bell pepper, finely
  chopped

1 clove garlic, minced, or
  ¼ teaspoon garlic powder

1. Micromelt margarine in a 3-quart dish on HIGH (100%) 1 minute. Add onion, bell pepper, and garlic. Sauté on HIGH (100%) 6 minutes or until tender.

2 tablespoons flour
2 heaping tablespoons undiluted
  cream of celery soup
1 (10-ounce) can Ro-tel tomatoes
  and green chilies, puréed with liquid

1 cup beer
2 teaspoons salt
1 teaspoon cayenne pepper

2. Add flour and celery soup. Stir in puréed Ro-tel, beer, salt, and pepper. Microwave on HIGH (100%) 6 minutes.

1 pound peeled crawfish

3. Add crawfish. Cover. Microwave on HIGH (100%) 4 minutes. Serve étouffée over rice. Serves 4.

Tout de Suite à la Microwave II (Louisiana)

★ **Editor's Extra:** I suggest starting with ⅛ teaspoon of cayenne pepper, adding more to taste. Arceneaux likes his étouffée hot!

★★★★★★★★★★★★★ ★★★★★★★★★★★★★

Memree's Soppin' Shrimp

Memree makes a special trip to the Florida panhandle around Memorial Day and gets the fresh shrimp for this memorable meal.

3 pounds raw shrimp, in shells
¼ pound butter
⅔ cup lemon juice
1 teaspoon grated lemon rind

1½ cups Italian dressing
2½ teaspoons black pepper, more
  to taste

Wash shrimp and remove heads, but leave in shell. Drain. In a medium saucepan, melt butter and add lemon juice, lemon rind, Italian dressing, and black pepper. Bring to a boil. Add shrimp and simmer for about 6 minutes or just until tender.

   Serve with crusty French bread. Ladle shrimp into individual bowls with plenty of sauce for soppin' the bread in. You peel your own shrimp, which guarantees the pleasure of slow eating. Serves 4.

Cross Creek Kitchens (Florida)

Shrimp Bisque in Puff Pastry

¼ cup grated onion
2 tablespoons grated green bell
  pepper
2 tablespoons butter or margarine
1 (10¾-ounce) can cream of
  potato soup
¾ cup light cream

½ cup grated sharp Cheddar
  cheese
2 teaspoons lemon juice
1½ cups shrimp, cooked and
  peeled or seafood of choice
1 (10-ounce) package frozen puff
  pastry shells

In a skillet, sauté onion and green pepper in butter. Blend in soup, cream, Cheddar cheese, lemon juice, and prepared seafood. Season to taste. Cook about 5-7 minutes. This may be stored in refrigerator or frozen until serving. When ready to serve, prepare puff pastry shells according to package directions. Thaw and heat seafood mixture thoroughly; pour into baked pastry shells. Serves 4-6.

Amazing Graces (Texas II)

Barbecue Shrimp

24 large shrimp, peeled and deveined   12 slices bacon

Peel and devein the shrimp, leaving the tails on. Cook the bacon halfway in a skillet, chill, and cut in half lengthwise. Wrap the shrimp in bacon, holding together with a toothpick.

BARBECUE SAUCE:
1½ cups orange juice concentrate
6 tablespoons soy sauce
1 cup ketchup
¾ cup molasses
4 teaspoons Worcestershire sauce
2 teaspoons Tabasco

1½ cup chili sauce
2 tablespoons Dijon mustard
2 cloves garlic, chopped fine
2 tablespoons fresh lemon juice
½ cup chicken broth
2 teaspoons salt

In a large bowl mix together all the ingredients for the BBQ sauce. Place the bacon-wrapped shrimp on a sheet tray. Ladle the BBQ sauce generously over each shrimp, leaving the tails un-sauced. Place the shrimp under a low-heat broiler; cook for 6 minutes. Turn shrimp and cook for another 6 minutes. To serve, place the shrimp on a large decorative platter, with napkins on the side. Yields 8 servings.
Recipe by Chef Chuck "Rocky" Rachwitz.

The Simply Great II Cookbook (Michigan)

★ **Editor's Extra:** You'll probably have extra barbeque sauce too yummy to not keep! So freeze or keep in fridge for next time.

★★★★★★★★★★★★   ★★★★★★★★★★★★

Spiedino Di Mare

1 pound medium shrimp (50 count)
½ cup virgin olive oil
Salt and pepper to taste

Seasoned bread crumbs
Lemon Butter Sauce
1 pound cooked pasta of your choice

Lightly brush peeled shrimp with oil and season with salt and pepper. Cover all sides with bread crumbs. Skewer shrimp and grill for about 3 minutes per side. Divide shrimp and pasta among 6 plates. Cover with Lemon Butter Sauce.

LEMON BUTTER SAUCE:

2 teaspoons finely chopped
 garlic
2 teaspoons finely chopped
 onion
1 ounce clarified butter

½ cup white wine
¼ cup lemon juice
½ cup cold unsalted butter
Salt and white pepper to
 taste

Sauté garlic and onion in clarified butter over medium heat until onions are soft. Add wine and lemon juice; turn the flame to high and reduce by three-fourths. Lower flame and slowly add cold butter one small pat at a time. Shake the pan continuously to blend the sauce. Add salt and pepper to taste.

Raspberry Enchantment House Tour Cookbook (New Mexico)

Boiled Shrimp

Technique based on some research done at LSU. Excellent!

3 pounds unpeeled raw
 shrimp
1 large onion, peeled and quartered
3 cloves garlic
½ cup vegetable oil
½ cup catsup (optional)

½ teaspoon Tabasco
½ teaspoon black pepper
1 lemon, sliced
¼ cup vinegar
1 tablespoon liquid crab boil
¾ cup salt

Wash shrimp. Half-fill a 6-quart pot with water; bring to a boil. Add all ingredients except shrimp, crab boil, and salt; return to a boil; add shrimp and crab boil. Boil 5 minutes; remove from heat. Add salt; stir to dissolve. Let set, covered, for 30 minutes for shrimp to absorb flavor. Remove shrimp. May be served immediately or chilled. (The water may be used for boiling potatoes.)

'Tiger Bait' Recipes (Louisiana)

Pascagoula Shrimp Boil
with Peppy Seafood Sauce

3 ounces prepared shrimp boil
  (commercial spice mix)
1 small onion, sliced
1 lemon, sliced

1 clove garlic, sliced
1 gallon water
½ cup salt
5 pounds shrimp, fresh or frozen

Tie the shrimp boil, onion, lemon and garlic in a piece of cheesecloth. Place water in large container. Add salt and bag of seasonings. Cover and bring to boiling point over a hot fire. Add shrimp and return to boiling point. Cover and cook 5 minutes or until shrimp are tender. Drain.

Note: If shrimp is to be used for salad or cocktails, cook as above, remove from water, peel, devein, and chill.

PEPPY SEAFOOD SAUCE:

½ cup chili sauce
½ cup catsup
3 tablespoons freshly squeezed
  lemon juice
1 tablespoon horseradish
1 tablespoon mayonnaise or salad
  dressing

1 teaspoon Worcestershire sauce
½ teaspoon onion, grated
¼ teaspoon salt
3 drops Tabasco sauce
Dash pepper

Mix ingredients well. Serve with shrimp.

Dixie Dining (Mississippi)

Gulf Shrimp Divine

Simply divine!

⅔ cup olive oil (no substitute)
½ cup lemon juice
½ teaspoon salt
⅛ teaspoon pepper
3 tablespoons butter (no substitute)
1 clove garlic, crushed

2 pounds fresh shrimp, shelled and
  deveined
1 cup blanched slivered almonds
Dash of hot pepper sauce
½ cup dry vermouth

Make marinade of olive oil, lemon juice, and seasonings. Marinate shrimp for at least 2 hours. Melt butter in large skillet; add garlic and shrimp. Reserve marinade. Stir-fry shrimp over medium heat until pink. Discard garlic; remove shrimp to a hot platter. Sauté slivered almonds in butter until brown; add marinade, hot pepper sauce, and vermouth. When well blended, pour sauce over shrimp. Serve over saffron rice mixed with chopped chives or finely chopped green onions. Serves 6-8.

Suncoast Seasons (Florida)

Shrimp Stir-Fry with Lemon

½ pound peeled raw shrimp
¾ cup thinly sliced celery
½ medium green pepper, cut in
  strips
2 scallions, sliced, including tops
½ cup bamboo shoots
1 (4-ounce) can sliced mushrooms
  (drained, reserve liquor)

2 or 3 pimentos, cut in strips
1 tablespoon oil
1½ tablespoons cornstarch
1½ teaspoons soy sauce
1 tablespoon lemon juice
1 chicken bouillon cube
Salt and pepper to taste
½ teaspoon grated lemon peel

Stir-fry the shrimp, celery, green pepper, scallions, bamboo shoots, mushrooms, and pimentos in oil for 3 minutes in a 10-inch skillet. Add enough water to mushroom liquid to make 1 cup. Combine liquid with cornstarch, soy sauce, lemon juice, bouillon cube, salt, pepper and lemon zest. Cook until sauce is clear and thickened, 1-3 minutes. Stir sauce into shrimp mixture. Serve over hot rice.

Heritage Fan-Fare (New England)

Deviled Crab

½ stick margarine
½ small onion, chopped
1 stem celery, chopped
½ bell pepper, chopped
3 eggs, beaten
12 Ritz crackers, crumbled slightly
1 heaping tablespoon mayonnaise

1 teaspoon prepared mustard
1 tablespoon Worcestershire sauce
1 dash Tabasco sauce
½ teaspoon salt
Black pepper
¼ cup milk
1 pound claw crabmeat

Melt margarine in heavy saucepan. Sauté onion, celery, and pepper until tender, but not browned. Beat eggs, add all other ingredients, and toss together lightly until well mixed. Turn into 1-quart greased casserole, sprinkle with additional cracker crumbs and paprika. Bake at 325° about 25-30 minutes or until firm. Serves 6.

Strictly for Boys (South Carolina)

Shrimp and Crabmeat au Gratin

1 stick butter, divided
3 heaping tablespoons flour
2 cups milk
Sherry to taste
2 tablespoons sugar
1 teaspoon salt

½ teaspoon pepper
½ pound shrimp, cooked
½ pound crabmeat
1 cup sharp cheese, grated
1 tablespoon paprika
Slivered almonds

Melt ⅔ stick butter in saucepan and gradually add flour, milk, sherry, sugar, salt and pepper. Allow it to come to a boil and keep warm. Grease a casserole dish with remaining butter. Place half of shrimp and crab in casserole and half of the cheese, followed by a layer of sauce. Repeat layers and sprinkle top with paprika and almonds. Bake at 325° for approximately 45 minutes.

Bay Leaves (Florida)

★★★★★★★★★★★ ★★★★★★★★★★★

Crabmeat à La Landry

1 cup finely chopped onions
1/3 cup finely chopped celery
1/4 pound oleo or butter
Pinch sage
Pinch thyme
Pinch nutmeg
Pinch oregano
Pinch marjoram

1 teaspoon salt
1/2 teaspoon cayenne
1 tablespoon flour
1 can evaporated milk
1 cup cornflakes
1 pound white crabmeat
1 cup Ritz crackers, crumbled
3 tablespoons butter

Sauté onions and celery in oleo or butter until onions are wilted. Add sage, thyme, nutmeg, oregano, marjoram, salt, cayenne, and flour. Add milk, stirring constantly.

Toast the cornflakes (bake 5 minutes at 375° on cookie sheet) and crumble; then mix with the crabmeat. Mix well. Combine crabmeat with the spices and put into ramekins or casserole. Sprinkle with crumbled Ritz crackers. Add pats of butter and bake for 20-25 minutes at 375°. Serves 6.

Secrets of the Original Don's Seafood & Steakhouse (Louisiana II)

Pawleys Island Inn Crab Cakes

1 cup mayonnaise
1/8 teaspoon cayenne pepper
1 egg white
Juice of 1/2 lemon
3 tablespoons extra-fine cracker
  meal

1 pound fresh lump crabmeat
1 stick butter
Fresh breadcrumbs

Blend mayonnaise, pepper, egg white, lemon juice, and cracker meal; then fold lightly into crabmeat. Shape into patties and roll in fresh bread crumbs. Sauté in heavy skillet with butter until evenly browned. Drain on absorbent towel before serving. Yields 8-10 cakes.

Blessed Isle—Recipes from Pawleys Island (South Carolina)

Meats

The National Route 66 Museum in Elk City, Oklahoma, offers a classic walk through the 2,400 miles and eight states that make up the "Mother Road." Route 66 was the first truly cross-country national highway.

My Sunday Roast

Fit for a king!

1 (5 to 6-pound) rump roast
2 teaspoons Lawry's seasoning salt
1 teaspoon black pepper

1½ teaspoons Accent (optional)
½ stick oleo
3 cups water

Preheat oven to 325°. Season roast generously with salt, pepper, and Accent. Place in a 2-inch-deep baking pan and cut oleo in pats to go under your roast. Cook for 2 hours. Remove roast from oven and pour grease out of pan (this is good for Yorkshire pudding). Add water and mix well with "dregs" in pan, scraping bottom of pan. Put roast back in gravy and baste. Cook another hour. Taste your gravy during the last hour to see if you need more salt. (Accent enhances the flavor.) When done, take roast out of gravy to be sliced. Serve with rice, as this gravy is true pan gravy. My family loves it.

Variation: Add a can of mushrooms and juice to gravy and reheat. If you like a thick gravy, take 1½ tablespoons of grease and brown 2 tablespoons flour in it. Add 1 cup water and cook until smooth. Add this to your pan gravy last hour of cooking.

YORKSHIRE PUDDING:
**⅓ cup of hot beef grease drippings
  from a rib roast or rump roast**
1½ cups flour
2 teaspoons baking powder

½ teaspoon salt
2 eggs, separated
1 cup milk

Sift together flour, baking powder, and salt. Add beaten egg yolks, then milk, and mix well. Fold in stiffly beaten egg whites. Pour into 1-quart baking dish containing hot beef drippings. Swirl grease in dish so it will be all over. Bake in hot oven at 475°. Also good served with prime rib.

The Country Gourmet (Mississippi)

Texas Brisket

Best brisket I've ever eaten. I didn't use a knife, it was so tender.

1 (4 to 5-pound) brisket
2 teaspoons meat tenderizer
1 bottle (4 ounces) liquid smoke
1 teaspoon celery salt
1 teaspoon paprika

¼ teaspoon nutmeg
¼ teaspoon garlic powder
1 teaspoon onion salt
1 tablespoon brown sugar

Sprinkle brisket with meat tenderizer; cover with liquid smoke. Refrigerate overnight, covered with foil. Next day, sprinkle brisket with mixture of remaining ingredients. Cover tightly with foil, bake 2 hours at 300°. Loosen foil, bake 5 hours more at 200°. Remove meat from pan; set aside 1 hour before slicing. Strain any grease from pan juices (or chill in deep freeze for easy removal). Slice brisket very thin across grain. Serve with hot degreased liquid or barbecue sauce of your choice. Serves 5 or 6.

Cook 'em Horns (Texas)

Working Man's Roast

1 (3-pound) rump roast
¼ teaspoon garlic powder
¼ teaspoon seasoned salt
⅛ teaspoon salt

⅛ teaspoon pepper
1 package onion soup mix
2 tablespoons Worcestershire sauce
1 can cream of mushroom soup

Put foil in a cake pan and put roast in pan. Mix together garlic powder, seasoned salt, salt, pepper, onion soup mix, Worcestershire sauce, and soup. Pour over roast. Seal foil and bake at 200° from 7:00 a.m. to 5:00 p.m., or for 10 hours.

Recipes from the Heart (Great Plains)

St. Louis Cathedral, established as a parish in 1720, is the oldest cathedral still in use in the United States. Situated along the banks of the Mississippi River opposite Jackson Square, this impressive structure is a New Orleans landmark.

Easy Italian Beef

1 (3 to 4-pound) roast beef (rump
  roast or sirloin tip)
1 jar pepperochini peppers
  (juice and all)

1 can beer
1 (10¾-ounce) can beef bouillon

Combine all ingredients in a large crock pot. Cook on high for 30 minutes; reduce heat to low. Cook till beef is tender. (For supper, start cooking before leaving for work. It's ready to eat when you get home. For a luncheon, start cooking before you go to bed, allowing it to cook while you sleep!)

   Remove meat from juices, slice thinly and return to pot. Serve on hoagie buns. Dip sandwiches in juices.

Carol's Kitchen (Illinois)

Pepper Steak

1 pound thin sliced beef round
1 tablespoon paprika
2 tablespoons butter or margarine
2 cloves garlic (or equivalent of
  garlic powder), crushed
1½ cups beef broth
1 large onion, cut in eighths

1 green pepper, cut in strips
2 tablespoons cornstarch
¼ cup water
¼ cup soy sauce
1 box frozen pea pods (optional)
2 ripe tomatoes, cut in eighths
3 cups cooked rice

Cut beef into thin strips and sprinkle with paprika; let stand while cutting up other ingredients. Brown meat in butter. Add garlic and broth. Cover and simmer 20-30 minutes. Stir in onion and green pepper. Cook 5 minutes more. Blend cornstarch, water, and soy sauce. Stir into meat mixture. Cook, stirring until thickened. Add pea pods; cook 2 minutes and add tomatoes. Stir gently to heat through. Serve over rice. Serves 4.

The Philadelphia Orchestra Cookbook (Pennsylvania)

Elegant Filet Mignon

Topped with a superb butter sauce!

**4 filets mignon (approximately
  1½ to 2 inches thick)**
**2-3 teaspoons freshly cracked black
  pepper**
2 teaspoons extra virgin olive oil
4-7 tablespoons butter, divided

3-6 shallots, sliced in half
½ cup beef bouillon
2-3 tablespoons red wine vinegar
**1-2 tablespoons Worcestershire
  sauce**
Sliced green onions, for garnish

Dry filets and sprinkle each side generously with ½ teaspoon pepper; press pepper into beef. Place on plate and cover; refrigerate 2-3 hours. In a skillet, heat olive oil and add 1 tablespoon butter; cook filets quickly on each side (approximately 4-6 minutes per side). Place meat on a warm platter; keep warm.

Pour excess pan drippings from skillet; add 2-3 tablespoons butter to pan. Sauté shallots for 1 minute over medium heat; add beef bouillon. Increase heat and boil to reduce pan juices to 2 tablespoons. Be sure to scrape bottom of pan well while sauce is cooking; add red wine vinegar and Worcestershire sauce; boil 1 minute. Add remaining 2-3 tablespoons butter and mix with pan juices; pour over filets. Garnish with sliced green onions. Serve immediately. Serves 4. Do not overcook this elegant beef dish!

Note: Sliced mushrooms can be substituted for shallots. Use only extra-virgin olive oil for this recipe.

Words Worth Eating (Virginia)

Mock Filet

1 pound ground beef
1 cup cracker crumbs
1 egg, beaten
⅓ cup catsup
¼ cup lemon juice

1 cup grated cheese
¼ cup chopped green pepper
2 tablespoons chopped onion
Salt and pepper to taste
Bacon slices – *omit*

Combine all ingredients except bacon. Preheat oven to 400°. Make into patties and wrap ½ slice bacon around each patty. Bake 15-20 minutes.

The Mississippi Cookbook (Mississippi)

★ **Editor's Extra:** My grandson, Patrick, loves these. He comes in the door saying, "Can we have Mock Filets, Mimi?"

Lone Star Chicken-Fried Steak

No Texas cookbook can claim authenticity without including a chicken-fried steak recipe. There are many variations, but they are all breaded, tenderized steak, fried and served with cream gravy.

1½ pounds round steak, tenderized	2 eggs, slightly beaten
1 cup flour	½ cup milk
1 teaspoon salt	Oil for frying
Pepper	

GRAVY:

6 tablespoons bacon or pan drippings	3 cups hot milk
6 tablespoons flour	Salt and pepper

Trim steak and cut into 5 pieces. Combine flour, salt and pepper. Dredge all steak pieces in flour mixture until lightly coated. Combine eggs and milk. Dip steak into egg mixture and dredge again in flour. Heat ½ inch of oil in a heavy skillet. Place steaks in skillet and fry until golden brown on both sides.

To make gravy, remove steaks to warm oven, retaining 6 tablespoons of drippings (or use bacon drippings). Add flour. Cook and stir until flour begins to brown. Add hot milk and stir until thickened. Season with salt and pepper to taste and pour over warm steaks. Serves 5.

Tastes & Tales from Texas...with Love (Texas)

★ **Editor's Extra:** Try chicken this way, too!

 Texas is the nation's largest producer of cattle, most of which are beef breeds, as opposed to the dairy varieties. The cattle industry actually began in Texas with long-horn cattle, which were driven by cattlemen to Kansas and Missouri for shipment by railroad.

Beef Stroganoff

3 tablespoons flour
1½ teaspoons salt
¼ teaspoon pepper
1 pound beef tenderloin, ¼ inch
  thick
1 clove garlic, cut
¼ cup butter or margarine

½ cup minced onions
¼ cup water
1 (10½-ounce) can condensed
  chicken soup, undiluted
1 pound sliced mushrooms
1 cup commercial sour cream
Snipped parsley, chives, or dill

Combine flour, salt, and pepper. Trim fat from meat. Rub both sides of meat with garlic. With rim of saucer, pound flour mixture into both sides of meat. Cut meat into 1½- or 1-inch strips. In hot butter in Dutch oven or deep skillet, brown meat strips, turning them often. Add onions; sauté until golden. Add water, stir to dissolve brown bits in bottom of Dutch oven. Add soup and mushrooms; cook, uncovered, over low heat, stirring occasionally, until mixture is thick and meat is fork-tender, about 20 minutes.

Just before serving, stir in sour cream; heat but do not boil. Sprinkle with parsley. Serve with hot fluffy rice or wild rice, boiled noodles, or mashed potatoes. Makes 4-6 servings.

Hospitality Heirlooms (Mississippi)

Stuffed Cabbage Rolls

1 large head cabbage
1 pound hamburger
2 eggs
½ cup rice (uncooked)

1 teaspoon salt
¼ teaspoon pepper
1 small onion, finely chopped

Simmer cabbage leaves to soften. Combine remaining ingredients and mix well. Place mixture into cabbage leaves and roll up. Place layer of cabbage leaves in bottom of pan. Place rolls on top. Make Sauce.

SAUCE:
1 large onion, chopped
2 (8-ounce) cans tomato sauce
2 (1-pound, 13-ounce) cans tomatoes
2 tablespoons lemon juice

¼ teaspoon pepper
1 teaspoon salt
1 teaspoon Worcestershire sauce
½ to 1 cup brown sugar

Bring sauce to a boil and pour over rolls. Place in 375° oven, covered, for 1 hour. Bake uncovered at 250° for 2 hours.

Country Cookbook (Michigan)

Beef Tips in Wine

Perfect open-hearth recipe! Try it some cold winter Saturday in a black iron pot swung from a cooking crane in an open fireplace. A very successful recipe.

4 pounds sirloin tip, or eye of round, cubed
1 teaspoon salt
1 teaspoon coarse-grind black pepper
½ cup flour
1 clove garlic, crushed
3 medium onions, sliced thin
2 (4-ounce) cans sliced mushrooms, drained
1 cup chopped celery hearts with tops
1 teaspoon Worcestershire sauce
2 teaspoons tomato paste
1 (10-ounce) can beef broth
3 tablespoons flour
¼ cup dry red wine
Buttered noodles

Toss beef cubes with salt, pepper, and ½ cup flour until thoroughly coated. Place in bottom of large slow cooker or iron pot. Add garlic, onions, mushrooms, and celery. Stir Worcestershire sauce and tomato paste into beef broth. Pour over meat and vegetables; mix together well. Cover and cook slowly 5-6 hours in fireplace or 7-12 hours in slow cooker on low setting.

One hour before serving, turn cooker to high or move pot to hotter place over fire. Make smooth paste of 3 tablespoons flour and wine. Stir into meat and vegetables; cook only until thickened. If using iron pot, empty immediately into covered soup tureen, as wine should not stand in iron. Serve over hot buttered noodles. Serves 8-10.

The Historic Roswell Cook Book (Georgia)

French Oven Beef Stew

2 pounds stew beef, cubed
2 medium onions, sliced thin
3 stalks celery, sliced
4 medium carrots, sliced
1 cup tomato juice
⅓ cup tapioca
1 tablespoon sugar
1 tablespoon salt
¼ teaspoon pepper
½ teaspoon basil
2 or 3 potatoes, cubed in medium pieces

Combine all but potatoes in a 2½-quart casserole. Cover. Bake at 325° for 3½ hours. Put potatoes on last hour. Stir occasionally. Excellent!

Thoroughbred Fare (South Carolina)

Veal Parmigiana

1 onion, minced
3 garlic cloves, finely minced
4 tablespoons olive or salad oil,
  divided
1 (16-ounce) can tomatoes
1¼ teaspoon salt
¼ teaspoon pepper
1 (8-ounce) can tomato sauce
¼ teaspoon thyme

1 egg
¼ cup packaged dried bread
  crumbs
½ cup grated parmesan cheese,
  divided
1 pound thin veal cutlets cut into
  8 pieces—about 2x4½ inches
½ pound mozzarella or muenster
  cheese

About 1 hour before serving, sauté onion and garlic in 3 tablespoons of oil until golden. Add tomatoes, salt and pepper. Break tomatoes apart with spoon and simmer uncovered 10 minutes. Add tomato sauce and thyme and simmer uncovered 20 minutes more. Beat egg well with fork. Combine bread crumbs and ¼ cup of the parmesan cheese. Dip each piece of veal into egg, then into crumb mixture, and cook in 1 tablespoon of hot oil.

Sauté a few pieces at a time until golden brown on both sides. Arrange slices in 9x13x2-inch baking dish. Place thinly sliced mozzarella on top of veal pieces and spoon tomato mixture over. Sprinkle with ¼ cup parmesan. Bake, uncovered in a preheated 350° oven for 30 minutes or until fork tender. Yields 4 generous servings.

Boarding House Reach (Georgia)

Smothered Steak Daufuskie Style

A delicious and quick one-dish meal.

Steak (any kind and any amount)
Raw potatoes, enough sliced to
  cover steak
Sliced onions, enough to cover
  potatoes

Salt and pepper to taste
Soy sauce, if desired

Salt, pepper, and flour favorite steak and brown in a little oil in skillet. Take steak up and remove most of grease from pan. At this point, a little brown gravy may be made, then put the steak in gravy (or just put steak back into pan). Cover steak with sliced Irish potatoes and top with sliced onions. A shake of salt and pepper over the whole thing, and maybe a dash of soy sauce improves the flavor. Cover and simmer (20-30 minutes) until all is done.

Stirrin' the Pots on Daufuskie (South Carolina)

★★★★★★★★★★★★ ★★★★★★★★★★★★

Barbecued Meatballs

1 (13-ounce) can evaporated milk
3 pounds hamburger
2 cups 1-minute oatmeal, uncooked
2 eggs
1 cup chopped onion
¼ teaspoon garlic powder
2 teaspoons chili powder
2 teaspoons salt
½ teaspoon pepper

Mix together and shape with ice cream scoop.

SAUCE:
2 cups catsup
1½ cups brown sugar
2 teaspoons liquid smoke
1½ teaspoons garlic powder
½ cup chopped onion

Mix and pour over meatballs and bake at 350° for 1 hour.

Note: Marinate meatballs in sauce overnight in refrigerator to enhance flavor.

A Century in His Footsteps (Great Plains)

★ **Editor's Extra:** This makes enough to feed a party! Easy to halve for your family, or freeze some for later.

Venison Meat Balls

1½ pounds ground venison
2 cups grated raw potatoes (or run them through the meat grinder after venison)
1 tablespoon chopped onion
1½ cups soda cracker crumbs
1½ teaspoons salt
⅛ teaspoon pepper
1 egg
¼ cup milk
¼ cup butter
3 cups water, divided
½ package Lipton Beefy Onion Soup Mix
2-3 tablespoons flour

Combine venison, potatoes, onion, crackers, salt, pepper, egg, and milk; shape into 1½-inch balls. Brown balls slowly in butter in large skillet. Add ½ cup water and soup mix; cover. Simmer for 20 minutes or until done. Remove meatballs.

To make gravy, add ½ cup cold water to flour, combine well, and add to pan with remaining water. Simmer until thick. Add meatballs. Heat.

Marketplace Recipes Volume I (Wisconsin)

Meatballs Diablo

2 tablespoons bacon drippings
  or olive oil
1 medium onion, finely chopped
1 pound lean ground beef
½ pound ground pork
3 eggs
2 dashes of Tabasco or to taste

½ cup dried bread crumbs
½ teaspoon ground cumin
1 clove garlic, minced
½ teaspoon ground nutmeg
1 tablespoon chopped fresh parsley
Cooking oil

Heat the bacon drippings or oil in a frying pan, and cook the onion until soft. Mix together the ground beef and ground pork in a mixing bowl and stir in the onions. Lightly beat the eggs and add to the meat mixture. Stir in the Tabasco, bread crumbs, cumin, garlic, nutmeg, and parsley and form into balls approximately the size of walnuts. Fry the meatballs in the cooking oil over medium heat until well browned and done through. Place meatballs in Red Chile Sauce and serve with rice. Yields 2 dozen meat balls.

RED CHILE SAUCE:

2 tablespoons butter
2 tablespoons all-purpose flour
1½ cups beef stock or broth
¼ cup red wine
1 clove garlic, finely minced

1 teaspoon ground New Mexico
  red chile
½ teaspoon salt
½ teaspoon freshly ground
  black pepper

Melt the butter, stir in the flour and stir constantly, letting the flour brown slightly. Slowly stir in the beef stock and wine. Stir until the sauce starts to thicken, then turn down the heat to simmer. Stir in the garlic, chile, salt and pepper. Let cook over low heat, until just heated through.

Billy the Kid Cook Book (New Mexico)

Excellent Meat Loaf

MEAT LOAF:
1½ pounds ground beef
½ can tomato soup
1 cup Pepperidge Farm Herb
  Stuffing
2 ribs celery
1 egg

1 large onion, chopped
½ cup American cheese, grated
½ cup bell pepper, chopped
1½ teaspoons salt
¼ teaspoon black pepper
Bacon slices

SAUCE:
2 tablespoons butter, melted
2 tablespoons soy sauce
1 (8-ounce) can tomato sauce

¼ cup water
¼ cup vinegar
½ cup brown sugar

Mix all meat loaf ingredients except bacon; form into loaf and top with bacon slices to cover meat loaf. Pour sauce over top and cook at 350° for 1 hour and 15 minutes. Baste with sauce every 5 minutes.

The Bonneville House Presents (Arkansas)

Cheeseburger Pie

Pastry for 1 (9-inch) one-crust pie,
  unbaked
1 pound ground beef
½ teaspoon ground oregano
½ cup crushed soda crackers

1 (8-ounce) can tomato sauce
¼ cup chopped onion
¼ cup chopped green pepper
¾ teaspoon salt
¼ teaspoon pepper

Brown meat. Drain. Stir in remaining ingredients and pour into pastry shell.

CHEESE TOPPING:
1 egg, beaten
¼ cup milk
½ teaspoon salt

½ teaspoon dry mustard
½ teaspoon Worcestershire sauce
2 cups grated Cheddar cheese

Combine egg and milk. Stir in seasonings and cheese. Spread topping evenly over filling. Cover edge of pie crust with 2-3-inch strip of aluminum foil to prevent excessive browning. Remove foil the last 15 minutes of baking. Bake in 425° oven for 30 minutes. Serves 6-8.

Amarillo Junior League Cookbook (Texas)

Taco Pie

1 deep-dish frozen pie crust
1 pound ground beef
1 medium onion, chopped
1 package taco seasoning mix
1 (16-ounce) can refried beans
1 small jar taco sauce, divided

2 cups shredded Cheddar cheese
12 nacho chips, crushed
Chopped lettuce
Chopped tomatoes
Sour cream

Preheat oven to 400°. Thaw pie crust 10 minutes. Prick bottom and sides of pie crust with fork. Bake pie crust for 10 minutes. Remove from oven and reduce temperature to 350°.

In skillet, brown hamburger and onion until brown. Drain fat. Add taco seasoning mix. In small bowl, combine refried beans and ⅓ cup taco sauce.

Layer ⅓ of refried bean mixture into pie crust; cover with ½ hamburger mix, then 1 cup Cheddar cheese and crushed nacho chips. Repeat layers, except nachos. Bake an additional 20-25 minutes. Remove from oven and top with lettuce, tomato, and additional taco sauce or sour cream.

Our Best Home Cooking (Illinois)

Ranch Hand Mexican Pie

Enough prepared mashed potatoes
   for 4 servings
1 egg, slightly beaten
¼ cup sliced green onions
   (with tops)
1 pound ground beef
½ cup chopped onion

1 (8-ounce) can tomato sauce
¼ cup sliced ripe olives
2-3 teaspoons chili powder (to taste)
¼ teaspoon salt
¼ teaspoon garlic powder
1 cup shredded Cheddar or
   Monterey Jack cheese

Heat oven to 425°. Grease 9-inch pie plate. Place mashed potatoes in a bowl; stir in egg and green onions. Spread and press potato mixture evenly against bottom and side of pie plate. Bake 20-25 minutes or until light brown. Cook ground beef and chopped onion in 10-inch skillet, stirring occasionally, until beef is brown; drain thoroughly. Stir in remaining ingredients except cheese. Cover and cook over low heat 5 minutes, stirring occasionally. Spoon into shell; sprinkle with cheese. Bake 2-3 minutes or until cheese is melted. If desired, garnish with sour cream, green bell pepper, tomato, and avocado.

Down-Home Texas Cooking (Texas II)

Green Enchiladas

½ to ¾ pound ground beef
½ medium onion, finely chopped
1 clove garlic, finely chopped
1 teaspoon chili powder (increase to taste)
Salt and pepper to taste
Salad oil
1 dozen corn tortillas
1 large onion, chopped

1½ cups grated Velveeta or Monterey Jack cheese
¼ cup margarine
3 tablespoons flour
½ teaspoon salt
2 cups milk
1 (4-ounce) can chopped green chilies

Brown meat, the half onion, and garlic together until meat is thoroughly cooked. Add chili powder, salt, and pepper, and set aside. Soften tortillas by frying in ½ inch of hot salad oil for only a few seconds. Do not allow them to become crisp. They may be stacked as they are cooked.

To prepare enchiladas, place a spoonful of meat mixture on a tortilla. Add a tablespoon each of onion and cheese. Roll up and place seam-side-down in a 9x13-inch baking dish. Prepare remaining tortillas in the same manner. Any remaining meat or cheese may be sprinkled on top of enchiladas. More cheese may be used if desired. Melt margarine on medium heat and add flour and salt. Stir until bubbly and add milk. Stir until smooth and only slightly thickened. Add green chilies and remove from heat. Pour over enchiladas and bake the casserole at 350° for 10-15 minutes, or until thoroughly heated. Enchiladas may be prepared the day before serving or may be frozen. If preparing ahead, add sauce just before cooking in oven. Serves 4-6.

San Angelo Junior League Cookbook (Texas)

Shepherd's Pie

1 tablespoon vegetable oil
1 medium-size onion, chopped
1 pound ground beef (lean)
1 teaspoon basil, dried
½ pound green beans (fresh), steamed until tender

1 cup canned tomatoes (garlic flavored), chopped
2 medium-size potatoes, cooked until tender
1 egg, beaten
½ cup water

Heat oil in large skillet and sauté onion until golden. Add beef and basil and cook until browned. Stir in green beans and tomatoes, then turn mixture into casserole. Preheat oven to 350°. Mash potatoes together with egg and water; spoon evenly over meat mixture and bake for 15 minutes.

Down Home Cooking from Hocking County (Ohio)

★★★★★★★★★★★★ ★★★★★★★★★★★★

Pork Loins and Fried Apples

Flour (about ⅔ cup)
Salt and pepper to taste
4 pork loins
Bacon drippings or butter for
  browning (2 tablespoons)

3 or 4 tart apples
½ cup brown sugar

Mix flour, salt, and pepper and dredge each piece of meat in this mixture. Melt fat in heavy skillet and brown each piece of meat on both sides. Turn heat low. Cut unpeeled cored apples into quarters and place around the meat. Sprinkle with brown sugar, cover, and simmer 45-60 minutes. Serves 4.

More Than Moonshine: Appalachian Recipes and Recollections
(Kentucky)

Pork Tenderloin

1 (2 to 3-pound) pork tenderloin
3 strips bacon
½ cup soy sauce
1 tablespoon grated onion

1 clove garlic, minced
1 tablespoon vinegar
⅛ teaspoon cayenne pepper
½ teaspoon sugar

Wrap tenderloin with bacon. Fasten with toothpicks. Mix remaining ingredients and pour over meat. Marinate 3 hours or overnight. Turn once. Bake at 300° for 2 hours or until tender, basting often. Serve over rice with juices.

Sharing Our Best / Home of the Good Shepherd (Minnesota)

Pork Tenderloin with Mustard Sauce

2 pounds whole pork tenderloin
  (1 to 1½ inches diameter)
1 clove garlic, cut in half
1½ teaspoons salt

1 cup red wine
½ teaspoon onion salt
½ teaspoon Beau Monde

MUSTARD SAUCE:
1 cup mayonnaise
1 tablespoon honey
1 tablespoon finely chopped
  fresh parsley

2 teaspoons prepared mustard
1 teaspoon curry powder
½ teaspoon paprika

Rub the tenderloin with the cut garlic thoroughly. Sprinkle with salt and bake in a shallow baking pan about 1¼ hours (until tender) at 325°. Combine the wine, onion salt, and Beau Monde and simmer 1 minute. Combine all ingredients for the Mustard Sauce. Slice the tenderloin, pour hot wine sauce over the slices, and serve Mustard Sauce in a separate dish. Serves 4-6.

Bravo! Applaudable Recipes (Alabama)

★ **Editor's Extra:** If you can't find Beau Monde, recipe is fine without it. The Mustard Sauce is so good, it can be used over vegetables and even as a dip!

Orange Pork Chops

Delicious served with fried rice.

6 thick pork chops
1 (11-ounce) can mandarin oranges
4 tablespoons brown sugar
½ teaspoon cinnamon
3 whole cloves

½ teaspoon salt
1 teaspoon prepared mustard
¼ cup catsup
1 tablespoon vinegar

Brown chops on both sides in large skillet. Add drained oranges to skillet, reserving juice. Combine ½ to ¾ cup of reserved liquid with remaining ingredients. Pour over pork chops. Cover and simmer gently until chops are done (about 45 minutes).

To Market, To Market (Kentucky)

★ ★ ★ ★ ★ ★ ★ ★ ★ ★ ★ ★   ★ ★ ★ ★ ★ ★ ★ ★ ★ ★ ★ ★

Pork Chops in Mushroom Gravy

2 (1-inch thick) loin pork chops
2 tablespoons all-purpose flour
1 teaspoon paprika
Salt and pepper
1 tablespoon vegetable oil

1 small onion, minced
½ green pepper, minced
6-8 mushrooms, chopped
1 cup milk
Juice of ½ lemon

Remove excess fat from edge of chops. Combine flour, paprika, salt, and pepper; dredge chops in mixture. Set aside remaining flour mixture. Brown chops in oil and remove to shallow casserole. Add onion, green pepper, and mushrooms to skillet; sauté until soft. Add reserved flour mixture; cook, stirring, 3 minutes. Blend in milk and cook until thickened, stirring constantly. Stir in lemon juice. Pour sauce over chops; cover and bake at 350° for 1 hour. Remove cover and bake 10 more minutes. Yields 2 servings.

Bell's Best 2 (Mississippi)

Wild Rice and Pork Chop Casserole

5-8 pork chops or pork loin
Flour
1 can Campbell's golden mushroom
  soup

1 can water
1 can Campbell's beef bouillon soup
1 box Uncle Ben's long grain and
  wild rice

Roll pork chops in flour and brown. Mix remaining ingredients together and put in casserole. Place browned pork chops on top and cover with lid or aluminum foil. Bake at 350° for 1 hour.

Seasoned with Love (Illinois)

★★★★★★★★★★★★   ★★★★★★★★★★★★

Stuffed Pork Chops

4 thick pork chops

FILLING:

2 apples, cored and chopped
½ cup raisins
¾ cup bread crumbs
1 tablespoon brown sugar
½ teaspoon black pepper
½ teaspoon salt

½ teaspoon cloves
2 tablespoons melted butter
2 tablespoons chopped chives
  or parsley
2 tablespoons butter
1 cup beef broth

Trim fat off chops. Make a slit in thick end of chop. In bowl, combine apples, raisins, bread crumbs, brown sugar, pepper, salt, and cloves. Add 2 tablespoons melted butter and chives or parsley; mix well. Stuff each chop with filling. Skewer with toothpick to close.

Heat 2 tablespoons butter in skillet. Brown chops slowly over medium heat on both sides. Add beef broth; bring to a simmer over low heat for about 30 minutes or until tender (cover, if broth does not cover chops). Remove toothpicks, put on platter, pour pan juice over chops, and serve with a green salad and steamed broccoli.

A Collection of Recipes from St. Matthew Lutheran Church (Illinois)

Pork Chops Hawaiian

1 cup soy sauce	2 tablespoons vinegar
1/2 cup water	1/2 cup pineapple syrup
1/4 cup brown sugar	1/2 cup sugar
8 (1-inch) boneless pork chops (trimmed) or boneless loin	1/4 cup ketchup
	1 small onion, sliced
2 tablespoons flour	1 small green pepper
1 teaspoon each, salt and pepper	5 slices pineapple, cut in wedges

About 6 hours before serving, bring soy sauce, water, and brown sugar to a boil. Cool slightly and pour over meat. Turn every hour for 4 hours. Remove and pat meat dry. Mix flour, salt, and pepper. Coat meat and brown in oiled skillet. Remove to baking dish. Combine vinegar, pineapple syrup (pour the syrup of the canned pineapple and add sugar to make syrup), ketchup, onion, green pepper chunks, and pineapple chunks. Pour over meat. Cover and bake for 1 1/2 hours at 350°. Serve over rice.

Seasoned Cooks II (Michigan)

Pork Fajitas

Fast and fabulous.

1 teaspoon olive oil	1/2 teaspoon ground cumin
1 pound pork tenderloin, julienned	2 teaspoons fresh lime juice
1/2 teaspoon salt	8 (6-inch) flour tortillas, warmed
1/4 teaspoon pepper	1/2 cup prepared salsa of your choice
1 red bell pepper, thinly sliced	Garnishes: shredded lettuce, chopped tomatoes, avocado slices, cilantro, and olives
1 green bell pepper, thinly sliced	
1 small onion, thinly sliced	
1 clove garlic, minced	

Heat oil in large skillet over high heat. Add pork; sprinkle with salt and pepper. Cook, stirring constantly, 2 minutes. Add peppers, onion, garlic, and cumin. Continue cooking until vegetables are crisp-tender, 3-4 minutes. Stir in lime juice. To serve, roll 3/4 cup pork mixture in each tortilla with 1 tablespoon salsa and garnishes, as desired. Makes 4 servings.

Palates (Colorado)

Barbequed Pork Loin Baby Back Ribs

1 slab pork loin baby back ribs

MARINADE:

½ cup chicken stock	**¼ cup vinegar**
½ cup soy sauce	**6 tablespoons sugar**
¼ cup oil	**2 cloves garlic, minced**

Combine marinade ingredients and marinate ribs in refrigerator for 2 hours to overnight.

Remove ribs from marinade and sprinkle with dry barbeque seasoning. Cook over medium coals (225°) until internal temperature registers 160° on a meat thermometer. Baste with marinade or sprinkle lightly with dry seasoning every 30 minutes during cooking process. Serves 2-3.

The Passion of Barbeque (Missouri)

Barbeque Rub

2 cups sugar	**½ cup salt**
¼ cup paprika	**2 teaspoons black pepper**
2 teaspoons chili powder	**1 teaspoon garlic powder**
½ teaspoon cayenne pepper	

Combine all ingredients and use as a rub for any barbeque meat. Yields about 3 cups.

The Passion of Barbeque (Missouri)

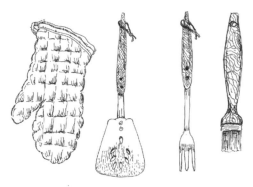

Finger Lickin' Spareribs

6 pounds country-style spareribs

½ cup each sherry and water

SAUCE:

1 teaspoon each chili powder and
  celery seed

3 cups water

½ cup chopped onion

1 teaspoon salt

1 cup catsup

¼ cup vinegar

¼ cup Worcestershire

¼ lemon, sliced thin

⅛ teaspoon pepper

½ cup brown sugar

In a large frying pan, brown spareribs (without flour). Then add sherry and ½ cup water, and cook (simmer), covered, for 1 hour. In another pan, combine all sauce ingredients and cook (simmer) for an hour. Let ribs cool in liquid long enough to skim off fat. Then remove ribs and drain. Lay drained ribs in large casserole, cover with sauce, and bake 1 hour at 300°.

Historic Kentucky Recipes (Kentucky)

Best Bar-B-Que

I have never seen this recipe in any recipe book. I have had it for 35 years and enjoy it every time we have a party or have a number of guests.

2 pounds beef roast
  (no fat, no bone)

2 pounds pork roast
  (no fat, no bone)

Boil together or in separate containers until very tender. Remove from broth. Let cool. Save broth. Do not cut meat, but tear apart with fingers or forks or both when cool. In separate pan, mix:

1 medium bottle tomato catsup

1 medium jar India relish

1 cup onions, diced finely

1 cup diced celery

1 cup diced bell pepper

Salt and pepper to taste

Mix ingredients with meat. Simmer (do not boil) for 1½ to 2 hours. Add some broth, just enough to make moist. (This can be served as sandwiches.) Makes a large amount for about 20 people.

Cooking on the Road (Missouri)

Apricot Baked Ham

Ham is a great choice for the Christmas Eve meal, because once it goes in the oven, it practically takes care of itself until dinnertime. The sugary crust makes the ham beautiful to serve.

1 (10-14-pound) whole ham, fully
  cooked, bone in
Whole cloves
⅓ cup dry mustard

1 cup apricot jam
1 cup light brown sugar, firmly
  packed

Trim skin and excess fat from ham. Place ham on a rack in a large roasting pan. Insert cloves in ham every inch or so. Be sure to push cloves into the ham surface as far as they'll go. Now combine the dry mustard and the jam. Spread over entire surface of the ham. Pat the brown sugar over the jam mixture. Bake uncovered at 325° for 2½ to 3½ hours, or until meat thermometer registers 140°. Count on 15-18 minutes per pound. The sugary crust that forms on the ham keeps the juices in. When ham is done, remove it from oven and let sit for 15-20 minutes before carving. Will serve 15 or more.

Christmas Thyme at Oak Hill Farm (Indiana)

Stromboli

Hungry teenagers will make this disappear.

1 loaf frozen bread dough
¼ pound provolone cheese, grated
¼ pound American cheese, grated
½ pound pepperoni or salami
1 large tomato, cut into chunk,
  (optional)

1 small onion, sliced thin
1 teaspoon oregano
½ teaspoon pepper
½ teaspoon garlic powder
½ cup parmesan cheese, grated
2 tablespoons olive oil

Defrost and let bread dough rise according to package directions. Roll out dough to ½-inch thickness. Spread provolone and American cheeses over dough, keeping ½ inch from edge. Spread pepperoni next. Top with tomato, onion rings, seasonings, and parmesan cheese. Sprinkle olive oil over all. Roll as you would a jelly roll and seal the edges. Rub with olive oil, puncture with fork, and place on oiled cookie sheet. Bake at 350° for 30-40 minutes. Yields 4-6 servings.

Hint: Add other sliced meats if you enjoy a meatier sandwich.

The Eater's Digest (Pennsylvania)

★ **Editor's Extra:** Frozen bread loaves come several in a package; this uses only one. It looks small frozen, but rises to a good-sized loaf.

Walking Taco

Fun, fun, fun—great for kid's parties.

1½ pounds hamburger
1 small onion, chopped
1 teaspoon garlic salt
Salt and pepper to taste
10 (2¾-ounce) bags Fritos or
  nacho cheese Doritos chips

2 cups shredded lettuce
1 cup chopped tomatoes
1 cup shredded Cheddar cheese
1 cup sour cream
1 can chopped black olives, drained
Taco sauce to taste

Brown hamburger, onion, garlic salt, salt and pepper. Cut ¼ inch off top of chip bags. Crush chips slightly. Fill bags with cooked hamburger mixture. Top with lettuce, tomatoes, cheese, sour cream, and olives. Stick fork in bag and serve. Offer taco sauce.

Recipes from the Heart (Great Plains)

★ **Editor's Extra:** Want a little more spice? Try putting taco seasoning in the ground meat.

Sloppy Joes

Perfectly simple—takes about 15 minutes from start to finish!

1 pound ground beef
1 onion, chopped
2 tablespoons chili powder
3 tablespoons barbecue sauce
Dash Worcestershire sauce
½ cup ketchup

1 tablespoon sugar
½ cup milk
2 tablespoons vinegar
1 tablespoon flour
Salt and pepper to taste

Brown beef and onion. Stir in other ingredients. Simmer for 5 minutes. Serve on toasted buns.

Kitchen Klatter Keepsakes (Oklahoma)

Stuffed Green Peppers

2 large green peppers
½ pound lean ground beef
¼ cup uncooked instant rice
1 (8-ounce) can tomato sauce, divided
2 tablespoons chopped onion
1 egg, beaten
½ teaspoon salt
1 tablespoon parmesan cheese
½ teaspoon Worcestershire sauce
Dash of pepper

Cut peppers in half lengthwise and remove seeds. Combine ground meat, rice, ¼ cup tomato sauce, and remaining ingredients. Stuff peppers with mix and place in a greased baking dish. Spoon remaining tomato sauce over stuffed peppers and then sprinkle with additional parmesan cheese. Cover and bake at 350° for 50-60 minutes. Yields 4 servings.

By Special Request (Louisiana II)

The Society Hill's Philadelphia Phenomenon Cheese Steak

1 (8-inch) round Italian roll
2 tablespoons vegetable oil
6 ounces thinly sliced steak
2 slices cheese (American, mozzarella, or provolone)
2 tablespoons or more water
1 tablespoon chopped, sautéed onions (optional)
1 tablespoon chopped, sautéed green peppers (optional)
1 tablespoon chopped, sautéed mushrooms (optional)
1 slice bacon, fried and crumbled (optional)
1 tablespoon chopped artichoke hearts (optional)
1-2 tablespoons commercial pizza sauce (optional)

Cut roll in half horizontally and hollow out. Heat roll in a 250° oven until warm, approximately 4-5 minutes. Heat oil on griddle or in frying pan. When oil is hot, sizzle steak. (Break steak apart for faster cooking.) When steak has cooked for 10-15 seconds, place cheese on top; add water to griddle or frying pan to aid cheese in melting. Remove from griddle or pan; stuff roll with steak and cheese and any or all of the optional toppings. Serves 1.

Pennsylvania's Historic Restaurants and Their Recipes (Pennsylvania)

Cakes

The Gateway Arch in St. Louis is our nation's tallest monument standing 630 feet tall. It was built in 1961-1965 to commemorate the westward growth of the United States between 1803 and 1890.

Old-Fashion Strawberry Shortcake

Just like Mom made...

2 pints fresh strawberries
½ cup, plus 3 tablespoons sugar,
  divided
2½ cups Bisquick

3 tablespoons butter, melted
½ cup milk
2 pints whipping cream
3-4 tablespoons powdered sugar

Wash and cap strawberries. Reserve about 6 of the best for decoration and slice the remainder. Sprinkle with ½ cup sugar and refrigerate overnight.

To make cake, mix Bisquick, 3 tablespoons sugar, butter, and milk into a dough and gently knead into a smooth ball. Pat into a disk about 8 inches in diameter and place on a baking sheet. Bake in a preheated 425° oven for about 15-20 minutes. Cool. Cut in half horizontally. Whip cream with the powdered sugar until stiff.

To assemble: Spoon some of the strawberry juice over the cut sides of the cake to moisten. Arrange ⅔ of the strawberry slices over the bottom half of the cake and spread with ⅓ of the whipped cream. Place the top on the cake and arrange the remaining ⅓ of the berries on the top. Spread the remaining whipped cream over the berries and garnish with the reserved whole berries. This is best if allowed to sit in the refrigerator a couple of hours before serving. Serves 6-8.

Birdies in the Oven / Aces in the Kitchen (Alabama)

★ **Editor's Extra:** This tastes like the delicious shortcake made every year at the Strawberry Festival in Ponchatoula, Louisiana. Pictured on the cover, it tastes even better than it looks!

Cakes

Melt-In-Your-Mouth Blueberry Cake

A wonderful light summer dessert and especially good for picnics. A family favorite!

2 eggs, separated
1 cup sugar, divided
½ cup margarine, softened
¼ teaspoon salt
1 teaspoon vanilla
1½ cups sifted flour plus
  1 tablespoon for coating blueberries

1 teaspoon baking powder
⅓ cup milk
1½ cups fresh blueberries
Cinnamon sugar for topping
  (1 tablespoon sugar mixed with
  ¼ teaspoon cinnamon)

Preheat oven to 350°. Beat egg whites until stiff. Beat in ¼ cup of sugar.

Cream margarine; add salt, vanilla, and remaining sugar gradually. Add egg yolks and beat until creamy.

Sift flour with baking powder. Add alternately to creamed mixture with milk. Fold in beaten egg whites. Coat blueberries with 1 tablespoon of flour. Fold in berries. Turn into a well-greased and floured 8x8-inch pan. Sprinkle cinnamon sugar on top. Bake in 350° oven 40-50 minutes. Cool on rack. Wrap any leftovers and store in refrigerator. May be frozen. Serves 8.

The Maine Collection (New England)

Simply Great Pineapple Cake

1 box yellow or lemon cake mix
  with pudding in the mix
¾ cup vegetable oil

4 eggs, unbeaten
1 (11-ounce) can mandarin oranges
  with juice

Mix ingredients in order given. Blend; beat with electric mixer, medium speed, for 2 minutes. Bake at 325° in 3 (8-inch) greased and floured pans for 20-25 minutes, or at 350° in 9x13-inch pan for 28-36 minutes. When cool, spread with the following icing.

ICING:
1 (13½-ounce) can crushed
  pineapple
1 (3½-ounce) package dry instant
  vanilla pudding mix

1 (12-ounce) container whipped
  topping
Dash of salt

Mix crushed pineapple and instant pudding. Fold in the topping and salt; spread over cake. Serves 15. Store cake in refrigerator.

Nutritional Analysis: Cal 370; Carbo 44g; Prot 4g; Fat 19.5g; Chol 73mg; Vit A 330IU; Vit C 11mg; Sod 234mg; Potas 119mg; Calc 66mg.

REC Family Cookbook (Great Plains)

★★★★★★★★★★★★   ★★★★★★★★★★★★

The Apple Barn Fresh Apple Pound Cake

Luscious apple all the way and easy to make.

3 cups all-purpose flour, spooned
  into cup
1 teaspoon baking soda
1 teaspoon salt
1½ cups corn oil
2 cups sugar

3 large eggs, room temperature
2 teaspoons vanilla extract
1¼ cups pecans, chopped
  medium-fine
2 cups pared apples, finely chopped
Brown Sugar Topping

Sift flour, soda, and salt onto a platter or waxed paper. In a large bowl, beat oil, sugar, eggs, and vanilla at medium speed of electric mixer for 3 or 4 minutes until well blended. Gradually add flour mixture; beat until smooth. Fold in pecans and apples. Pour batter into a greased and floured (10-inch) Bundt pan. Bake in a preheated 325° oven about 1 hour 20 minutes, or until cake tests done. Cool on wire rack 20 minutes.

For festive occasions, dribble brown sugar topping over warm cake. For an elegant dessert, slice cake and top each serving with baked custard. This cake is marvelous plain. Serve warm or cold. Store cake in foil or tin can for a day or two. To keep longer, refrigerate and bring to room temperature before serving. Fresh apples tend to mold easily. Yields 22-24 servings.

BROWN SUGAR TOPPING:
½ cup butter or margarine
½ cup light brown sugar, lightly
  packed

2 teaspoons milk

Combine all ingredients and bring to a boil over medium heat; cook 2 minutes, stirring constantly. Spoon hot sugar mixture over warm cake.

The Apple Barn Cookbook (Tennessee)

Pineapple Upside Down Cake

3 tablespoons butter or margarine
1 cup brown sugar
1 large can sliced pineapple, drained
8 maraschino cherries
1½ teaspoon baking powder
Pinch salt

3 eggs
1½ cups sugar
½ cup water (or juice from
  pineapple)
1 teaspoon vanilla
1½ cups flour

Put butter and brown sugar in a (10-inch) iron frying pan. Let simmer a couple of minutes and add sliced pineapple. Place a maraschino cherry in center of each pineapple slice. Remove from heat. Make a batter of the remaining ingredients and pour over pineapple slices. Heat oven to 400°. Put skillet in oven for 10 minutes. Reduce heat to 350° and bake an additional 50 minutes or until cake is done. Turn out of pan on a large platter. Serve plain or with whipped cream.

Treasured Recipes Book II (Missouri)

Carrot Cake

1½ cups salad oil
2 cups sugar
2½ cups flour
2 teaspoons baking powder
1 teaspoon baking soda
1 teaspoon salt

2 teaspoons cinnamon
4 eggs
2½ cups grated carrots
1 cup crushed pineapple
1 teaspoon vanilla
1 cup chopped pecans or walnuts

Combine oil and sugar; mix well. Sift dry ingredients; mix alternately with the eggs (1 at a time) to the oil and sugar mixture. Add carrots, pineapple, and vanilla; mix well. Add nuts (reserve some for garnish). Bake at 350° for 1 hour in 10-inch angel food cake pan or 3 (9-inch) round pans.

FROSTING:

1 (8-ounce) package cream cheese
3½ cups powdered sugar

½ cup margarine, softened
2 teaspoons vanilla

Mix all ingredients. Spread on cool cake. Garnish with nuts.

Susie's Cook Book (Pennsylvania)

Hummingbird Cake

3 cups all-purpose flour
2 cups sugar
1 teaspoon salt
1 teaspoon soda
1 teaspoon cinnamon
3 eggs, beaten

1½ cups salad oil
1½ teaspoons vanilla
1 (8-ounce) can crushed pineapple, drained
2 cups chopped bananas
1 cup chopped nuts

Mix well by hand. Combine dry ingredients; add eggs and salad oil and stir until well mixed. Add vanilla, pineapple, bananas, and nuts. Spoon batter into large greased and floured sheet pan. Bake at 350° for 40-45 minutes.

ICING:

1 box confectioners' sugar
½ cup margarine
1 (8-ounce) package cream cheese

1 teaspoon vanilla
1 cup chopped nuts

Combine first 4 ingredients. Sprinkle chopped nuts on top of icing.

Calling All Cooks (Alabama)

Aunt Judy's Italian Cake

1 fudge marble cake mix
  (Duncan Hines)
2 pounds ricotta cheese

4 eggs
1 cup sugar
1 teaspoon vanilla

Mix cake mix per instructions on the box. Put into 9x13-inch pan, but do not bake yet. Mix ricotta cheese, eggs, sugar, and vanilla together. With large spoon, spoon the cheese mixture over the top of the cake batter. It should cover the entire surface. Bake at 350° for 1 hour and 5 minutes. Let cool well!

TOPPING:

1 (3-ounce) package instant
  chocolate fudge pudding

1 cup milk
1 (12-ounce) container Cool Whip

Mix pudding with 1 cup milk and add this to Cool Whip. Spread on the cake as frosting. This cake is best when baked the day before needed. Refrigerate.

Cookin' with Friends (Illinois)

A Very Special Rum Cake

A rich, wonderful cake that will make discernible waves. Try it and see.

CAKE:

1 cup chopped walnuts
1 (18½-ounce) package yellow
  cake mix with pudding
3 large eggs

½ cup cold water
½ cup vegetable oil
½ cup any 80-proof dark rum

This cake does well in a (12-cup) Bundt pan, but you can also bake it in a 10-inch tube pan. Grease the pan well, sprinkle flour over it. Spread the chopped nuts over the bottom of pan. Preheat oven to 325°.

Put remaining ingredients in mixing bowl. Beat on medium speed for about 5 minutes or until well blended. Pour the batter over the nuts. Bake for one hour or until a fork comes out dry when cake is pierced near the center. When cake is cool, invert it on a large plate. Prick as many holes in top as you can without ruining the cake.

GLAZE AND TOPPING:

1 stick unsalted butter
¼ cup water
1 cup sugar

½ cup 80-proof rum
1 cup heavy cream
3 tablespoons chopped walnuts

Melt butter in small pan, put in water and sugar. Boil for 5 minutes, stirring often. Remove from heat source and stir in rum.

Using a pastry brush, brush tops and sides of cake with mixture. Pour some into the holes you have made in cake. Repeat the procedure, using the liquid that has collected on bottom of plate. Repeat again and again until all the liquid is absorbed by the cake. This cake will taste better if you leave it for some hours to absorb the rum. You can do the next step at the last minute.

Whip the cream. Add sugar if desired, or a bit of rum flavoring. Put it on top of the cake, also in the hole in center. Do this immediately before serving. Put walnuts on top of whipped cream. Serves 8 elegantly.

Viva Italia (Ohio)

Earthquake Cake

1 cup coconut
1 cup chopped pecans
1 box German chocolate cake mix
1 stick margarine, softened

1 (8-ounce) package cream cheese, softened
2 cups powdered sugar

Grease and flour a 9x13-inch cake pan. Put coconut and pecans in bottom of pan; spread evenly. Mix cake mix as directed on box (with eggs, water, etc.). Pour cake mix over coconut and nuts. Mix margarine, cream cheese, and powdered sugar. Spoon on top of cake mix (in dollops). Bake at 350° for 50 minutes. May be served with whipped cream.

College Avenue Presbyterian Church Cookbook (Illinois)

Coconut-Sour Cream Layer Cake

1 (18½-ounce) box butter-flavored cake mix
2 cups sugar
1 (16-ounce) carton sour cream

1 (12-ounce) package frozen coconut, thawed
1½ cups frozen non-dairy whipped topping, thawed

Prepare cake mix according to package directions, making 2 (8-inch) layers. When completely cool, split both layers. Combine sugar, sour cream, and coconut, blending well. Chill. Reserve 1 cup sour cream mixture for frosting and spread remainder between layers of cake. Combine reserved sour cream mixture with whipped topping; blend until smooth. Spread on top and sides of cake. Seal cake in an airtight container and refrigerate for 3 days before serving. This cake can also be prepared in a 9x13-inch sheet cake pan. Stores well.

Mountain Laurel Encore (Kentucky)

★★★★★★★★★★★★★   ★★★★★★★★★★★★★

Comptroller of Public Accounts
Lemon Gold Cake

This should be kept in a vault!

2 cups sifted Swans Down Cake Flour
2 teaspoons Calumet Baking Powder
½ cup butter, softened (or shortening)
1 cup sugar
3 egg yolks, beaten until thick
  and lemon-colored

¾ cup milk
1 teaspoon vanilla (or ½ teaspoon
  lemon extract)

Sift flour once, measure, add baking powder, and sift together 3 times. Cream butter thoroughly, adding sugar gradually, and cream together until light and fluffy. Add egg yolks and beat well. Add flour alternately with milk, a small amount at a time. Add extract. Beat well. Bake in 2 greased 9-inch layer pans in moderate oven (375°) 25-30 minutes. Spread Luscious Lemon Frosting between layers and on top and sides of cake. Double recipe to make 3 (10-inch) layers.

LUSCIOUS LEMON FROSTING:

3 teaspoons grated orange rind
Dash of salt
3 tablespoons butter, softened

3 cups confectioners' sugar
2 tablespoons lemon juice
1 tablespoon water

Add orange rind and salt to butter; cream well. Add part of sifted sugar gradually, blending after each addition. Combine lemon juice and water; add to creamed mixture alternately with remaining sugar, until of right consistency to spread. Beat after each addition until smooth. Makes enough frosting to cover tops and sides of 2 (9-inch) layers. For a deeper yellow frosting, tint with yellow food coloring.

Ma's in the Kitchen (Texas II)

★ **Editor's Extra:** A recipe that looks good, tastes great, and is so impressive. "Treat yourself to a start-from-scratch cake," says noted food stylist, Bobbi Cappelli. "This one is definitely worth it!"

★★★★★★★★★★★★★★   ★★★★★★★★★★★★★★

Chocolate Cake

There is no other!

1 cup butter
2 cups sugar
4 eggs
2 cups flour, sifted
¼ teaspoon salt
1½ teaspoons soda

⅔ cup buttermilk
1 teaspoon vanilla extract
3 (1-ounce) squares unsweetened
   chocolate, melted in ⅔ cup
   boiling water

Preheat oven to 325°. Cream butter and sugar with electric beater until light and fluffy. Add eggs, one at a time, and beat well after each addition. Sift flour with salt. Mix soda with buttermilk and add alternately with flour to creamed mixture, starting and ending with flour. Add vanilla and melted chocolate with water; stir until smooth. Grease a 9x13-inch pan. Pour batter into pan and bake 50-55 minutes. Cool in the pan. While slightly warm, frost with Chocolate Frosting. Makes about 20 (2-inch) squares. The cake freezes well.

CHOCOLATE FROSTING:

½ cup margarine
1½ cups sugar
⅓ cup milk

¾ cup semisweet chocolate pieces
1 cup chopped pecans or walnuts
   (optional)

In a heavy saucepan, cook margarine, sugar, and milk to a full rolling boil. Boil for 2 minutes. Remove from heat; add chocolate pieces and nuts. Blend quickly. Beat until a spreading consistency. (It won't take more than a minute or two.) Spread at once over chocolate cake.

Cook and Deal (Florida)

★★★★★★★★★★★★ ★★★★★★★★★★★★

Wasp's Nest Cake

1 (3-ounce) box cook-and-serve
  vanilla pudding
2 cups milk

1 yellow cake mix
1 (12-ounce) package butterscotch
  morsels

On the stovetop mix pudding with milk and bring to a boil. Dump in box of cake mix. Stir and pour into a greased 9x13-inch pan. Sprinkle on butterscotch morsels. Bake in 350° oven for 30 minutes. Let cool; serve.

Taste & See (Indiana)

Hurricane Oatmeal Cake

Good to have on hand for "hurricane watches."

1 cup oatmeal
1¼ cups boiling water
2 eggs
1 cup brown sugar
1 cup granulated sugar

½ cup vegetable oil
1½ cups flour
1 teaspoon soda
1 teaspoon salt
1 teaspoon cinnamon

Combine oatmeal and boiling water; set aside. Beat together eggs, sugars, and oil until blended. Add sifted flour, soda, salt, and cinnamon; add oatmeal mixture.

Pour into greased 9x13-inch baking pan. Bake at 350° for 30-35 minutes.

TOPPING:

1 cup coconut
1 cup brown sugar
6 tablespoons melted margarine

½ cup chopped pecans
¼ cup evaporated milk

Mix together topping ingredients until moist. Spread over cake; broil until topping is light brown and crunchy—about 2 minutes.

Island Born and Bred (North Carolina)

On July 4th, 1776, Congress adopted the Declaration of Independence, and the United States of America was born. On that day, we declared independence from England and it was the beginning of a journey full of struggles and woes, defeats and accomplishments, enabling us to become the strong nation we are today.

Turtle Cake

Cake version of turtle candy.

1 German chocolate cake mix
1 stick margarine, softened
1½ cups water
½ cup oil

1 can Eagle Brand milk, divided
1 (1-pound) bag caramels
Chopped pecans

Combine and mix well cake mix, margarine, water, oil, and ½ can Eagle Brand milk. Pour ½ of the batter into a greased and floured 9x13x2-inch baking dish. Bake in a preheated 350° oven for 20-25 minutes.

Melt and mix together caramels and ½ can Eagle Brand milk. Spread over the baked layer. Sprinkle generously with pecans. Cover with remaining cake batter. Bake 25-35 minutes longer. Frost with Turtle Cake Frosting.

TURTLE CAKE FROSTING:

1 stick margarine
3 tablespoons cocoa
6 tablespoons evaporated milk

1 box powdered sugar
1 teaspoon vanilla

Melt in a small saucepan margarine, cocoa, and evaporated milk. Remove from heat and add powdered sugar and vanilla. Spread over cool cake.

Calf Fries to Caviar (Texas)

Texas Pecan Torte

3 cups pecans
6 eggs, separated
1½ cups sugar
3 tablespoons flour
1 teaspoon salt

3 tablespoons rum, divided
½ cup whipping cream
2 tablespoons powdered sugar
1 cup chocolate chips
½ cup sour cream

Chop pecans very finely in a blender, 1 cup at a time. Beat egg yolks until light and beat in sugar, flour, salt, 2 tablespoons rum, and nuts. Set aside. Beat egg whites until stiff and fold into the nut mixture. Pour into 3 (8-inch) or 2 (10-inch) layer cake pans, buttered and lined with waxed paper. Bake for 25 minutes in 350° oven. Allow to cool. (May be kept overnight.) A few hours before serving time, whip cream with powdered sugar and 1 tablespoon of rum. Spread filling between layers. Melt chocolate chips, fold in sour cream, and spread over the cake for icing.

San Antonio Cookbook II (Texas)

★★★★★★★★★★★ ★★★★★★★★★★★

Burning Love Chocolate Cream Cake

3 squares unsweetened chocolate
2¼ cups sifted flour
2 teaspoons baking soda
½ teaspoon salt
½ cup butter or margarine,
 softened
2¼ cups firmly packed light
 brown sugar

3 eggs
1½ teaspoons vanilla
1 cup dairy sour cream
1 cup boiling water
Whipped Cocoa Cream

Melt chocolate in a small bowl over hot (not boiling) water and cool. Grease and flour two (9x1½-inch) pans. Tap out excess flour.

Sift flour, baking soda, and salt onto waxed paper. Preheat oven to 350°. Beat butter, sugar, and eggs in a large bowl with electric mixer on high speed until light and fluffy. Beat in vanilla and cooled chocolate. Stir in dry ingredients, alternating with sour cream and beating well with a spoon until smooth. Stir in water. (Batter will be thin.) Pour into pans. Bake for 35 minutes or until centers spring back when lightly pressed with fingertips. Cool in pans 10 minutes, then turn on wire racks and cool completely. Split each layer in half crosswise to make 4 thin layers. Fill and frost with Whipped Cocoa Cream. Refrigerate.

WHIPPED COCOA CREAM:
⅔ cup confectioners' sugar
1 teaspoon vanilla

1 pint heavy cream
½ cup unsweetened cocoa powder

Whip ingredients in a medium bowl until stiff.

Elvis Fans Cookbook II (Tennessee)

209

★★★★★★★★★★★   ★★★★★★★★★★★★

Better Than Sex Cake

1 (6-ounce) package chocolate chips
¾ cup pecans, chopped
1 box yellow butter cake mix
  (without pudding)
4 eggs

½ cup oil
¼ cup water
1 teaspoon vanilla
1 small box instant vanilla pudding
1 (8-ounce) carton sour cream

Coat chocolate chips and pecans with a little of the dry cake mix. Mix remainder of cake mix, eggs, oil, water, vanilla, vanilla pudding, and sour cream thoroughly. Fold in chocolate chips and pecans. Pour into a greased and floured tube pan and bake for about 50 minutes at 350°. Cool before frosting.

CHOCOLATE FROSTING:
1 (16-ounce) box powdered sugar
3 squares baking chocolate, melted

¾ stick margarine, softened
Milk

Prepare chocolate frosting by combining all ingredients except milk. Add enough milk to make the frosting of a spreading consistency. Frost and serve—then judge for yourself!!

Ready to Serve (Texas)

Chocolate Chip Cake

1 yellow cake mix
1 (3½-ounce) package instant
  chocolate pudding
1 (8-ounce) carton sour cream
¾ cup oil

3 eggs
¾ cup water
1 (6-ounce) package milk chocolate
  chips

In a large bowl, blend all ingredients except chocolate chips. Beat for 4 minutes. Fold in the chips. Pour into a well-greased and floured Bundt pan. Bake at 350° for 50 minutes. Allow cake to cool completely before removing from pan. Yields 12-16 servings.

Our Country Cookin' (Oklahoma)

Apricot Nectar Cake

CAKE:
1 (18½-ounce) box yellow cake mix
4 eggs
¾ cup oil

¾ cup apricot nectar
3 teaspoons lemon extract

LEMON GLAZE:
1½ cups powdered sugar

2 lemons, juiced, rind grated

Preheat oven to 325°. In a medium mixing bowl, combine cake mix, eggs, oil, apricot nectar, and lemon extract. Beat with electric mixer at medium speed for 4 minutes. Pour into a greased and floured 9-inch tube or Bundt pan. Bake for 55 minutes. Let stand 5 minutes. Turn out onto a serving dish. Prick holes in cake with an ice pick or skewer. Prepare Lemon Glaze and spread over warm cake. Yields 14 servings.

Cooking on the Wild Side (Ohio)

Pumpkin Pie Cake

1 large can pumpkin	½ teaspoon ginger
1 can condensed milk	½ teaspoon salt
3 eggs	2 teaspoons cinnamon
1 cup sugar	1 yellow cake mix
1 teaspoon nutmeg	1 cup nuts
½ teaspoon cloves	2 sticks margarine, melted

Mix together like making a pumpkin pie the pumpkin, milk, eggs, sugar, nutmeg, cloves, ginger, salt, and cinnamon. Pour into a 9x13-inch pan. Sprinkle cake mix over pie mixture and press well. Sprinkle nuts on top and pour margarine over top. Bake at 350° for 50 minutes.

A Taste of Christ Lutheran (Wisconsin)

Elsie's Gingerbread

There is no doubt in our minds that this is the world's best gingerbread. Moist and sweet and dark, tinged with molasses but not too molasses-y. Sprinkled with a crisp streusel topping, this is outstanding—perhaps one of our ten all-time favorite recipes. Try it plain, with ice cream, with whipped cream, accompanying a baked apple or pear; make it with a few variations, as muffins; try it as upside-down cake. A wonderful, can't-go-wrong dessert, perfect for fall.

1½ cups unbleached white flour	1 egg, well beaten
1 cup sugar	3 tablespoons molasses
2 teaspoons ginger	1 teaspoon baking soda
1 teaspoon cinnamon	1 scant teaspoon salt
½ cup butter or shortening	1 cup buttermilk

Preheat oven to 350°. Combine flour, sugar, ginger and cinnamon. Cut in butter or shortening. Reserve ¼ cup of this crumbled mixture for topping. Add egg to the flour mixture. Stir in molasses. Dissolve soda and salt in buttermilk. Add to the other mixture. Pour into a greased 9-inch square pan, sprinkle with the reserved topping, and bake for 30 minutes.

The Dairy Hollow House Cookbook (Arkansas)

Delectable Sour Cream Pound Cake

This is a soft, velvety pound cake that keeps better than any pound cake I know. It has a delicious crunchy top that comes from being baked in low heat—not from an overload of sugar. This cake is just as delicious when the sugar is cut, which makes it especially delightful for breakfast or tea with a dish of strawberries. Bake it both ways. You will love this cake.

3 cups sifted all-purpose flour
¼ teaspoon baking soda
¼ teaspoon salt
1 cup (2 sticks) butter, cut into pieces
3 cups sugar (2¾ cups for cakes to
  be served with fruit)

6 large eggs, separated
1 cup sour cream
1½ teaspoons vanilla extract or
  cognac vanilla or ⅔ teaspoon
  ground mace

Preheat the oven to 325°. Combine the sifted flour with the baking soda and salt, and sift again. Cream the butter and sugar thoroughly with an electric mixer. Add the egg yolks and beat hard until you have a fairly smooth mixture. This will not "ribbon" with just the yolks.

Add the flour mixture in batches, alternating with the sour cream, blending by hand with a rubber spatula or a whisk. Blend in the vanilla or mace.

Beat the egg whites until they hold a stiff peak but are not dry and grainy. Gently fold them into the cake batter. Spoon the batter into a greased and lightly floured heavy 9- or 10-inch tube pan, or two 8x4x3-inch loaf pans, filling the pans not more than three-quarters full. Bake until the cake springs back at once when lightly touched, about 1 hour and 15 or 20 minutes (this will vary with the pans used). A cake tester or skewer inserted into the cake should come out clean. Remove the cake from the oven and allow it to rest 5 minutes. Run a thin knife around the edges of the pan to loosen the cake, and unmold it onto a rack. Turn the cake right-side-up to cool. Store in a tightly closed plastic or tin box. Serves 10-15.

The Heritage of Southern Cooking (Kentucky)

★★★★★★★★★★★★   ★★★★★★★★★★★★

Chocolate Raspberry Cheesecake

1½ cups (18) finely crushed creme-
   filled chocolate cookies
2 tablespoons butter, softened
4 (8-ounce) packages cream cheese,
   softened, divided
1¼ cups sugar
3 eggs

1 cup sour cream
1 teaspoon vanilla
1 cup (6 ounces) semisweet
   chocolate chips, melted
⅓ cup seedless raspberry preserves
1-2 packages frozen raspberries

Mix cookies and butter and press into bottom of a buttered 9-inch springform pan. Combine 3 packages cream cheese and sugar until well blended. Add eggs, 1 at a time, mixing well after each. Blend in sour cream
and vanilla; pour over crust. Combine remaining package cream cheese
and melted chocolate until smooth and well blended. Add preserves and
mix well. Drop spoonfuls of chocolate onto plain batter. Do not swirl.
Bake at 325° for 1 hour 20 minutes. Cool before removing rim from pan.
Serve with sieved raspberry sauce (1-2 packages frozen raspberries
pushed through food mill or strainer to remove seeds). Serve 2 tablespoons sauce per slice of cheesecake.

Y Winners...Cookbook of Champions (Great Plains)

Kahlúa Mousse Cheesecake

CRUST:
1 cup chocolate wafer crumbs   ¼ cup butter or margarine, melted

Combine crumbs and butter. Press onto bottom of 9-inch springform pan. Chill.

FILLING:
1 envelope unflavored gelatin   1 teaspoon lemon juice
½ cup cold water   ⅓ cup Kahlúa
3 (8-ounce) packages cream cheese   1 teaspoon vanilla extract
1 cup sugar   ¾ cup heavy or whipping cream,
1 can evaporated milk   whipped

In small saucepan, sprinkle gelatin over cold water; let stand 1 minute. Stir over low heat until completely dissolved; set aside.

In large bowl, beat cream cheese and sugar until fluffy. Gradually add evaporated milk and lemon juice. Beat till mixture is very fluffy. Gradually beat in gelatin mixture, Kahlúa, and vanilla until thoroughly blended. Fold in whipped cream. Pour into crust. Chill 8 hours or overnight.

Cheesecakes et cetera (Colorado)

Quick Lemon Cheesecake

CRUST:
1¼ cups graham cracker crumbs   6 tablespoons melted butter
¼ cup sugar

Combine crumbs, sugar, and butter. Press firmly on bottom and sides of an 8-inch square pan or 9-inch round pie pan. Chill while preparing filling.

FILLING:
1 (8-ounce) package cream cheese,   ½ teaspoon vanilla
   softened   1 (3¾-ounce) package instant
2 cups milk, divided   lemon pudding
1 tablespoon sugar

Beat cream cheese until soft. Blend in ½ cup milk. Add remaining milk, sugar, vanilla, and pudding mix; mix well. Pour into crust. Chill until firm. Garnish with whipped cream and strawberries or cherries.

St. Joseph's Parish Cookbook (Iowa)

Cheesecake Pie

Easy and delicious!

1 (8-ounce) package cream cheese, softened
¾ cup sugar
1 cup sour cream
2 teaspoons vanilla
1 (8-ounce) carton of Cool Whip

1 (9-inch) graham cracker pie crust
1 small box frozen sweet strawberries, thawed, or 1 can blueberry pie filling, or 1 can cherry pie filling

Beat cream cheese until smooth; gradually beat in sugar. Blend in sour cream and vanilla. Fold in Cool Whip, blending well. Spoon into crust (the crust may be bought—makes it even easier). Chill at least 4 hours. Garnish with strawberries or other topping. Yields 6-8 servings.

Betty is Still "Winking" at Cooking (Arkansas)

With more geysers and hot springs than the rest of the world combined, Yellowstone National Park in Wyoming is the first and oldest national park in the world, and the largest park in the lower 48—2.2 million acres.

The World's Best Sugar Cookies!

1 cup Wesson (vegetable) oil
1 cup butter, softened
1 cup confectioners' sugar
1 cup granulated sugar
2 eggs
1 teaspoon vanilla

4 cups unsifted flour
1 teaspoon baking soda
1 teaspoon cream of tartar
½ teaspoon salt
Granulated sugar

Beat Wesson oil and butter. Add confectioners' sugar and 1 cup granulated sugar and beat well. Beat in eggs and vanilla. Sift flour, soda, cream of tartar, and salt. Stir into sugar mixture. Mix well. Chill at least 2 hours. Roll into balls and roll them in granulated sugar. Place on ungreased cookie sheet and flatten with bottom of glass dipped in sugar also. Don't flatten too thin. Bake at 375° for approximately 10 minutes (depends on your oven) until light brown at edges. Makes approximately 5 dozen.

A Casually Catered Affair (Texas II)

"Can't Stop" Cookies

Everyone loves these cookies.

2 cups sugar
2 cups butter or margarine, softened
3 cups flour
2 teaspoons cream of tartar

½ teaspoon salt
2 teaspoons baking soda
4 cups cornflakes
1 cup chopped pecans

Cream sugar and butter. Add dry ingredients. Then fold in cornflakes and nuts. Roll into balls, place on greased cookie sheets and bake at 350° for 10-15 minutes. Makes about 100 cookies.

The Second Typically Texas Cookbook (Texas II)

★★★★★★★★★★★ ★★★★★★★★★★★

Marie Wallace's World's Best Cookies!

Once in a while a really good and different recipe comes along, and this recipe falls into that category. There are interesting additions that you certainly wouldn't expect (cornflakes?!), but the cookie is buttery and very tender—not crisp. They literally melt in your mouth!

1 cup butter, softened
1 cup sugar
1 cup light brown sugar, firmly
 packed
1 egg, slightly beaten
1 cup salad oil (Crisco, Wesson,
 Puritan, etc.)
1 cup quick rolled oats
1 cup crushed cornflakes (measure
 after crushing)

3½ cups flour
1 teaspoon baking soda
1 teaspoon salt
1 teaspoon vanilla
½ cup coconut
1 cup pecans, chopped rather fine
Red or green glazed cherries for
 decoration (optional)

Cream butter with the sugars. Add the egg and the oil. Mix well. Add oats, cornflakes, flour, soda, salt, and vanilla. Mix well. Stir in coconut and nuts. Roll into 1-inch balls of dough and place on a lightly greased cookie sheet. Flatten the balls with a fork in a crisscross pattern. Dip fork in water between cookies. If desired, place glazed cherry half in the center of each cookie. Bake at 350° for about 10 minutes, or until light brown. Do not overbake. Makes 8-10 dozen cookies.

Christmas Thyme at Oak Hill Farm (Indiana)

Ginger Snaps

Bet you can't eat just one!

¾ cup shortening
1 cup sugar
¼ cup molasses
1 egg
2 cups flour

¼ teaspoon salt
2 teaspoons baking soda
1 teaspoon ginger
1 teaspoon cinnamon
1 teaspoon cloves

Mix shortening and sugar; add molasses and egg. Mix well. Add dry ingredients and mix. Roll into 1½-inch balls; flatten with bottom of glass dipped in sugar. Bake at 350° for 9-11 minutes. Very crispy and crunchy.

Wyndmere Community Alumni Cookbook (Great Plains)

White Chocolate Chunk Cookies

The yield on this cookie recipe (4 dozen large cookies) might seem like a lot. But one taste may cause you to think the recipe just might be too small. We think this will become a family favorite at your house.

1 cup butter, softened
1 cup packed brown sugar
1 cup granulated sugar
2 large eggs
1 teaspoon vanilla
2 tablespoons Irish Cream liquor
3 cups cake flour

1 teaspoon baking soda
½ teaspoon salt
1 cup chopped walnuts or
    macadamia nuts
1½ cups white chocolate chunks
    or white chocolate chips

In a medium bowl with electric mixer, cream the butter and sugars together until light and fluffy. Add eggs, vanilla, and Irish Cream liquor. Set aside. Sift together flour, soda, and salt; add to butter mixture.

In a separate bowl, combine walnuts and white chocolate chunks, then add to mixture, just to blend. Drop by heaping tablespoon onto parchment-paper-covered cookie sheet, 2-inches apart and bake in a preheated 375° oven for approximately 11-13 minutes. Cool on wire rack. Yields 4 dozen large cookies.

Masterpiece Recipes of the American Club (Wisconsin)

★ **Editor's Extra:** See page 13 for a simply divine homemade Irish Cream recipe.

Chocolate Chip Pudding Cookies

A soft cookie lover's delight!

1½ cups butter or margarine,
  softened
3 eggs
1 cup brown sugar
½ cup granulated sugar
1½ teaspoons vanilla

3⅓ cups flour
1½ teaspoons baking soda
2 (4-ounce) packages instant vanilla
  pudding powder
2 cups chocolate chips

Cream butter, eggs, sugars, and vanilla together and mix well. Sift flour, soda, and pudding powder together and add to creamed mixture. Add chocolate chips. Mix well. Drop by teaspoon onto ungreased baking sheets. Bake at 350° for 10-12 minutes just until golden; do not over-bake.

Note: Cook-and-serve pudding can also be used, but increase flour about ½ cup. Also, can use chocolate or tapioca.

Kelvin Homemakers 50th Anniversary Cookbook (Great Plains)

Old-Fashioned Oatmeal Cookies

1 cup seedless raisins
1 cup water
¾ cup soft shortening
1½ cups sugar
2 eggs
1 teaspoon vanilla
2½ cups flour

½ teaspoon baking powder
1 teaspoon baking soda
1 teaspoon salt
1 teaspoon cinnamon
½ teaspoon cloves
2 cups rolled oats
½ cup chopped nuts

Simmer raisins and water in saucepan over low heat until raisins are plump, 20-30 minutes. Drain raisin liquid into measuring cup. Add water to make ½ cup. Heat oven to 400°. Cream shortening, sugar, eggs, and vanilla. Stir in raisin liquid. Blend flour, baking powder, baking soda, salt, and spices. Stir in. Add rolled oats, nuts, and raisins. Drop rounded teaspoonfuls 2 inches apart onto ungreased baking sheet. Bake 8-10 minutes. Makes 6-7 dozen cookies.

Mountain Recipe Collection (Kentucky)

Peanut Butter Cookies

No flour. Easy and delicious!

1 egg	1 cup creamy or chunky
1 cup sugar	peanut butter
1 teaspoon baking soda	

Preheat oven to 350°. Cream egg and sugar. Stir in baking soda. Fold in peanut butter. Roll into 36 balls; place on cookie sheet and crease top of balls with fork. Bake for 10 minutes.

Dine with the Angels (Oklahoma)

★ **Editor's Extra:** For crispier cookies, leave on the cookie sheet about 5 minutes, then put on rack or brown paper.

"I Need a Hug" Peanut Butter Cookies

1 cup unsalted butter, softened	2 eggs
1 cup crunchy peanut butter	2½ cups flour
1 cup granulated sugar	1 teaspoon baking powder
1 cup firmly packed light brown	1½ teaspoons baking soda
sugar	½ teaspoon salt

Preheat oven to 375°. In a large bowl, cream butter, peanut butter, sugar, and brown sugar. Beat in eggs. Sift together flour, baking powder, baking soda, and salt. Stir into the batter. Cover bowl and refrigerate batter for 1 hour. Roll into 1-inch balls and place on ungreased baking sheets. Flatten balls with a fork, making a crisscross pattern. Bake on middle level of preheated oven about 10 minutes or until cookies begin to brown. Do not overbake. Remove immediately to cooling racks.

Note: For a softer cookie, substitute ⅓ of the 2 sugars with granulated fructose, a natural fruit sugar sold in supermarkets or health food stores.

Blissfield Preschool Cookbook (Michigan)

Benne Seed Wafers

The mix of flavors is sooo tasty!

1 cup sesame seeds
2½ cups light brown sugar
1 cup salad oil

2 eggs
1¼ cups self-rising flour
2 teaspoons vanilla extract

Place sesame seeds in heavy skillet over low heat and stir till golden. Set aside. Mix sugar, salad oil, and eggs in electric mixer at medium speed till light and fluffy. Add flour and mix thoroughly. Stir in vanilla and sesame seeds.

Drop by teaspoons on greased baking sheets and bake at 325° for about 10 minutes or until golden. Let stand on cookie sheet for 2 minutes before removing from pan. When cool, store in a covered container.

Fancy Foods & Flowers (Georgia)

Chocolate Kiss Cookies

1 cup butter, softened
⅔ cup sugar
1 teaspoon vanilla extract
1⅔ cups unsifted all-purpose flour
¼ cup cocoa

¾ cup finely chopped pecans
1 (9-ounce) package milk chocolate
 kisses
Powdered sugar

Cream butter, sugar, and vanilla in large mixing bowl. Combine flour and cocoa; blend into creamed mixture. Add pecans; blend well. Chill dough 1 hour. Unwrap kisses. Shape a scant tablespoon of dough around each kiss, covering completely. Shape into balls.

Place on ungreased cookie sheet. Bake at 375° for 10 minutes. Cool slightly; remove to wire rack; cool completely. Roll in powdered sugar. Yields 4½ dozen.

Peachtree Bouquet (Georgia)

Black Forest Cookies

½ cup butter or margarine,
  softened
1 cup sugar
1 egg
1 teaspoon vanilla
1½ cups flour

½ cup cocoa
¼ teaspoon salt
¼ teaspoon baking powder
¼ teaspoon baking soda
1 (10-ounce) jar maraschino
  cherries

In a large bowl, cream butter, sugar, egg, and vanilla until light and fluffy. Add remaining ingredients, except cherries, and blend at low speed until a stiff dough forms, about 1 minute. Shape dough into 1-inch balls, using a heaping teaspoon of dough for each. Place 2 inches apart on ungreased cookie sheet. Push one whole cherry halfway into each ball. When all cookies are molded and cherries are pushed in, prepare frosting and use immediately.

FROSTING:

1 (6-ounce) package semisweet
  chocolate chips (not milk chocolate)
½ cup sweetened condensed milk

¼ teaspoon salt
1 to 1½ teaspoons maraschino
  cherry juice

In small, heavy saucepan, melt chocolate and condensed milk over low heat, stirring constantly. Remove from heat. Add remaining ingredients and stir until smooth. Frost each cherry by spreading ½ teaspoon of frosting over each cookie. Bake frosted cookies for 8-10 minutes at 350° until puffy. Store tightly covered. Yields 4 dozen.

Ready to Serve (Texas)

Seven Layers of Sin Bars

1 stick butter, melted
1½ cups graham cracker crumbs
1 cup chocolate chips
1 cup butterscotch chips

1 cup chopped pecans
1 cup flaked coconut
1 (14-ounce) can sweetened
   condensed milk

First pour melted butter in bottom of 9x13-inch pan. Secondly, sprinkle graham cracker crumbs over butter. The third layer will be chocolate chips, followed by butterscotch chips. The fifth layer will be chopped pecans, the sixth will be flaked coconut. For the seventh layer, pour the milk over the top. Bake at 350° for 25 minutes.

Recipes & Remembrances (Great Plains)

Melt in Your Mouth
Chocolate Coconut Macaroons

Everybody's favorite.

1 cup sweetened condensed milk
4 cups coconut
⅔ cup mini semisweet chocolate bits

1 teaspoon vanilla extract
½ teaspoon almond extract

Preheat oven to 325°. Combine sweetened condensed milk and coconut. Mix well by hand—mixture will be gooey. Add chocolate bits, vanilla, and almond extract. Stir until all ingredients are well blended.

Lightly spray a nonstick (Teflon-coated) cookie sheet with a no-stick cooking spray. Drop by teaspoonfuls onto cookie sheet, 1 inch apart. Cook 12 minutes or until lightly brown on top.

Remove from pan with a Teflon-coated spatula and let cool. Store in an airtight container or in Ziploc freezer bags. Freezes well. Yields 50-55 cookies.

It's Christmas! (Missouri)

Orange Balls

Great for parties. Always a hit!

½ cup margarine, softened
1 (1-pound) box powdered sugar
1 (6-ounce) can frozen orange juice
  concentrate, thawed
½ cup coconut

½ cup chopped nuts
1 (12-ounce) box vanilla wafers,
  finely crushed
Powdered sugar, ground nuts, or
  fine coconut

Mix margarine and powdered sugar on low speed. Add orange juice, nuts, and coconut gradually. Blend in crushed vanilla wafers. Form 1-inch (or smaller) balls and roll in powdered sugar, nuts, or coconut. Store in tin or covered container. Yields 4 dozen balls.

Our Country Cookin' (Oklahoma)

Apricot Butter Bars

½ cup finely snipped dried apricots
¾ cup cold butter
1⅔ cups sifted flour
1 egg

½ cup brown sugar, firmly packed
½ teaspoon vanilla extract
½ cup chopped pecans
Lemon Glaze

LEMON GLAZE:
¾ cup confectioners' sugar
2 tablespoons lemon juice

¼ teaspoon lemon extract

Put snipped apricots into a heavy saucepan with a small amount of water, 5-6 tablespoons. Cover and cook over low heat until water is absorbed (about 15 minutes). If they are still in firm pieces, mash them with fork or give them a buzz in the food processor. Cool.

Cut butter into flour until particles are the size of a rice kernel. Press evenly into a 9x13-inch baking pan. Bake at 350° for 15 minutes. Beat egg, brown sugar, and vanilla until thickened. Stir into mixture of apricots and pecans. Spread evenly over partially baked layer in pan. Return to oven and bake about 20 minutes, or until light brown around the edge. Remove from oven and immediately drizzle blended Lemon Glaze over top. Cut when cool.

Eat Pie First...Life is Uncertain! (Missouri)

Romantic Raspberry Chocolate Meringues

Versatile because of Jell-O base—try experimenting with other flavors.

3 egg whites
1½ ounces raspberry Jell-O
¾ cup sugar
⅛ teaspoon salt
1 teaspoon white vinegar

1 (6-ounce) package semisweet
  chocolate chips
½ cup pecans or walnuts, finely
  chopped

Beat egg whites until they begin to get stiff. Add gelatin gradually, blending thoroughly. Add sugar a little at a time; beat until stiff peaks form. Beat in salt and vinegar. Fold in chocolate chips and nuts. Drop by half-full teaspoon on foil-lined baking sheets. Bake 20 minutes at 250°. Turn off heat and leave in oven 3 hours without opening door. To garnish, you may dip the tops in a little melted chocolate, or before baking, add a little shaved chocolate or a chocolate chip to top of cookie. These will hold their shape. Makes approximately 80.

Hors D'Oeuvres Everybody Loves (Mississippi)

Mint Julep Kisses

2 egg whites
¾ cup sugar
½ teaspoon peppermint extract

2 drops green vegetable coloring
6 ounces chocolate bits

Preheat oven to 325°. Beat egg whites until stiff, gradually adding sugar. Add peppermint and green coloring. Stir in chocolate bits. Drop by spoonfuls on cookie sheets. Put in preheated oven and turn off immediately. Leave in oven overnight or for several hours. Store in tin box. Yields 2 dozen.

The Kentucky Derby Museum Cookbook (Kentucky)

All-Time Favorite Lemon Squares

A tart-like cookie that is a real favorite—tastes like little lemon pies.

CRUST:

½ cup butter or margarine
1 cup flour

¼ cup confectioners' sugar

Combine butter, flour, and confectioners' sugar; blend together until mixture clings together (I use pastry blender). Pat evenly into a 9x9-inch pan. Bake at 350° for 20 minutes or until edges begin to brown.

FILLING:

2 eggs
1 cup sugar
1 tablespoon flour
2 tablespoons lemon juice

1 teaspoon grated lemon rind
Dash of salt
Confectioners' sugar

Beat together eggs, sugar, flour, lemon juice, lemon rind (if you don't use rind, add an extra tablespoon lemon juice), and salt. Pour over partially baked crust. Return to oven and bake 20 minutes longer or until set. Sprinkle with confectioners' sugar. Cool. Cut into squares (small ones for a tea).

Tip: Garnish tray with lemon twist and a sprig of mint. Cool looking.

Variation: To make Apricot-Lemon Squares, add ¾ cup finely chopped dried apricots (soaked in boiling water and drained) to filling above. Delightful.

Holiday Treats (Virginia)

Lemon Drop Cookies

M-M-M good!

1 box lemon supreme cake mix
2 eggs

1 small carton Cool Whip, soft
Powdered sugar

Mix first 3 ingredients together. Drop by teaspoon into powdered sugar. Make into small balls. Place on greased cookie sheet. Bake 10 - 12 minutes at 350°. (Try strawberry or chocolate cake mix, too!)

Recipes & Remembrances (Ohio)

Lemon Cream Cheese Bars

FIRST LAYER:

1 box lemon cake mix (Duncan Hines)
1 egg

1 stick margarine (room temperature)

Mix by hand and press in the bottom of a greased 9x13x2-inch pan.

SECOND LAYER:

1 (8-ounce) package cream cheese (room temperature)
3 cups powdered sugar

2 eggs
1 teaspoon vanilla
1 cup chopped nuts

Mix first four ingredients. This layer can be mixed with a mixer. Stir in nuts and spread over first layer. Bake 40 minutes at 350°. Sprinkle powdered sugar on top when taken from oven. Cool and cut into squares or bars.

Feeding the Faithful (South Carolina)

The Crazy Horse Memorial in South Dakota is the world's largest sculpture in progress. Now 50 years since the first blast, sculptor Korczak Ziolkowski was invited to the Black Hills by Lakota Chief Henry Standing Bear, whose invitation read: "My fellow chiefs and I would like the white man to know the red man has great heroes, too." It is not a federal or state project, but a non-profit educational and cultural undertaking now carried on by Ziolkowski's family and financed primarily from an admission fee. Open year round, it is located 17 miles from Mount Rushmore.

Chocolate Buttercream Squares

These absolutely divine squares remind you of a brownie combined with buttercream candy. Cut into very small pieces, since they are very rich.

COOKIE LAYER:

¼ cup butter
½ cup sugar
1 egg, beaten
1 ounce unsweetened chocolate,
  melted

½ cup flour
¼ cup chopped nuts (optional)

Preheat oven to 350°. Grease and flour an 8x8-inch pan. Cream butter, sugar, and egg. Add melted chocolate, flour, and nuts. Put in prepared pan and place in oven. Check after 10 minutes; it should be cooked. Do not overbake. Cool.

FILLING LAYER:

2 tablespoons margarine, softened
1 cup confectioners' sugar

1 tablespoon cream
½ teaspoon vanilla

Blend ingredients. Chill 10 minutes and spread over cookie layer.

ICING:

1 ounce unsweetened chocolate

1 tablespoon butter or margarine

Melt ingredients together and pour over filling. Chill in refrigerator. Cut into 24 small bars.

Virginia Hospitality (Virginia)

Shortbread Toffee Squares

¾ stick butter
4 tablespoons sugar
1 cup self-rising flour
½ stick butter
2 tablespoons sugar

1 (14-ounce) can condensed milk
¼ cup pecans, chopped
½ teaspoon vanilla
4 ounces German sweet chocolate,
  melted in 1 tablespoon water

Cream ¾ stick butter with 4 tablespoons sugar. Blend in flour. Spread onto greased 8-inch square pan and bake at 350° 20 minutes. Mix together next 4 ingredients and cook, stirring until mixture leaves the sides of the pan. Add vanilla. Pour over shortbread. Cool. Spread melted chocolate over toffee. Cool. Cut into squares. Makes 12-16.

The Twelve Days of Christmas Cookbook (Mississippi)

Half-Way-to-Heaven Bars

A brown sugar meringue crowns these chocolate chip bars, transforming them from the mundane to the ethereal. Perfect for holiday gift-giving.

½ cup (1 stick) butter
½ cup sugar
½ cup brown sugar
2 egg yolks
1 tablespoon water
1 teaspoon vanilla extract

2 cups flour
¼ teaspoon salt
¼ teaspoon baking soda
1 teaspoon baking powder
1 (12-ounce) package chocolate
  chips

In large bowl, cream together butter and sugars; add egg yolks, water, and vanilla. Mix well. Mix together flour, salt, baking soda, and baking powder. Add to butter mixture. Preheat oven to 350°. Lightly grease 15-inch jelly roll pan. Pat dough into pan. Sprinkle evenly with chocolate chips.

TOPPING:
2 egg whites   1 cup brown sugar

In small bowl of mixer, beat egg whites until stiff. Gradually beat in brown sugar. Spread mixture over top of chocolate chips. Bake 20-25 minutes. Cool, then cut into bars. Yields 4½ dozen bars.

Mystic Seaport's All Seasons Cookbook (New England)

Chattanooga Chew Chews

CRUST:

2 cups all-purpose flour
½ cup butter (no substitute),
  softened

1 cup brown sugar, firmly packed
1 cup chopped pecans

Preheat oven to 350°. Mix flour, butter and brown sugar. Press into ungreased 9x13-inch pan. Sprinkle pecans evenly over unbaked crust.

CARAMEL TOPPING:

1 cup butter (no substitute)
¾ cup brown sugar

1 (12-ounce) package semisweet
  chocolate chips

For Caramel Topping, melt butter and brown sugar in saucepan. Bring to a boil and boil for 1 minute, stirring constantly. Pour caramel mixture over crust and pecans. Bake for 20 or 25 minutes or until entire surface is bubbly. Remove from oven and sprinkle chocolate chips over hot surface. Gently swirl melted chocolate chips with spatula to give a marbled effect. Cool at least 5 hours. Cut into squares. Yields 32 squares.

Dinner on the Diner (Tennessee)

Sour Cream Cashew Drops

The best cookie we've tasted for the Christmas goodies tray.

2 cups sifted flour	½ cup butter, softened
1 teaspoon baking powder	1 cup brown sugar
¾ teaspoon baking soda	1 teaspoon vanilla
¼ teaspoon salt	½ cup sour cream
1 egg	1½ cups cashew nuts

Sift flour, baking powder, baking soda, and salt together into mixing bowl. Put egg, butter, brown sugar, vanilla, and sour cream in blender container. Cover and run on medium speed until smooth. Stop blender and add nuts. Cover and run on medium speed until nuts are coarsely chopped. Pour into flour mixture and stir to mix. Drop by teaspoonfuls onto lightly greased cookie sheets. Bake at 375° for 10 minutes or until golden brown. Cool and frost with a white butter frosting.

FROSTING:

4 tablespoons butter	2 cups powdered sugar
1 teaspoon vanilla	2 tablespoons cream

Cream butter and vanilla. Add remaining ingredients and beat until smooth. Can be frozen—frost before freezing. Makes 5 dozen.

Finely Tuned Foods (Missouri)

Praline Confection

20-24 graham crackers	1 cup light brown sugar (packed)
1 cup butter or margarine	1 cup chopped pecans

Line 10x15x1-inch jelly roll pan with whole graham crackers. Bring butter and sugar to rolling boil in medium saucepan. Boil for 2 minutes. Remove from heat. When bubbling has stopped, add nuts. Spoon over graham crackers. Bake at 350° for 10 minutes. Cut in squares. Keeps well in tightly covered container. Yields 40 squares.

Dixie Delights (Tennessee)

Glazed Honey Bars

1 cup sugar
2 cups flour
½ cup cooking oil
½ teaspoon salt
½ cup honey

1 egg
1 teaspoon baking soda
1 teaspoon cinnamon
1 cup nuts

Mix and press in greased cookie sheet. Cook 12 minutes at 350°. While hot, glaze.

GLAZE:

1 cup powdered sugar
2 tablespoons real mayonnaise

½ teaspoon vanilla
1 tablespoon water

Country Cooking (Oklahoma)

Cream Cheese Brownies

CREAM CHEESE BATTER:

2 tablespoons butter or margarine
1 (3-ounce) package cream cheese, softened
¼ cup sugar

1 egg
1 tablespoon flour
½ teaspoon vanilla

Blend butter and cream cheese. Gradually add sugar, beating well. Stir in egg, flour, and vanilla. Set aside.

CHOCOLATE BATTER:

4 ounces German sweet chocolate
3 tablespoons butter or margarine
2 eggs
¾ cup sugar
½ teaspoon baking powder

¼ teaspoon salt
½ cup flour
½ cup chopped nuts
1 teaspoon vanilla
¼ teaspoon almond extract

Preheat oven to 350°. Grease an 8- or 9-inch square pan. Melt chocolate and butter over very low heat. Set aside to cool.

Beat eggs until thick and light in color; slowly add sugar, beating well. Add baking powder, salt, and flour. Stir in melted chocolate mixture, nuts, vanilla, and almond extract. Spread about half of the chocolate batter in the pan. Add cheese mixture, spreading evenly. Top with spoonfuls of chocolate batter. Zigzag with a spatula to marble. Bake for 35-40 minutes. Yields 16 squares.

The Kimball Cookbook (Texas II)

Chocolate Sin Raspberry Truffle Brownies

BROWNIES:

1½ cups semisweet real chocolate
  morsels
½ cup margarine
¾ cup brown sugar
2 large eggs

1 teaspoon instant coffee crystals
2 tablespoons water
½ teaspoon baking powder
¾ cup all-purpose flour

In saucepan over low heat, melt morsels and margarine; cool slightly. In large mixing bowl, beat sugar and eggs. Add chocolate mixture and coffee dissolved in water. Mix well.

Stir in baking powder and flour; blend well. Spread in greased 9x9-inch pan. Bake at 350° for 30-35 minutes or until toothpick tests clean.

RASPBERRY TRUFFLE FILLING:

1 cup semisweet real chocolate
  morsels
¼ teaspoon instant coffee crystals
1 (8-ounce) package cream cheese,
  softened

¼ cup powdered sugar
⅓ cup seedless red raspberry
  preserves

Melt chocolate with coffee in pan over low heat. Set aside. In small mixing bowl, beat softened cream cheese until fluffy; add powdered sugar and preserves. Beat until fluffy. Beat in melted chocolate mixture until well blended. Spread over cooled brownie layer.

GLAZE:

¼ cup semisweet real chocolate
  morsels

1 teaspoon solid vegetable
  shortening

In small saucepan over low heat, melt chocolate and shortening. Drizzle over truffle layer. Chill 1-2 hours. Cut into bars.

The Marlborough Meetinghouse Cookbook (New England)

Heavenly Hash Cake

1 cup sugar	3 tablespoons cocoa
8 tablespoons margarine	1 teaspoon vanilla
2 eggs	1 cup pecans, chopped
¾ cup self-rising flour	1½ cups miniature marshmallows

Cream sugar and margarine. Add eggs and other ingredients except marshmallows. Bake in buttered 9x9x2-inch pan, 350° for 30-35 minutes. Test with toothpick. While cake bakes, make icing.

ICING:

2 tablespoons cocoa	2-4 tablespoons evaporated milk
2 tablespoons margarine	(icing will be thin)
½ box powdered sugar	

Remove cake from oven and while cake is hot, pour marshmallows over cake to cover. When completely cooled, put icing on cake in pan. Cut in 36 squares (1½ inches each).

Recipes and Reminiscences of New Orleans I (Louisiana)

Knock You Nakeds

Quite simply divine!

1 package German chocolate cake mix	¾ cup butter, melted
1 cup nuts, chopped	60 pieces caramel candy
⅓ cup evaporated milk	½ cup evaporated milk
	1 cup chocolate chips

Combine and mix well cake mix, nuts, ⅓ cup milk, and butter. Press half of mixture into the bottom of a greased 8x13-inch Pyrex dish; bake at 350° for 8 minutes. Melt caramel candy in top of double boiler with ½ cup of milk. When caramel mixture is well mixed, pour over baked mixture. Cover with chocolate chips and pour rest of dough on top of chips. Bake for 18 minutes at 350°. Cool before slicing. Yields 18-20 squares.

Great Flavors of Mississippi (Mississippi)

★★★★★★★★★★★★   ★★★★★★★★★★★★

Rocky Road

1 (12-ounce) package semisweet
  chocolate chips
1 (14-ounce) can sweetened
  condensed milk
2 tablespoons margarine

1 (10½-ounce) package (5½ cups)
  miniature marshmallows
1 (8-ounce jar) (1 ⅔ cups) unsalted
  roasted peanuts

In saucepan combine chocolate chips with sweetened condensed milk and margarine. Heat over low heat till chocolate is melted; remove from heat. In a large bowl, combine marshmallows and peanuts. Fold in chocolate mixture. Spread in a 9x13x2-inch pan whose sides and bottom have been lined with waxed paper. Chill 2 hours or till firm. Remove from pan. Peel off waxed paper and cut into 1-inch squares with a wet knife. Wrap pieces in plastic wrap. Makes 8 dozen.

The Sevier County Cookbook (Tennessee)

Microwave Candy Bark

A great quick gift; do ahead and easy.

¾ cup pecan chips or slivered
  almonds
1 cup sugar
½ teaspoon salt

1 stick unsalted butter
¼ cup water
1 (4-ounce) Hershey chocolate bar

Butter cookie sheet and sprinkle nuts on sheet. Combine sugar, salt, butter, and water in medium-size microwave bowl (such as Pyrex or Corningware; not plastic) and cook in microwave for 8-8½ minutes on full power. Pour over nuts. In separate microwave bowl, cook chocolate bar for 2¼ minutes on level 6. Spread melted chocolate over nuts and caramelized sugar. Put in freezer for 20 minutes or refrigerate for 45-60 minutes. Break in pieces, bag, and refrigerate. Serves 8.

Culinary Arts & Crafts (Florida)

Buckeyes

Ohio is known as the Buckeye State, and these candies are made to resemble the buckeye seed. (The real buckeye is reputedly poisonous.)

½ cup (1 stick) butter or margarine,
  room temperature
1 (1-pound) box confectioners'
  sugar
1½ cups peanut butter

1 teaspoon vanilla extract
1 (12-ounce) package real
  chocolate chips
¼ stick paraffin (optional)

Cream the butter, confectioners' sugar, peanut butter, and vanilla. Form into small (buckeye-sized) balls and refrigerate overnight. Melt the chocolate chips and paraffin in the top of a double boiler. Stick a toothpick in the candy ball and dip it in the chocolate mixture. Leave part of the ball uncovered so that it resembles a buckeye, but cover the toothpick hole. Place on waxed paper to cool and harden. These candies can be frozen. Yields 3-4 dozen.

Cincinnati Recipe Treasury (Ohio)

★ **Editor's Extra:** Paraffin takes longer to melt than chocolate, so start it melting first. This can be made without paraffin—softer, but equally delicious.

Almond Crunch

1 cup blanched slivered almonds
½ cup butter

½ cup sugar
1 tablespoon light corn syrup

Line bottom and sides of an 8- or 9-inch cake pan with aluminum foil. Set aside. Combine all ingredients in 10-inch skillet. Bring to a boil over medium heat, stirring constantly. Boil until mixture turns golden-brown—about 6 minutes. Quickly spread in prepared pan.

Cool about 15 minutes. Break into bite-sized pieces. This makes a great homemade gift item!

Arkansas Favorites Cookbook (Arkansas)

Louisiana Pralines Microwave

2 cups sugar
2 cups pecan halves
¾ cup buttermilk

2 tablespoons butter
⅛ teaspoon salt
1 teaspoon (baking) soda

Combine first 5 ingredients in a 4-quart glass casserole. Microwave on HIGH for 12 minutes, stirring every 4 minutes. Add soda, stirring well as it foams. Microwave on HIGH 1 minute longer; beat mixture until thickened and loses its gloss (about 1 minute). Drop candy by teaspoonfuls onto waxed paper; let stand until firm.

Note: You may need to adjust cooking time with your microwave oven. Soft failures are just as delicious to eat as firm pralines.

Foods à la Louisiane (Louisiana)

Candy-Pecan Clusters

This has got to be the best chocolate candy recipe in the whole wide world—makes a bunch!

1 (7-ounce) jar marshmallow creme
1½ pounds Hershey's milk
  chocolate kisses (no substitute)
5 cups of sugar

1 (13-ounce) can evaporated milk
½ cup butter or margarine
6 cups pecans

Place marshmallow creme and kisses in a large bowl; set aside. Combine sugar, milk and butter in a saucepan. Boil mixture to a high point; let boil 8 minutes (until soft ball stage). Pour over marshmallow creme and kisses; blend well. Add pecans and mix. Drop by teaspoonful on waxed paper. An easy, never-fail recipe. Makes 12 dozen clusters.

Collectibles II (Texas)

3-Minute Microwave Fudge

1 pound powdered sugar
  (3¾ cups)
½ cup cocoa
1 stick margarine (½ cup)

¼ cup milk
1 teaspoon vanilla
½ cup chopped peanuts
  (dry roasted)

Combine powdered sugar and cocoa in a 2-quart microwave-safe bowl. Place the stick of margarine on top of the mixture. Pour the milk over all. Do not stir! Microwave on HIGH (100%) for 3 minutes. Stir well and add the vanilla and peanuts. Pour into a greased 8x8-inch pan. Cool 20 minutes. Cut into squares. Yields 64 pieces.

Easy Livin' Microwave Cooking: The New Primer (Great Plains)

★ **Editor's Extra:** Bake for 3½ minutes if your microwave is not powerful.

Pies & Other Desserts

★★★★ ★★★★

Many layers of rock, nearly 3,000 feet deep in some areas, have been exposed by the constant cutting force of the Colorado River, which rushes through the bottom of the Grand Canyon. It is an awe-inspiring sight.

Topsy Turvy Pecan Apple Pie

½ stick butter, softened
Pecan halves
⅔ cup brown sugar, packed
2-crust pastry

6 cups apples, sliced, mixed with
  ½ cup sugar and sprinkles of
  apple pie seasonings (flour,
  cinnamon, nutmeg)

Smooth butter around sides and bottom of pie pan. Stick pecans in butter, then press brown sugar evenly over pecans. Then put on 1 layer of crust extending about an inch beyond edge of pan. Add apple mixture next, and then top crust. Lap extended crust over top crust and flute edges.

Prick top with fork. Bake 10 minutes at 450° then reduce heat to 350° and continue baking 30-45 minutes or until done. Flip upside down to serve.

Home Cookin' is a Family Affair (Illinois)

★ **Editor's Extra:** For ease in turning out, loosen around sides of crust with a knife.

Phyllis' Race Day Pie

¼ cup butter
1 cup sugar
3 eggs, beaten
½ cup chocolate chips
¾ cup white corn syrup
¼ teaspoon salt

1 teaspoon vanilla
½ cup chopped nuts (pecans
  are best)
2 tablespoons bourbon (or
  2 teaspoons vanilla)
1 (9-inch) unbaked pie shell

Cream butter and sugar together. Stir in other ingredients. Pour in unbaked pie shell and bake at 375° for 40-50 minutes. Serve topped with whipped cream.

Somethin's Cookin' at LG&E (Kentucky)

★★★★★★★★★★★★ ★★★★★★★★★★★★★

The Best Pecan Pie

1 stick butter
1 cup light Karo
1 cup sugar
3 large eggs, beaten
½ teaspoon lemon juice

1 teaspoon vanilla
1 dash of salt
1 cup chopped pecans
1 (8 or 9-inch) pie shell

Brown butter in saucepan until it is golden brown; do not burn. Let cool. In separate bowl add ingredients in order listed; stir. Blend in browned butter well. Pour in unbaked pie shell and bake at 425° for 10 minutes, then lower to 325° for 40 minutes.

The Cotton Country Collection (Louisiana)

★ **Editor's Extra:** The secret is browning the butter.

Pecan Tassies
(or Lemon Tassies)

Nutty rich—a real favorite.

PASTRY:
1 (3-ounce) package cream cheese, softened
1 stick margarine, softened

1 cup flour
Dash of salt

Blend together cream cheese, margarine, flour, and salt. Shape into 24 balls; press each ball into 1¾-inch muffin tins (press dough in bottom and sides with fingers; do not leave any holes).

FILLING:
2 eggs, beaten
1 cup brown sugar
2 tablespoons margarine, melted

1 teaspoon vanilla
Dash of salt
1 cup pecans, chopped

Combine eggs, brown sugar, margarine, vanilla, and salt. Mix well (do not beat with beater, or tops will be crusty instead of nutty). Divide pecans evenly in pastry shells. Pour filling in shells, filling two-thirds full. Bake at 350° for 20-25 minutes. Cool slightly before removing from pans. Cool on wire rack. Makes 24.

Lemon Tassies: Substitute white sugar for brown; omit pecans and add 2 tablespoons lemon juice and 1 teaspoon lemon rind.

Granny's Kitchen (Virginia)

Heavenly Pie
(Lemon Ice Box Meringue)

SHELL:

1 cup granulated sugar
¼ teaspoon cream of tartar

4 egg whites at room temperature
3 tablespoons shredded coconut

Sift 1 cup sugar and cream of tartar together; separate eggs. Beat whites in stiff peaks but not dry. Slowly add sugar, beating constantly. Spread meringue over bottom and sides of well-greased pie pan; make bottom about ¼-inch thick, sides thicker. Sprinkle 2 tablespoons coconut on top. Bake in 275° oven for 1 hour. Cool.

FILLING:

4 egg yolks
½ cup sugar
3 tablespoons lemon juice
1 tablespoon grated lemon rind

⅛ teaspoon salt
1 pint heavy cream
  (use for top and filling)

Beat 4 egg yolks slightly in double boiler, stir in ½ cup sugar, lemon juice, rind and salt. Cook, stirring over boiling water until thick (about 8 minutes). Cool, add 1 cup whipped cream to custard. Pour into cooked shell. Spread on rest of whipped cream (unsweetened); sprinkle on 1 tablespoon toasted coconut. Chill at least 12 hours.

Cabbage Patch: Famous Kentucky Recipes (Kentucky)

Holly's "Best" Apple Pie

The best apple pie that you will ever eat. The secret is soaking the apples in the melted butter. Serve warm to get the best rich butter flavor.

4 cups sliced apples
½ cup melted butter or margarine
⅔ cup sugar
2 tablespoons flour

¾ teaspoon ground cinnamon
¼ teaspoon nutmeg
1 (9-inch) unbaked pastry shell

TOPPING:
½ cup flour
¼ cup brown sugar
¼ cup butter or margarine (leftover
  from filling)

½ cup chopped pecans (optional)

Pour melted butter over sliced apples and soak a few minutes. Combine sugar, flour, and spices. Remove apples from butter (reserve any that is left and use in topping). Coat apples with sugar mixture and pour into pastry shell. Combine topping ingredients and crumble over apples. Bake at 400° for 40-45 minutes, or until brown and apples are tender. Serve warm with a scoop of vanilla ice cream.

Holiday Treats (Virginia)

Apple Cream Pie

You won't believe how good this is!

1½ cups sugar
4 tablespoons flour
2 cups whipping cream
Dash of salt
1 or 2 apples, cored, peeled, and
  sliced thin

1 (9-inch) pie shell, unbaked
1 tablespoon butter
Ground nutmeg to sprinkle on top

Combine sugar, flour, cream, and salt. Mix well, but don't beat air into it—just combine well. Add sliced apples (my favorite is Rome Beauty, but you may use any kind). Stir apples into batter. Pour into the prepared crust. Dot with butter and sprinkle nutmeg on top. Bake at 325° for 1 hour and 10-15 minutes. After this amount of time, gently shake pie—if it's still liquid in the center, bake another 10 minutes or so. If it shakes like custard, it's done.

Another time, leave out the apples for the best old-fashioned cream pie you ever tasted!

It's About Thyme (Indiana)

★★★★★★★★★★★ ★★★★★★★★★★★★

Sweet Potato Pie

1½ cups sugar
3 eggs
1½ cups mashed sweet potatoes
1 teaspoon vanilla extract

1 stick butter, melted
½ cup milk
1 deep (9-inch) pie shell, unbaked

Beat together sugar and eggs. Add potatoes, vanilla extract, and melted butter. Mix, then add milk. Cook in unbaked pie shell for 1 hour at 350°.

A Taste of Georgia (Georgia)

Pumpkin Chiffon Pie with Peanut Crust

CRUST:
½ cup (1 stick) butter
1 ⅔ cups all-purpose flour
½ cup finely chopped peanuts or
  other nuts

Pinch of salt
3-4 tablespoons water

Preheat oven to 400°. With a pastry blender or two knives, cut the butter into the flour, nuts, and salt until mixture resembles coarse crumbs. Add water, 1 tablespoon at a time, tossing lightly with a fork. Gather dough into a ball. Roll dough out thinly on a floured board and fit into a deep-dish 9-inch pie pan. Prick crust; bake in preheated oven until lightly browned, 10-12 minutes.

FILLING:
2 cups canned pumpkin
3 eggs, divided
¼ cup granulated sugar
½ cup milk
½ teaspoon salt

1 tablespoon cinnamon
1 package unflavored gelatin
¼ cup cold water
¼ cup granulated sugar
1 pint whipping cream, whipped

Thoroughly whisk together pumpkin, egg yolks, sugar, milk, salt, and cinnamon in a saucepan. Cook over medium heat until thickened, about 10-15 minutes. Dissolve gelatin in cold water. Remove pumpkin mixture from heat and mix in the dissolved gelatin. Let cool.

  In a mixing bowl, beat egg whites, gradually adding more sugar. Continue beating until stiff peaks form. Fold beaten egg whites into pumpkin mixture. Pour into cooled crust. Chill. Top with whipped cream before serving.

A Cook's Tour of Iowa (Iowa)

Chocolate Meringue Pie

2½ cups milk, divided
¾ cup sugar
4 tablespoons cornstarch
½ teaspoon salt
4 tablespoons cocoa
  (slightly heaped)

3 eggs, separated
1 teaspoon vanilla
Gob of butter (about 2 tablespoons)
8 or 9-inch pie shell, baked
6 tablespoons sugar

Heat 2 cups milk over medium heat until scalding. In the meantime blend ½ cup milk, the sugar, cornstarch, salt, cocoa and egg yolks. Add to warm milk, cook until thick, stirring constantly. Remove from heat, add vanilla and butter, pour in pie shell. Make meringue with 3 egg whites and 6 tablespoons sugar. Beat egg whites on high speed with mixer. When they begin to foam up good, start adding sugar 1 tablespoon at a time. When it stands in a peak, place on top of pie and bake in 350° oven until brown.

Coconut Cream Pie: Leave out the cocoa and add coconut when you add the vanilla and butter. Top meringue with coconut.

Banana Cream Pie: Leave out the cocoa, place bananas in bottom of crust, fill with about half the filling, more bananas, and finish with filling.

Plain Cream Pie: Leave out the cocoa. Sometimes, I want one cream pie and one chocolate pie, so I double the recipe, leaving out the cocoa, fill the crust for the cream pie, and add either semisweet chocolate chips or unsweetened chocolate to the remainder to make a different chocolate pie.

Peanut Butter Pie: Make cream pie filling plus 1 or 2 tablespoons peanut butter until it looks and tastes right.

A Collection of Recipes from the Best Cooks in the Midwest (Missouri)

Coconut Pie

This pie makes its own crust.

4 eggs
1¾ cups sugar
½ cup flour
2 cups milk

¼ cup melted butter
1½ cups coconut
1 teaspoon vanilla

Combine all the ingredients, in order, in a blender. Mix until smooth. Pour the mixture into a greased 10-inch pie pan. Bake for 45 minutes at 350°, or until a tester inserted into the middle comes out clean.
Recipe from The Leadville Country Inn, Leadville, Colorado.

Distinctly Delicious (Colorado)

Iowa Pride Chess Pie

Delicious warm or chilled.

1 cup granulated sugar
½ cup light brown sugar, firmly
  packed
1 tablespoon flour
1 tablespoon yellow cornmeal
⅛ teaspoon salt
3 large eggs

½ cup melted butter
3 tablespoons milk or light cream
1½ teaspoons white vinegar
1 teaspoon vanilla
1 unbaked 9-inch pie shell (or plain
  or butter-flavored ready crust)

Toss sugars, flour, cornmeal, and salt together with a fork. Add eggs, melted butter, milk or cream, vinegar, and vanilla. Beat mixture with electric beater until smooth. Pour into unbaked pie shell. Cover edges of crust with narrow strips of foil for first 25 minutes of baking to prevent overbrowning. Bake at 350° for 35-40 minutes or until a clean knife inserted in the center comes out clean. Can be frozen. Serves 6.

Recipes from Iowa with Love (Iowa)

Buttermilk Pie

A smooth, creamy, delicious pie, and a recipe worth trying—despite any preconceived notions you may have about buttermilk. Originally this pie was a makeshift dessert for times when the pantry or cellar was bare and there were no fruits in season. It has now become much more—a classic Texas dessert.

4 tablespoons flour
1¾ cups sugar
½ teaspoon salt
½ cup butter, melted
3 eggs, beaten
1 cup buttermilk
½ teaspoon vanilla
½ teaspoon lemon extract
1 (9-inch) unbaked pie shell
Cinnamon and nutmeg to taste (optional)

Combine flour, sugar, and salt in a mixing bowl. Add melted butter and beaten eggs and stir with a whisk or fork until well blended. Stir in buttermilk, vanilla, and lemon extract, and mix well. Pour into unbaked pie shell and dust with cinnamon or nutmeg, if desired.

Bake in center of 350° oven for 55-60 minutes, or until filling is set and lightly browned.

Cooking Texas Style (Texas)

Pineapple Pie

My aunt, Bonnie Robertson, is one of the most thoughtful ladies in the world. I couldn't count how many of these pies she has made, and most of them were to fill the need of another. She always has one for my husband when we visit her.

1 (9-inch) pie shell, unbaked
4 eggs (separate one)
1 stick butter
1½ cups sugar
2 tablespoons flour
1 small can crushed pineapple, well drained

Prepare pie shell and brush with a small amount of slightly beaten egg white. Set aside. Cream butter and sugar; add eggs, 1 at a time, beating well after each addition. Stir in flour. Add pineapple and mix until all ingredients are well blended. Pour mixture into pie shell and bake at 350° 30-40 minutes. Shake pan gently every few minutes during the last several minutes of baking time. The center should just be beginning to seem firm, but should still move. Remove from oven and set on a solid surface for pie to continue to set. Serves 6-8.

Of Magnolia and Mesquite (Texas)

Key Lime Pie

The tart and the sweet alternate on the tongue to delight and refresh.

1 can sweetened condensed milk
3 egg yolks
½ cup fresh key lime juice
1 baked pie shell

3 egg whites
¼ teaspoon cream of tartar
6 tablespoons superfine sugar
½ teaspoon vanilla

Beat first three ingredients together until thick and smooth. Pour mixture into pie shell. Make meringue (beat egg whites with cream of tartar; gradually add sugar and beat till stiff; add vanilla) and spread over pie filling. Bake at 400° 8-10 minutes to brown, then chill before serving.

Note: A key lime pie that is green is not a key lime pie. The Florida Cracker purist insists on the yellow pie made from true key limes. The trick is to squeeze them while they're in season, freeze the juice in ice cube trays, store them in freezer bags, and you'll have Key Lime Pie all year round.

Maurice's Tropical Fruit Cook Book (Florida)

★ **Editor's Extra:** Try substituting lemon—wonderful.

Margarita Pie

Tastes just like its namesake.

CRUST:
1½ cups crushed pretzel sticks
¼ cup sugar

¼ pound butter, melted

Combine crushed pretzels and sugar. Add melted butter. Press into 9-inch buttered pie plate and chill.

FILLING:
1 (14-ounce) can sweetened
  condensed milk
⅓ cup fresh lime juice
2 tablespoons tequila

2 tablespoons Triple Sec
1-2 drops green food coloring
1 cup heavy cream, whipped

Combine sweetened condensed milk, lime juice, tequila, and Triple Sec. Add food coloring, if desired. Fold whipped cream into mixture. Pour into chilled crust and freeze for 3-4 hours or until firm. (Can be stored in freezer for several days.) Before serving, garnish each piece with thin slice of lime. Serves 8-10.

Sunny Side Up (Florida)

Lemon Pie with Blueberry Sauce

Light and simple to prepare.

CRUST:

1 cup all-purpose flour	**2 tablespoons sugar**
½ cup butter	**¼ teaspoon salt**

Preheat oven to 375°. In a food processor mix flour, butter, sugar, and salt until crumbly. Place ⅓ cup of the crumb mixture in a small baking dish; press remaining mixture into a greased and floured 9-inch pie plate. Bake both 12-15 minutes. Cool.

FILLING:

2 egg whites	**2 teaspoons grated lemon peel**
⅔ cup sugar	**1 cup heavy cream, whipped**
¼ cup fresh lemon juice	

Combine egg whites, sugar, and lemon juice; beat to stiff peaks. Fold lemon peel and whipped cream into egg white mixture. Turn entire mixture into pie shell. Top with baked crumbs. Chill. Serve with Blueberry Sauce.

BLUEBERRY SAUCE:

⅔ cup sugar	**⅔ cup cold water**
1 tablespoon cornstarch	**2 cups fresh blueberries**

In a saucepan combine sugar and cornstarch. Add water; cook and stir until thick. Cook 2 minutes more. Add blueberries. Return mixture to boiling. Remove from heat. Chill.

   This pie freezes well. Do not freeze sauce. Serves 8.

Gulfshore Delights (Florida)

Out-of-This-World Pie

Makes two beautiful pies.

1 large can cherry pie filling
1 large can crushed pineapple
  with juice
1 teaspoon red food coloring
¾ cup sugar
1 tablespoon cornstarch

1 small box raspberry Jell-O
6 bananas, sliced
1 cup chopped pecans
2 (10-inch) pie shells, baked
Whipped topping

In saucepan, combine first 5 ingredients. Cook until thick. Remove from heat and add Jell-O. Allow to cool. Add bananas and pecans. Pour into pie shells and top with whipped topping.

Heavenly Dishes (Ohio)

Sour Cream Raisin Pie

1 cup sour cream
½ cup sugar
2 egg yolks (save whites)
1 tablespoon flour

1 teaspoon cinnamon
½ teaspoon cloves
1 cup raisins
1 (8 or 9-inch) pie crust, baked

Combine all ingredients and cook (over medium heat) until thick, 5-7 minutes. Pour into baked pie shell. Use egg whites for meringue.

MERINGUE:
2 egg whites
¼ teaspoon cream of tartar

¼ cup sugar

Whip egg whites and cream of tartar until frothy. Add sugar gradually and beat until stiff. Pile on hot pie filling. Bake at 400° for 8-10 minutes.

Lutheran Church Women Cookbook (Iowa)

★ **Editor's Extra:** Sometimes called Funeral Pie because it is made from readily available ingredients, this pie is a treat for raisin lovers.

Mile-High Rhubarb Pie

Gives rise to lofty praise.

CRUST:
1 cup all-purpose flour   ½ cup butter
2 tablespoons powdered sugar   Pinch of salt

FILLING:
2½ cups cut-up rhubarb   2 tablespoons flour
1⅓ cups sugar   ⅓ cup milk
3 egg yolks

MERINGUE:
3 egg whites   6 tablespoons sugar
¼ teaspoon cream of tartar   ½ teaspoon vanilla

Heat oven to 350°. Mix crust ingredients together and press into 8-inch pie pan. Bake 20 minutes. Combine filling ingredients in saucepan; cook until thick and pour into baked crust.

Heat oven to 400°. Beat egg whites and cream of tartar until foamy; gradually add sugar and beat until stiff but not dry. Fold in vanilla. Spread over filling; seal edges of meringue to crust. Bake about 10 minutes, until meringue is browned.

From Minnesota: More Than A Cookbook (Minnesota)

Best-Ever Apple Cobbler

½ cup (1 stick) butter	1½ cups sifted self-rising flour
2 cups sugar	⅓ cup milk
2 cups water	1 teaspoon cinnamon
½ cup shortening	2 cups apples, finely chopped

Heat oven to 350°. Melt butter in 9x13x2-inch baking pan. In a saucepan, heat sugar and water until sugar melts. Meanwhile, cut shortening into flour until particles are like fine crumbs. Add milk and stir with fork only until dough leaves the side of the bowl. Turn out on floured board; knead until smooth. Roll dough into a large rectangle about ¼ inch thick. Sprinkle cinnamon over apples, then sprinkle apples evenly over dough. Roll up dough like a jelly roll. Dampen the edge with a little water to seal. Slice dough into about ½-inch-thick slices. Place in pan of melted butter. Pour sugar syrup carefully around rolls. (This looks like too much liquid, but the crust will absorb it.) Bake 55-60 minutes.

Variation: This cobbler may be made with other fresh, frozen, or canned fruits such as blackberries, blueberries, cherries, or peaches. If packed in liquid, drain and substitute for part of sugar syrup. Always use 2 cups of liquid. An all-time favorite, this swirled cobbler is moist and juicy, yet flaky on top.

Auburn Entertains (Alabama)

Southern Peach Cobbler

½ cup sugar
½ cup water

6 or 7 peaches, peeled
4 tablespoons margarine

Mix together sugar and water and boil for a few minutes to make syrup. Slice peaches into syrup. Put margarine into Pyrex (ovenproof) dish; melt in 375° oven.

CRUST:

½ cup sugar
1½ teaspoons baking powder
½ cup milk

½ cup plain flour
½ teaspoon salt

Mix all ingredients together. Pour into Pyrex dish over melted butter. Pour peaches and syrup over this. Bake at 375° for 30-40 minutes until brown. The crust will rise.

Traditionally Wesleyan (Georgia)

★ **Editor's Extra:** A 28-ounce can of drained fruit will do in a pinch. Also a dash of cinnamon and nutmeg adds interest for spice lovers.

Tollville Strawberry Pie

1 (3-ounce) package cream cheese, room temperature
2-3 tablespoons milk
1 (9-inch) baked pie crust
1 quart ripe fresh strawberries, washed, capped, and drained

¾ cup sugar
2 tablespoons cornstarch
⅓ cup water
Red food coloring
Whipped cream

Mix (whisk) cream cheese with milk until smooth. Spread on baked pie crust with back of teaspoon until entire pie crust is covered. Cut half of the strawberries in half and put in a saucepan with sugar, cornstarch, and water. Cook over medium heat until thickened, adding a few drops of red food coloring. Place remaining strawberries (save a few for garnish) in the pie crust and pour cooled berry mixture over whole berries. Chill. Serve with whipped cream or Cool Whip.

Prairie Harvest (Arkansas)

Bing Cherry Pie

Always gets great reviews.

1 (14-ounce) can sweetened
  condensed milk
1 (16-ounce) can dark sweet cherries,
  drained
¾ cup pecan pieces, toasted

½ cup lemon juice
½ teaspoon red food coloring
1 cup whipping cream, whipped
1 (9-inch) graham cracker crust,
  baked and cooled

In a mixing bowl, combine and mix together the milk, cherries, pecans, lemon juice, and red food coloring. Whip the cream until it stands in peaks, and gently fold into the other mixture. Place in graham cracker crust, chill, and serve.

Leaving Home (Texas)

Traverse City Cherry Berry Pie

Traverse City is the capital of Michigan's fabulous cherry-producing region.

2 unbaked (9-inch) pie crusts
10 ounces frozen raspberries,
  thawed
3 tablespoons cornstarch
½ teaspoon salt

¾ cup sugar
2 cups pitted fresh red tart cherries
½ teaspoon ground cinnamon
1 quart vanilla or cinnamon ice
  cream

Preheat oven to 425°. Line a pie plate with one of the pie crusts. Drain raspberries, reserving syrup. Add water to syrup to make 1 cup. In a saucepan, combine the cup of liquid with the cornstarch, salt, and sugar. When cornstarch is dissolved, add the cherries. Cook over low heat, stirring, until mixture is thick and clear. Stir in raspberries and cinnamon. Pour filling into pastry shell. Top with second crust, crimping the edge and venting the top. Bake for 30 minutes or until the filling is hot and the crust is golden. Cool and serve with a scoop of ice cream. Serves 6-8.

Cranbrook Reflections (Michigan)

Raspberry Cream Cheese Pie

Good combination of flavors.

30 vanilla wafers, crushed
½ cup butter, melted
1 (8-ounce) package cream cheese,
  softened
1 cup powdered sugar

1 teaspoon vanilla extract
1 cup non-dairy whipped topping
1 (10-ounce) box frozen raspberries,
  drained
3-4 chocolate toffee candy bars

Preheat oven to 325°. Combine wafers and butter; pat into 9-inch pie plate. Bake 15 minutes. Turn off oven and leave crust in oven for 10 minutes; remove and cool.

Mix cream cheese, powdered sugar, vanilla, and whipped topping. Pour in raspberries. Fold and pour into crust. Crush candy bars in blender (or food processor); sprinkle on top of pie. Chill 1 hour before serving. Yields 6-8 servings.

Great Beginnings, Grand Finales (Indiana)

Blueberry Delight

1¼ sticks butter
2 tablespoons sugar
2 cups graham cracker crumbs
1 cup confectioners' sugar
1 (8-ounce) package cream cheese

3 tablespoons milk
1 to 1½ cups chopped pecans
1 can blueberry pie filling
1 giant (16-ounce) carton
  Cool Whip

Melt butter and add sugar and crumbs. Press into 9x13-inch pan and bake at 350° for 8 minutes. Cool. Whip confectioners' sugar, cream cheese, and milk until smooth. Spread on cooled crust. Sprinkle with nuts and then spread blueberry pie filling on top of nuts. Top with Cool Whip. Chill thoroughly.

Carolina Cuisine Encore! (South Carolina)

★ **Editor's Extra:** This recipe is also delicious subbing a 6-ounce package of chocolate, lemon or vanilla instant pudding, using 3 cups milk, or cherry pie filling for the blueberry.

★★★★★★★★★★★★   ★★★★★★★★★★★★

Wild Strawberry Dessert

One of the best of the fresh strawberry desserts in our collection.

CRUST:

1 cup flour

½ cup butter, melted

2 tablespoons powdered sugar

⅓ cup chopped pecans

Combine crust ingredients; pat in 9x13-inch pan and bake 20 minutes at 350°. Cool.

FIRST LAYER:

1 (8-ounce) package cream cheese, (Neufchatel) softened

¾ cup powdered sugar

1 cup Cool Whip

Mix and spread on chilled crust. Chill again.

SECOND LAYER:

1 cup sugar

3 tablespoons cornstarch

Pinch of salt

1½ cups 7-Up (or Sprite)

½ cup water

1 (3-ounce) package wild strawberry Jell-O

1 quart or more sliced fresh strawberries

Whipped cream

Jumbo strawberries for garnish

Combine in saucepan the sugar, cornstarch, salt, 7-Up, and water. Cook until thickened. Remove from heat and add Jell-O. Cool. Then add strawberries. Put over first layer. Refrigerate. Cut in squares and top each with a dollop of whipped cream and a jumbo strawberry.

Dorthy Rickers Cookbook: Mixing & Musing (Minnesota)

Amaretto Cheese Pie

This is so good it almost takes your breath away!

CRUST:

1½ cups chocolate wafers,
  crushed into fine crumbs
1 cup blanched almonds, crushed
  into fine pieces
⅓ cup sugar
1 stick butter, melted

Make a crust by mixing the chocolate wafers, almonds, sugar, and butter. Press into two greased Pyrex pie pans.

FILLING:

1 (8-ounce) package soft cream
  cheese
1 cup sugar
3 egg yolks
1 tablespoon amaretto liqueur
½ pint whipping cream
3 egg whites
1 small package blanched sliced
  almonds

In a mixing bowl, cream the cream cheese with sugar. Beat until fluffy. Add egg yolks and amaretto. In a separate bowl, whip the whipping cream until stiff and fold into the cheese mixture. In a separate bowl, beat the egg whites until stiff and fold into the cheese mixture. Pour into the chocolate crusts. Freeze. When ready to serve, sprinkle the top of each pie with sliced almonds browned in butter. Pour 1 tablespoon amaretto over each slice. (Makes two pies.)

Gazebo Gala (Tennessee)

Mousse in a Minute

1 (6-ounce) package chocolate chips
¾ cup scalded milk
2 tablespoons strong coffee
2 eggs
4 teaspoons dark rum (or sherry,
  Grand Marnier, or creme
  de menthe)

Put all ingredients in blender. Whirl for 1½ minutes. Pour into 4-6 serving dishes. Refrigerate at least 2 hours. Top with whipped cream and serve.

Culinary Contentment (Virginia)

★★★★★★★★★★★★ ★★★★★★★★★★★★

French Silk Pie

This is our favorite Saturday night dessert. So you jog that extra mile—it's worth it!

MERINGUE:

3 egg whites, room temperature	**½ teaspoon vanilla**
Pinch of salt	**¾ cup sugar**
¼ teaspoon cream of tartar	**⅓ cup finely chopped walnuts**

Preheat oven to 275°. Beat egg whites with salt, cream of tartar, and vanilla until just fluffy, then gradually add the sugar. Beat until meringue is light and firm. Spread into an ungreased 9-inch pie pan. Using a small rubber spatula, build a free-form rim of meringue at least ½ inch higher than rim of pie pan; it should resemble a mountain panorama, with some peaks here and there. Sprinkle rim and bottom with walnuts. Bake meringue for 1 hour, then turn off heat, and leave the meringue in the oven to cool and dry.

FILLING:

2 ounces unsweetened chocolate	**1½ cups sugar**
1 cup butter, room temperature	**2 teaspoons vanilla**
4 eggs	

Melt 2 ounces of chocolate in a small double boiler. Briefly beat the softened butter in the food processor. Add the eggs, sugar, vanilla, and melted chocolate, and process for 15 minutes (color will change from a light to a dark brown). Empty filling into a bowl, cover, and chill for at least 4 hours to set. An hour before serving, fill the meringue shell with the now firm chocolate cream.

TOPPING:

1 cup heavy cream	**Semisweet chocolate shavings**
1 tablespoon creme de cacao	**for garnish**

Whip the heavy cream with the creme de cacao and spread over the pie. Sprinkle with chocolate shavings and serve. Serves 8.

Recipes from a New England Inn (New England)

★★★★★★★★★★★★   ★★★★★★★★★★★★

Killer Peanut Butter and Fudge Ripple Pie

1 (8-ounce) package cream cheese,
  softened
¾ cup powdered sugar
¼ cup peanut butter
1 teaspoon vanilla
2 eggs

1 cup whipping cream, whipped
1 pre-made chocolate crumb pie
  crust
½ cup semisweet chocolate chips,
  melted

In a bowl, combine cream cheese, powdered sugar, peanut butter, and vanilla; beat at medium speed until smooth and well blended. Add eggs, 1 at a time, beating well after each addition. Fold in whipped cream. Spoon into crust. Spoon melted chocolate randomly over the filling. Gently pull knife through the chocolate to marble. Freeze. When ready to serve, let stand at room temperature about 15 minutes before serving. Serves 8-10.

What's Cookin' (Michigan)

★ **Editor's Extra:** If this does kill you, you'll die happy!

Hot Brownie with Fudge Sauce

This is the chocoholic's dream come true! And easy—you can even mix this in the same dish you are going to cook it in!

1 cup instant biscuit baking mix
1 cup sugar, divided
3 tablespoons plus ⅓ cup cocoa,
  divided

½ cup milk
1 teaspoon vanilla
1 ⅔ cups hot water

Mix biscuit mix, ½ cup sugar, and 3 tablespoons cocoa in 8x8-inch glass baking dish. Stir in milk (you can use skim milk if you think it will help) and vanilla until blended. Sprinkle with remaining ⅓ cup cocoa and ½ cup sugar. (Do not stir.) Pour water over top and DO NOT STIR! Bake at 350° for 40 minutes. Top will look and taste like a brownie. Underneath is this heavenly chocolate syrup. Spoon in dessert dishes and top with whipped cream. This recipe should be outlawed! It is just not right to be this easy and taste so GOOD!

One Course At A Time (South Carolina)

★★★★★★★★★★★★   ★★★★★★★★★★★★

Moon Bars

1 cup water
1 stick oleo
1 cup flour
4 eggs
2 packages instant vanilla pudding
4 cups milk

1 (8-ounce) package cream cheese, softened
1 (8-ounce) carton Cool Whip
Chocolate syrup
Nuts (optional)

Boil water and oleo. Add flour and stir well. Add eggs one at a time. Stir well. Spread out in jelly roll pan and bake at 400° for 30 minutes. Cool. Mix pudding according to directions. Add softened cream cheese. Mix and put on baked crust. Cool. Add Cool Whip. Drizzle with chocolate. Top with nuts, if desired.

Trinity Lutheran Church Centennial Cookbook (Iowa)

Dirt Cake

Use two new 8-inch plastic flowerpots or three 6-inch pots.

2 (8-ounce) packages cream cheese
2 cups confectioners' sugar
3 cups milk
2 (6-serving) boxes instant vanilla pudding

1 teaspoon vanilla
1 (16-ounce) carton Cool Whip
2 (16-ounce) packages Double Stuff Oreo Cookies

Beat cream cheese and sugar until smooth. Beat milk and pudding until smooth and thick. Combine vanilla and Cool Whip. Blend into cream cheese and pudding mixture. Crush Oreo cookies in blender just a few at a time. Put waxed paper circles in bottom of pots to cover holes. Layer pudding and crushed Oreos into flowerpots, ending with Oreos on top. Decorate with a few silk flowers.

WYVE's Cookbook/Photo Album (Virginia)

★ **Editor's Extra:** A delicious fun dessert—just watch the expressions when you dip into the potted plant and eat "dirt"!

Chocolate Éclairs

A step-by-step New Orleans classic.

1 cup water
1 stick butter or margarine
1 cup flour
¼ teaspoon salt
4 large eggs

1 small box vanilla pudding
 (regular or instant)
2 cups cold milk
Chocolate Topping

Boil water in heavy pot; add butter and stir until melted. Add flour and salt all at once, stirring and cooking a minute or so until mixture forms soft ball that does not separate. Remove from heat, cool 10 minutes, and add eggs, 1 at a time, beating vigorously after each.

Form 12-15 spoonfuls batter into smooth capsule shapes on a greased cookie sheet. Bake in 450° oven 15 minutes, then lower to 325° and bake another 25 minutes. While éclairs are baking, prepare and refrigerate pudding (per package directions) and Chocolate Topping.

When éclairs are cool, slice top third off with sharp knife. Fill each eclair with about 2 tablespoons pudding. Replace top. Frost with Chocolate Topping. Refrigerate loosely covered (with sheet of waxed paper).

CHOCOLATE TOPPING:
2 (1-ounce) squares unsweetened
 baking chocolate
3 tablespoons butter

1¼ cups powdered sugar
1 teaspoon vanilla
2-3 tablespoons milk

Melt chocolate in microwave on HIGH for 2 minutes (or over hot water on stovetop). Add butter; stir to melt. Add powdered sugar, vanilla, and milk for thin consistency. Beat with spoon until glossy.

Note: Easier than you imagined, I'll bet. Cream Puffs are similar, but round and sprinkled with powdered sugar. Try chocolate or lemon filling or stiffly whipped cream.

The Little New Orleans Cookbook (Louisiana II)

Death by Chocolate

1 (19.8-ounce) family-size fudge
  brownie mix
¼ to ½ cup Kahlúa or coffee liqueur*
3 (3.5-ounce) boxes chocolate mousse
  or milk chocolate pudding

8 Skor or Heath bars
1 (12-ounce) carton Cool Whip

Bake brownies according to directions on package. Cool. Punch holes in brownies with fork and pour Kahlúa over brownies.

Whip up chocolate pudding (or mousse) according to package directions. Break Heath bars into small pieces with hammer (in the wrapper). Break up half the brownies and place in the bottom of a large glass trifle dish. Cover with half the pudding, half the candy, and half the Cool Whip. Repeat layers.

*Instead of liqueur, you may substitute a mixture of 1 teaspoon sugar and 4 tablespoons black coffee.

Covered Bridge Neighbors Cookbook (Missouri)

★ **Editor's Extra:** A devil's-food cake mix with vanilla pudding subs well— a softer death. This is awesome!

Ice Box Pudding

This is a great favorite with men!

1½ cakes German sweet chocolate
3 tablespoons water
3 tablespoons confectioners' sugar
5 eggs
1 teaspoon almond or vanilla
  flavoring

1 teaspoon powdered coffee
2 packages ladyfingers
1 cup whipped cream

Melt the chocolate over hot water (or microwave on HIGH 2 minutes) in the combined water and confectioners' sugar. Separate the eggs, adding the yolks to the chocolate mixture. Beat the whites until stiff and fold into mixture. Flavor with almond and the powdered coffee.

In dish used to serve (must have sides at least 3 inches deep), place the ladyfingers around in upright position. Then cover bottom of dish with ladyfingers. Pour mixture into dish. Refrigerate 24 hours. Before serving, cover with whipped cream.

High Hampton Hospitality (North Carolina)

★ **Editor's Extra:** Try this with torn pieces of angel food cake instead of ladyfingers.

★★★★★★★★★★★★ ★★★★★★★★★★★★

Tiramisù

The name Tiramisù means "pick me up," so get ready! This recipe was on the cover of Cooking Light Magazine's *March 1995 issue. If you've never had Tiramisù, this is the perfect time to try making it. I know it requires using a few bowls, but it is worth the effort. You can find instant espresso coffee at the grocery store to make espresso without any special appliances.*

½ cup espresso coffee
¼ cup plus 1 tablespoon sugar
3 tablespoons coffee liqueur
1 (8-ounce) package light cream
  cheese, softened
¾ cup confectioners' sugar

1½ cups light frozen whipped
  topping, thawed and divided
3 large egg whites
20 ladyfingers, split
Cocoa, for sprinkling

In a small bowl, combine the espresso coffee, one tablespoon sugar, and the coffee liqueur; set aside. In a mixing bowl, combine the cream cheese with the confectioners' sugar, beating until well blended. Fold in one cup frozen whipped topping. In another mixing bowl, beat the egg whites until soft peaks form, add the remaining ¼ cup sugar, and continue beating until stiff peaks form. Fold into the cream cheese mixture.

In a 9x9x2-inch dish, place a layer of the split ladyfingers across the bottom of the dish. Drizzle with half of the espresso mixture, half of the cream cheese mixture, and repeat the layers, beginning with split ladyfingers and ending with the cream cheese mixture. Spread with the remaining ½ cup whipped topping in a thin layer on top of the dessert and sprinkle with cocoa. Refrigerate until well chilled. Makes 16 servings.

Cal 147; Fat 5g; Cal from Fat 30.6%; Sat Fat 3.5g; Sod 102mg; Chol 57mg.

Trim & Terrific American Favorites (Louisiana II)

Piña Colada Wedges

1 (8-ounce) package cream cheese, softened
⅓ cup sugar
2 tablespoons rum or ½ teaspoon rum extract
3½ cups thawed whipped topping, divided

1 (8¼-ounce) can crushed pineapple in syrup
2 ⅔ cups (7 ounces) coconut flakes, divided

Beat cream cheese with sugar and rum until smooth. Fold in 2 cups of the whipped topping, pineapple with syrup, and 2 cups of the coconut. Spread in 8-inch round layer pan lined with plastic wrap. Invert pan onto serving plate; remove pan and plastic wrap. Spread with remaining whipped topping and sprinkle with remaining coconut.

Freeze until firm, about 2 hours. Cut into wedges. Garnish with pineapple and cherries, if desired.

First Christian Church Centennial Cookbook (Iowa)

Orange Charlotte

A scrumptious orange cloud for dessert!

1⅓ tablespoons unflavored gelatin
⅓ cup cold water
⅓ cup boiling water
1 cup sugar
3 tablespoons fresh lemon juice
1 cup fresh orange juice

1 cup heavy cream
2 teaspoons vanilla flavoring
3 egg whites, beaten stiffly
Cherries and nuts, if desired, for garnish

Soften gelatin in cold water. Dissolve in boiling water. Add sugar and stir until dissolved, over low heat, if necessary. Add lemon juice and orange juice to mixture. Chill in refrigerator until mixture begins to congeal slightly.

Whip cream, flavor with vanilla, and fold into juice mixture. Fold in beaten egg whites. Return to refrigerator until firm. Garnish with cherries and nuts. May be served in individual dishes or crystal bowl. Makes 6-8 servings.

Note: Use a sweet and juicy orange for the best taste. Orange juice made from frozen concentrate may be used in place of fresh orange juice.

Puttin' on the Peachtree (Georgia)

Lemon Cup Cake Pudding Quickie

2½ tablespoons flour
¾ cup sugar
¼ teaspoon salt
1 tablespoon butter

2 eggs, separated
1 cup sweet milk
Grated lemon peel
¼ cup lemon juice

Combine flour, sugar and salt with softened butter. Add egg yolks, milk, lemon peel and juice; stir. Fold in stiffly beaten egg whites. Pour into casserole and place it in a pan of warm water. Bake about 35 minutes at 350°. Will form a delicate cake-top layer with a custard sauce. Serve warm or chilled. Serves 6.

Gourmet of the Delta (Mississippi)

Beehives

If peaches happen to be out of season at the time you read this recipe, save it in a very special place for use the next year. We think you will declare it well worth the wait! Prepare this recipe in the cool of the morning, as we do in the inn, and then pop dessert into the oven while you enjoy your dinner.

8 extra large perfect peaches   **Double recipe of pie crust**

Roll pie crust into an oblong shape and cut strips 1-inch wide. Wash and dry 8 extra-large, perfect peaches. They must be *perfect*. Wrap the strips of pie crust around starting from the bottom until the peach is entirely covered. Pat and patch the crust as you go along so there are no holes. Seal the edges. Place "beehives" on a cookie sheet and bake for 40 minutes at 400°. Serve hot with hard sauce.

To eat: Break the "beehive" in half, remove the stone, and spoon a heaping tablespoon of hard sauce into the cavity. The peach skin has disappeared! What an absolutely divine dessert!

HARD SAUCE:

4 tablespoons sweet butter	**1 teaspoon vanilla**
1 unbeaten egg	**Nutmeg**
2 cups powdered sugar	**1 tablespoon brandy**

Cream butter. Add egg and mix well. Gradually work in 2 cups or more powdered sugar. The definite amount of sugar you add will depend upon whether you like tight or not-so-tight hard sauce. Flavor with brandy. Pile sauce into peach cavity and sprinkle with nutmeg. Serves 8 lucky people.

From the Inn's Kitchen (New England)

Pears Melba

3 cups water
1 (3-inch) cinnamon stick
1 teaspoon pure vanilla extract
1½ tablespoons fresh lemon juice
   (reserve ½ teaspoon)
1 (1x3-inch) piece lemon rind
4 large pears, stems intact, peeled,
   halved, and cored

1 tablespoon cornstarch
10 ounces frozen raspberries,
   thawed, drained (reserve juice)
1 cup low-fat cottage cheese
2 teaspoons sugar
Mint leaves

In large skillet combine water, cinnamon stick, vanilla, 1 tablespoon lemon juice, and rind. Bring water to high simmer; add pears and poach, covered, 10 minutes. (Can be prepared up to this point, covered, and chilled overnight.) Add cornstarch to reserved raspberry juice; heat until slightly thickened. Add berries; cool.

Purée cottage cheese, reserved lemon juice, and sugar until smooth and creamy. Matching halves, fill each pear half with 2 tablespoons cheese mixture; stand upright on plate and press halves together. Level bottom, if necessary, by cutting off thin slice. Spoon 2 tablespoons raspberry sauce over each pear. Place mint leaf at each stem. May be chilled several hours. Yields 4 servings.

Note: If fresh pears are not available, canned pear halves can be substituted.

Sounds Delicious! (Oklahoma)

Easy Boiled Custard

This dessert tastes like you may have spent a long time stirring it over a hot stove. We add apricot brandy to it for flavoring.

1 (3¾-ounce) package French
   vanilla instant pudding mix
½ cup sugar
1 teaspoon vanilla

4 cups milk
1 (8-ounce) carton Cool Whip
   whipped topping

Add pudding mix, sugar and vanilla to milk. Stir until smooth. Fold in whipped topping. Chill until very, very cold.

Curtis Grace, Encore (Kentucky)

★★★★★★★★★★★   ★★★★★★★★★★★

Hotel Natchez Bread Pudding
with Bourbon Sauce

The cooks of Natchez learned the secret of bread pudding: stale French bread and a good whiskey sauce. During the Yankee occupation of the city, many a Northern heart was stolen by this treat.

1 loaf French bread	3 tablespoons vanilla
1 quart milk	½ cup chopped pecans
3 eggs	1 cup raisins
2 cups sugar	1 tablespoon oleo

Soak bread in milk and work with back of a wooden spoon until it is well mixed. Add beaten eggs, sugar, vanilla, pecans, and raisins and combine well. Pour melted oleo in bottom of a heavy 7x11-inch oblong cake pan or similar baking dish. Bake at 350° for 1½ hours or until very firm. Cool. Slice into squares. Top with Bourbon Sauce.

BOURBON SAUCE:

½ cup butter	1 egg
1 cup sugar	3 tablespoons bourbon whiskey

Cream butter and sugar together and cook in the top of a double boiler until the mixture is very hot and the sugar dissolves. Pour into a blender and add egg at top speed so that egg doesn't scramble. Cool. Add bourbon just before serving. Spoon sauce over bread pudding. Heat under broiler. Serves 8-10.

Cook with a Natchez Native (Mississippi)

Bread Pudding with Glazed Cream
(from Le Ruth's)

½ stick butter, softened
4 eggs
2½ cups sugar
1 quart milk
1 tablespoon vanilla

¼ teaspoon mace
¾ cup raisins
½ loaf stale poor boy bread, cut
    into slices 1 inch thick

TOPPING:
½ cup whipping cream
⅓ cup sugar

½ stick butter

Spread soft butter over 12-inch round (or similar size; 9x13 will do) baking pan. Mix eggs, sugar, milk, vanilla, and mace. Stir in raisins. Add bread and allow to soak 10 minutes. Pour into pan. Bake at 375° until pudding is almost firm (about 40-45 minutes). Remove from oven. Increase oven temperature to 425°. Carefully pour liquid whipping cream over top (no substitutes), then sprinkle with ⅓ cup sugar and pieces of butter. Return to oven and bake 10-15 minutes to allow cream to set. Serves 6-8.

Paul Naquin's French Collection II (Louisiana)

★ **Editor's Extra:** Try serving bread pudding for breakfast—it may become a standard, like it has for us.

Flan Café

3 eggs, slightly beaten
6 tablespoons sugar
¼ teaspoon salt
3 tablespoons instant coffee
  granules

1 teaspoon vanilla extract
3 cups milk, scalded
6 tablespoons coffee-flavored
  liqueur (optional)
½ cup whipped cream

In a mixing bowl, combine eggs, sugar, salt, coffee and vanilla. Mix thoroughly. Gradually add scalded milk, stirring vigorously. Pour mixture into 6 custard cups. Place in pan of hot water and bake at 375° for 25-40 minutes or until firm. Chill thoroughly. To serve, spoon liqueur over flan and top with whipped cream.

Simply Simpatico (New Mexico)

Baked Lemon Pudding

This baked pudding is very easy to make and can be served warm or cold. Be sure to use fresh lemon juice for best flavor. While pudding is baking, it separates into a thin bottom layer of lemon sauce with a fluffy cake-like layer on top.

¾ cup sugar, divided
5 tablespoons flour
¼ teaspoon baking powder
⅛ teaspoon salt
2 eggs, separated

3 tablespoons fresh lemon juice
Grated zest of 1 lemon
1½ tablespoons butter, melted
1 cup milk

Preheat oven to 375°. Combine ½ cup sugar with flour, baking powder, and salt. Beat egg yolks until light; add lemon juice, zest, butter, and milk. Set aside. Beat well with a spoon. Stir in dry ingredients until smooth. Beat egg whites until foamy; gradually beat in remaining ¼ cup sugar until stiff, but not dry. Fold into flour mixture.

Transfer mixture to a 1-quart baking dish. Put baking dish in a larger pan filled with warm water. Bake at 375° for 40-45 minutes until top is firm and nicely browned. Makes 6 servings.

50 Years of Regal Recipes (Wisconsin)

Alabama Banana Pudding

¾ cup sugar
Dash of salt
¼ cup flour
3 egg yolks, beaten

½ teaspoon vanilla
2 cups milk
2-4 bananas, sliced
15 vanilla wafers

Combine sugar, salt, and flour; add to egg yolks and vanilla. Heat milk in saucepan; slowly add egg mixture. Cook until thick. Arrange wafers and bananas in shallow 1½-quart baking dish. Add pudding.

MERINGUE:
3 egg whites
6 tablespoons sugar

½ teaspoon vanilla

To make meringue, beat egg whites till frothy, then gradually add sugar, then vanilla and beat until very stiff. Spread over pudding and bake at 400° until golden brown. Serve warm or cold. Serves 8.

Huntsville Heritage Cookbook (Alabama)

Toffee Ice Cream Pie

PIE:

12 (¾-ounce) Heath bars
1¼ cups chocolate wafer crumbs

¼ cup butter, melted
½ gallon vanilla ice cream

Put Heath Bars in freezer to harden. Mix crumbs and butter. Line 9x13-inch pan. Press mixture evenly into pan. Put into refrigerator to harden. Crush Heath bars and mix with softened ice cream. Put in crust and freeze overnight.

SAUCE:

1 stick butter
1 (12-ounce) package chocolate
  chips

2 cups powdered sugar
1 (13-ounce) can evaporated milk
2 teaspoons vanilla

Melt butter and chocolate chips. Add sugar and milk. Cook about 8 minutes or until thick, stirring constantly. Add vanilla. Serve warm over pie. The sauce can be made early in the day and heated at the last minute. Serves 8-10.

Note: Oreos may be substituted for chocolate wafers if the filling is scraped off.

Tea-Time at the Master's (Georgia)

Buster Bars

BARS:

1 package Oreo cookies
⅓ cup melted butter

½ gallon vanilla ice cream
2 cups peanuts

Crush Oreos. Mix with butter. Put in 9x13-inch pan. Spread ice cream over crust. Put peanuts over ice cream, then the Fudge Sauce. Freeze until firm.

FUDGE SAUCE:

1 can Eagle Brand Condensed Milk   2 cups chocolate chips

Microwave until melted. Cool slightly and put on Buster Bars.

Country Cupboard (Wisconsin)

Aunt Pittypat's Homemade Peach Ice Cream

2 cups sugar
2 tablespoons flour
4 eggs, slightly beaten
2 cups half-and-half

2 cans undiluted evaporated milk
12 overripe peaches, peeled,
 crushed, and sweetened with
 1 cup sugar

Mix sugar and flour. Add eggs and half-and-half. Cook in double boiler, stirring constantly, until mixture steams. Remove from heat. Add evaporated milk. Pour into ice cream freezer. When mixture reaches mushy consistency, add peaches. Continue freezing until firm. To serve, place scoops of ice cream in large bowl. Let guests help themselves.

Betty Talmadge's Lovejoy Plantation Cookbook (Georgia)

Fruit Pizza

1 package sugar cookie mix (or
  1 roll refrigerated sugar
  cookie dough)
1 (8-ounce) package cream cheese
⅓ cup sugar

½ teaspoon vanilla
Sliced fruit of choice (fresh or
  canned)
½ cup peach or apricot preserves
2 tablespoons water

Prepare cookie mix according to directions and pat out in a sprayed 14-inch pizza pan. Bake and cool. Blend softened cream cheese, sugar, and vanilla. Spread over cooled cookie crust. Arrange fruit over cream cheese layer (use any combination of fresh or drained canned fruit). Glaze with preserves mixed with water. Chill.

Note: If using fruits that brown (such as bananas), dip slices into lemon juice before placing on pizza to keep them from turning brown.

Cooking with the Warriors (Indiana)

Amaretto Cake

1 ready-to-eat angel food cake
  (loaf or tube-type)
12 tablespoons Amaretto, divided

½ gallon ice cream (any flavor)
1 large carton Cool Whip

Split cake into 3 sections horizontally. Place first section on cake plate. Drizzle 3 tablespoons amaretto over cake. Cover with 2 inches of ice cream.

Place second section of cake on top of ice cream layer. Drizzle with 3 tablespoons of amaretto. Cover with 2 inches of ice cream. Place third section of cake on top of ice cream. Drizzle with 3 tablespoons of amaretto. Fold 3 tablespoons of amaretto into large carton of Cool Whip. Ice cake. Freeze.

Note: Amaretto keeps cake from freezing hard, so you can remove it from freezer and serve immediately.

Cooking on the Go (South Carolina)

★★★★★★★★★★★★   ★★★★★★★★★★★★

Dee's Baked Alaska

This is very easy and quick and can be made several days ahead of time and kept in freezer. Everyone—all ages—loves it!

SAUCE:

3 tablespoons cornstarch
3 tablespoons Chocolate-Raspberry liqueur

1½ cups Hershey's chocolate syrup

Combine cornstarch and liqueur in saucepan; stir in chocolate syrup. Cook, stirring constantly, until mixture thickens and bubbles 3 minutes. Remove from heat and cool completely.

1 baked (10-inch) pie shell, cooled
½ gallon vanilla ice cream
Chopped nuts (optional)
Chopped cherries (optional)
4 egg whites

¼ teaspoon cream of tartar
¼ teaspoon salt
½ cup sugar
½ teaspoon almond flavoring

Drizzle several spoonfuls of sauce into bottom of pie shell.* Scoop ice cream with a large serving spoon—make a layer over sauce, drizzle more sauce and nuts and/or cherries, if desired. Continue layers, ending with ice cream. Smooth ice cream, making a higher mound in the center. Freeze while making meringue.

Beat egg whites with cream of tartar and salt until foamy and double in volume. Beat in sugar gradually, until meringue forms stiff peaks. Add almond flavoring. Frost ice cream with meringue, sealing to pastry edge. Make swirls. Freeze until serving time. Bake at 475° for 3 minutes or until meringue is touched with brown.

Heat remaining sauce. Cut into wedges, drizzle with sauce, and serve.

*You usually have sauce left—if not, it only takes minutes to make more.

Best of Friends (Texas II)

Abraham Lincoln, our 16th president, guided our country through the most devastating experience in its national history—the Civil War. He is considered by many historians to have been the greatest American president.

Listed below are the cookbooks that have contributed recipes to *The Recipe Hall of Fame Cookbook,* along with copyright, author, publisher, city and state. The information in parenthesis indicates the BEST OF THE BEST cookbook in which their recipe originally appeared.

All About Bar-B-Q Kansas City Style ©1995, 1997 Pig Out Publications, by Rich Davis and Shifra Stein, Pig Out Publications, Kansas City, MO (Great Plains)

Amarillo Junior League Cookbook ©1979 Amarillo Junior League Publications, Amarillo Junior League, Amarillo, TX (Texas)

Amazing Graces ©1993 The Texas Conference Ministers Spouses Association, The Texas Conference United Methodist Ministers' Spouses Association, Houston, TX (Texas II)

The American Gothic Cookbook ©1996 Penfield Press, Penfield Press, Iowa City, IA (Iowa)

Amish Country Cookbook III ©1993 Bethel Publishing, by Das Dutchman Essenhaus, Evangel Publishing House, Nappanee, IN (Indiana)

Angels and Friends Favorite Recipes II ©1991 Angels of Easter Seals, Angels of Easter Seals, Youngstown, OH (Ohio)

Another Blue Strawbery ©1983 James Haller, by James Haller, The Harvard Common Press, Boston, MA (New England)

The Apple Barn Cookbook ©1983 The Apple Barn and Cider Mill, The Apple Barn, Sevierville, TN (Tennessee)

Arkansas Favorites Cookbook ©1991 J and J Collections, by Judy Giddings and June Simmons, Hot Springs, AR (Arkansas)

Asbury United Methodist Church Cook Book ©1990 Asbury United Methodist Church, Asbury United Methodist Church, Magnolia, AR (Arkansas)

Auburn Entertains ©1983, 1986 Auburn Entertains, by Helen Baggett, Jeanne Blackwell and Lucy Littleton, Rutledge Hill Press, Nashville, TN (Alabama)

The Authorized Texas Ranger Cookbook ©1994 Harris Farms Publishing, by Johnny and Cheryl Harris, Hamilton, TX (Texas II)

Back Home Again ©1993 The Junior League of Indianapolis, Inc., Junior League of Indianapolis, Indianapolis, IN (Indiana)

Bay Leaves ©1975 The Junior Service League of Panama City, Inc., Panama City Junior Service League, Panama City, FL (Florida)

Bell's Best 2 ©1982 Telephone Pioneers of America-Mississippi Chapter #36, Telephone Pioneers of America, Jackson, MS (Mississippi)

Best of Friends ©1985 Dee Reiser and Teresa Dormer, by Dee Reiser and Teresa Dormer, Kingwood, TX (Texas II)

The Best of Friends ©1976 Fort Morgan Museum, Fort Morgan Museum, Fort Morgan, CO (Colorado)

The Best of South Louisiana Cooking ©1983 Bootsie John Landry, by Bootsie J. Landry, Lafayette, LA (Louisiana)

The Best of the Bushel ©1987 The Junior League of Charlottesville, Inc., Junior League of Charlottesville, Inc., Charlottesville, VA (Virginia)

Bethany Lutheran Church Celebrating 125 Years, Bethany WELCA, Jackson, MN (Minnesota)

Betty Groff's Up-Home Down-Home Cookbook ©1987 Betty Groff, by Betty Groff, Pond Press, Mount Joy, PA (Pennsylvania)

Betty is Still "Winking" at Cooking, by Betty J. Winkler, Little Rock, AR (Arkansas)

Betty Talmadge's Lovejoy Plantation Cookbook ©1983 Betty Talmadge, by Betty Talmadge, Atlanta, GA (Georgia)

Billy the Kid Cook Book ©1998 by Lynn Nusom, by Lynn Nusom, Golden West Publishers, Phoenix, AZ, (New Mexico)

Birdies in the Oven/Aces in the Kitchen ©1986 Patricia Y. Leverett, by Trish Leverett, Birmingham, AL (Alabama)

Birthright Sampler, Birthright of Johnstown, Inc., Johnstown, PA (Pennsylvania)

Blessed Isle—Recipes from Pawleys Island ©1998 All Saints Waccamaw Episcopal Church, Church Women of All Saints Waccamaw Episcopal Church, Pawleys Island, SC (South Carolina)

Blissfield Preschool Cookbook, Blissfield Preschool Co-Op, Blissfield, MI (Michigan)

Boarding House Reach ©1981 Dot Gibson Publications, Dot Gibson Publications, Waycross, GA (Georgia)

The Bonneville House Presents ©1990 The Bonneville House Association, The Bonneville House Association, Fort Smith, AR (Arkansas)

Bountiful Harvest Cookbook ©1987 Lancaster Bible College Women's Auxiliary, Lancaster Bible College Women's Auxiliary, Lancaster, PA (Pennsylvania)

Bountiful Ohio ©1993 by Susan Failor, by James Hope and Susan Failor, Gabriel's Horn Publishing Co., Inc, Bowling Green, OH (Ohio)

Bouquet Garni ©1989 Independence Regional Health Center, Independence Regional Health Center Auxiliary, Independence, MO (Missouri)

Bravo! Applaudable Recipes ©1977 Mobile Opera Guild, Mobile Opera Guild, Mobile, AL (Alabama)

By Special Request © 1993 Leu Wilder, by Leu Wilder, Shreveport, LA (Louisiana II)

C-U in the Kitchen ©1983 Champaign-Urbana Hadassah, Champaign-Urbana Hadassah, Champaign, IL (Illinois)

Cabbage Patch: Famous Kentucky Recipes ©1952, 1954, 1956, 1972 Cabbage Patch Circle, Cabbage Patch Circle, Louisville, KY (Kentucky)

Cafe Oklahoma ©1994 Junior Service League, Junior Service League of Midwest City, Midwest City, OK (Oklahoma)

Calf Fries to Caviar ©1983 Jan-Su Publications, by Janel Franklin and Sue Vaughn, Jan-Su Publications, Lamesa, TX (Texas)

Calling All Cooks ©1982 Telephone Pioneers of America-Alabama Chapter No. 34, Telephone Pioneers of America, Alabama Chapter #34, Birmingham, AL (Alabama)

Canyon Echoes ©1994 Texas Panhandle Star Co., by Prairie Dog Pete, Clarendon, TX (Texas II)

Carol's Kitchen ©1993 Carol J. Moore, by Carol J. Moore, Galesburg, IL (Illinois)

Carolina Cuisine Encore! ©1981 The Junior Assembly of Anderson, The Junior Assembly of Anderson, Anderson, SC (South Carolina)

A Casually Catered Affair ©1980 Carole C. Curlee, by Carole Curlee, Lubbock, TX (Texas II)

Celebration, A Taste of Arkansas ©1985 Sevier County Cookbook Committee, Sevier County, Lockesburg, AR (Arkansas)

Centennial Cookbook ©1986 Arispe Centennial Cookbook Committee, Arispe Centennial Cookbook Committee, Arispe, IA (Iowa)

A Century in His Footsteps ©1991 Mullen United Methodist Church, Mullen United Methodist Church, Mullen, NE (Great Plains)

Changing Thymes ©1995 Austin Junior Forum, Inc., Austin Junior Forum Publications, Austin, TX (Texas II)

Charleston Receipts ©1950 The Junior League of Charleston, Inc., The Junior League of Charleston, Inc., Charleston, SC (South Carolina)

Charleston Receipts Repeats ©1989 The Junior League of Charleston, Inc., The Junior League of Charleston, Inc., Charleston, SC (South Carolina)

Cheesecakes et cetera ©1989 Shirley Michaels, by Shirley Michaels, Loveland, CO (Colorado)

Chickadee Cottage Cookbook II, by Donna Hawkins, Mahtomedi, MN (Minnesota)

Christmas in New Mexico ©1991, 1997 Lynn Nusom, by Lynn Nusom, Golden West Publishers, Phoenix (New Mexico)

Christmas Thyme at Oak Hill Farm ©1994 Thyme Cookbooks, by Marge Clark, West Lebanon, IN (Indiana)

Cincinnati Recipe Treasury ©1983 Ohio University Press, by Mary Anna DuSablon, Ohio University Press, Athens, OH (Ohio)

Coastal Cuisine, Texas Style ©1993 Junior Service League of Brazosport, Junior Service League of Brazosport, Lake Jackson, TX (Texas II)

Collectibles II ©1983 Mary Pittman, by Mary Pittman, Van Alstyne, TX (Texas)

Collection of Recipes from St Matthew Lutheran Church, A, St. Matthew Lutheran Church, Galena, IL (Illinois)

A Collection of Recipes from the Best Cooks in the Midwest, by Nellie Ogan, Richmond, MO (Missouri)

College Avenue Presbyterian Church Cookbook, Presbyterian Women of College Avenue Church, Aledo, IL (Illinois)

Colorado Collage ©1995 The Junior League of Denver, Inc., The Junior League of Denver, Inc., Denver, CO (Colorado)

Company's Coming ©1984 The Alliance of The University of Texas Institute of Texan Cultures, The Institute of Texan Cultures, San Antonio, TX (Texas)

Connecticut Cooks III ©1988 American Cancer Society, CT Division, American Cancer Society, Connecticut Division, Wallingford, CT (New England)

Convertible Cooking for a Healthy Heart ©1991 Joanne D'Agostino, Frank D'Agostino, by Joanne D'Agostino, Easton, PA (Pennsylvania)

Cook 'em Horns ©1981 The Ex-Students Association of the University of Texas, The Ex-Students' Association of The University of Texas, Austin, TX (Texas)

Cook and Deal ©1982 D.J. Cook, by D.J. Cook, Vero Beach, FL (Florida)

Cook, Line & Sinker, Rocky River Junior Women's Club, Rocky River, OH (Ohio)

Cook with a Natchez Native ©1977 Myrtle Bank Publishers, by Bethany Ewald Bultman, Myrtle Bank Publishers, Natchez, MS (Mississippi)

A Cook's Tour of Iowa ©1988 University of Iowa Press, by Susan Puckett, University of Iowa Press, Iowa City, IA (Iowa)

A Cook's Tour of Shreveport ©1964 The Junior League of Shreveport, Inc., Junior League of Shreveport, Shreveport, LA (Louisiana II)

Cookin' in the Spa, Hot Springs Junior Auxiliary, Hot Springs, AR (Arkansas)

Cookin' Wise ©1980 YWCA of Texarkana, YWCA, Texarkana, TX (Texas)

Cookin' With Friends, Friends of the Graves-Hume Library, Mendota, IL (Illinois)

Cooking on the Go ©1982 NTW Enterprises, by Nancy Welch, Greer, SC (South Carolina)

Cooking on the Road, by Montana Whitfield, Steele, MO (Missouri)

Cooking on the Wild Side ©1995 Zoological Society of Cincinnati, Cincinnati Zoo and Botanical Garden, Cincinnati, OH (Ohio)

Cooking Texas Style ©1983, 1993 by the University of Texas Press, by Candy Wagner and Sandra Marquez, University of Texas Press, Austin, TX (Texas)

Cooking to Your Heart's Content ©1990 Barbara Taylor, by Barbara Taylor, The University of Arkansas Press, Fayetteville, AR (Arkansas)

Cooking with Colorado's Greatest Chefs ©1995 Marilynn A. Booth, by Marilynn A. Booth, Westcliffe Publishers, Englewood, CO (Colorado)

Curtis Grace, Encore ©1998 Curtis Grace, by Curtis Grace, McClanahan Publishing House, Inc., Kuttawa, KY (Kentucky)

Cooking with Daisy's Descendants ©1994 Elaine Gilbert Davis, by Elaine Gilbert Davis, Fairmount, IL (Illinois)

Cooking with H.E.L.P., Help Elevate Local Politics, York, ME (New England)

Cooking with Kiwanis, The Kiwanis Club, Los Alamos, NM (New Mexico)

Cooking with the Warriors, Whiteland Community High School, Whiteland, IN (Indiana)

Cooking With the Groundhog ©1958, 1983 Adrian Hospital, by Punxsutawney Hospital Auxiliary, Punxsutawney, PA (Pennsylvania)

Cooks and Company ©1988 Muscle Shoals District Service League, by Muscle Shoals District Service League, Sheffield, AL (Alabama)

Cordon Bluegrass ©1988 The Junior League of Louisville, Inc., The Junior League of Louisville, Inc, Louisville, KY, (Kentucky)

The Cotton Country Collection ©1972 Junior Charity League, Monroe, LA, Junior League of Monroe, Monroe, LA (Louisiana)

Cotton Country Cooking ©1972 The Decatur Junior Service League, Inc., Junior League of Morgan County, Inc., Decatur, AL (Alabama)

Country Classics ©1995 Ginger Mitchell and Patsy Tompkins, by Ginger Mitchell and Patsy Tompkins, Karval, CO (Colorado)

Country Cookbook, Marilla Historical Society, Copemish, MI (Michigan)

Country Cooking ©1996 Port Country Cousins, Port Country Cousins, Sentinel, OK (Oklahoma)

Country Cupboard, by Lois Krueger, Washington Island, WI (Wisconsin)

The Country Gourmet ©1987 Miriam G. Cohn, by Miriam G. Cohn, Alexandria, LA (Mississippi)

The Country Mouse ©1983 Quail Ridge Press, Inc., by Sally Walton and Faye Wilkinson, Quail Ridge Press, Brandon, MS (Mississippi)

Covered Bridge Neighbors Cookbook ©1990 Circulation Service, Inc., Covered Bridge Neighbors, St. Peters, MO (Missouri)

Cowtown Cuisine ©1980 St. Joseph's Hospital Guild, St. Joseph's Hospital Guild Volunteer Office, Fort Worth, TX (Texas)

Cranbrook Reflections ©1991 Cranbrook House & Gardens Auxiliary, Cranbrook House and Gardens Auxiliary, Bloomfield Hills, MI (Michigan)

Creme de Colorado ©1987 The Junior League of Denver, Inc., The Junior League of Denver, Inc., Denver, CO (Colorado)

Cross Creek Kitchens ©1983 Sally Morrison, by Sally Morrison, Triad Publishing Co., Inc., Gainesville, FL (Florida)

The Crowning Recipes of Kentucky ©1986 Madonna Smith Echols, by Madonna Smith Echols, Marathon International Book Co., Madison, IN (Kentucky)

Culinary Arts & Crafts ©1984 The Park Maitland School, Inc., The Park Maitland School, Maitland, FL (Florida)

Culinary Contentment ©1984 Virginia Tech Faculty Women's Club, Virginia Tech Faculty Women's Club, Blacksburg, VA (Virginia)

Cypress Garden Cookbook ©1970 St. Agnes Welfare Guild, St. Paul's Episcopal Church, St. Agnes Guild—St. Paul's Episcopal Church, Winter Haven, FL (Florida)

The Dairy Hollow House Cookbook ©1986 Crescent Dragonwagon, by Crescent Dragonwagon, Cato & Martin Publishers, Eureka Springs, AR (Arkansas)

Dine with the Angels, St. Michael's Catholic Youth, Henryetta, OK (Oklahoma)

Dinner on the Diner ©1983 Junior League of Chattanooga, Inc., Junior League of Chattanooga, Chattanooga, TN (Tennessee)

Distinctly Delicious ©1997 The Distinctive Inns of Colorado, by David J. Richardson, Stars End Creations, Greenwood Village, CO (Colorado)

Dixie Delights ©1983 St. Francis Hospital Auxiliary, St. Francis Hospital Auxiliary, Memphis, TN (Tennessee)

Dixie Dining ©1982 Mississippi Federation of Women's Clubs, Inc., GFWC-Mississippi Federation of Women's Clubs, Jackson, MS (Mississippi)

Dorthy Rickers Cookbook: Mixing & Musing, by Dorthy Rickers, The Cows' Outside, Worthington, MN (Minnesota)

Down Home Cooking from Hocking County, Hocking County, Logan, OH (Ohio)

Down-Home Texas Cooking ©1994 Gulf Publishing Company, by James Stroman, Gulf Publishing Company, Houston, TX (Texas II)

Dr. Martin Luther Church 100th Anniversary Cookbook, Dr. Martin Luther Church, Oconomowoc, WI (Wisconsin)

Easy Livin' Microwave Cooking: The New Primer ©1989, 1991 Karen Kangas Dwyer, by Karen Kangas Dwyer, Ohama, NE (Great Plains)

Easy Recipes for 1, 2 or a Few ©1994 Anna Aughenbaugh, by Anna Aughenbaugh, Starlite Publications, Fort Collins, CO (Colorado)

Eat Pie First...Life is Uncertain! ©1990 Joan Jefferson, by Joan Jefferson, Freeman, MO (Missouri)

Eat To Your Heart's Content, Too!, by Woody and Betty Armour, The Heart Rock Cafe, Hot Springs, AR (Arkansas)

The Eater's Digest, Scranton Preparatory School Parent's Club, Scranton, PA (Pennsylvania)

Elsah Landing Heartland Cooking ©1981 The Elsah Landing Restaurant, Inc., by Helen Crafton and Dorothy Lindgren, Grafton, IL (Illinois)

Elvis Fans Cookbook ©1984 R & M Crafts and Reproductions, edited by Wilma K. Wooten, Winston-Salem, NC (Tennessee)

Elvis Fans Cookbook II ©1986 R & M Crafts and Reproductions, edited by Wilma K. Wooten, Winston-Salem, NC (Tennessee)

Extra! Extra! Read All About It! ©1995 Corinne H. Cook, by Corinne H. Cook, Baton Rouge, LA (Louisiana II)

Family Favorites ©1976 Black Rock Retreat, Black Rock Retreat Auxiliary, East Petersburg, PA (Pennsylvania)

Fancy Foods & Flowers ©1980 Federated Garden Clubs of Macon, Federated Garden Clubs of Macon, Inc., Macon, GA (Georgia)

Favorite Fare II, The Woman's Club of Louisville, Inc., Louisville, KY (Kentucky)

Feasts of Eden ©1990 Apple Cooks Inc., by Ruby C. Thomas, August House Publishers, Little Rock, AR (Arkansas)

Feeding the Faithful ©1983 The Women of Mauldin United Methodist Church, United Methodist Women of Mauldin United Methodist Church, Mauldin, SC (South Carolina)

Ferndale Friends Cook Book, Ferndale Friends, Ferndale, MI (Michigan)

15 Minute Storage Meals ©1996 Jayne Benkendorf, by Jayne Benkendorf, Ludwig Publishing, Edmond, OK (Oklahoma)

The Fifth Generation Cookbook, by Carol L. Wise, Findlay, OH (Ohio)

50 Years of Regal Recipes ©1995 Regal Ware, Inc., Amherst Press, Amherst, WI (Wisconsin)

Finely Tuned Foods ©1987 Symphony League of Kansas City, Symphony League of Kansas City, Leawood, KS (Missouri)

Fire Gals' Hot Pans Cookbook ©1996 Garrison Emergency Service Auxiliary, Garrison Emergency Service Auxiliary, Garrison, IA (Iowa)

First Christian Church Centennial Cookbook, First Christian Church, Mason City, IA (Iowa)

Five Loaves and Two Fishes II, First United Methodist Church Women, Springfield, IL (Illinois)

Flaunting Our Finest ©1982 Junior Auxiliary of Franklin, Junior Auxiliary of Franklin, Franklin, TN (Tennessee)

Florida Flavors ©1984 Environmental Studies Council, Inc., Environmental Studies Council, Inc., Jensen Beach, FL (Florida)

Foods a la Louisiane ©1980 Louisiana Farm Bureau Women, Louisiana Farm Bureau Federation, Baton Rouge, LA (Louisiana)

For Crying Out Loud... Let's Eat! ©1988 The Service League of Hammond, Inc., The Service League of Hammond, Hammond, IN (Indiana)

A Fork in the Road ©1998 Mimbres Region Arts Council, Mimbres Region Arts Council, Silver City, NM (New Mexico)

Four Seasons Cookbook ©1993 by Avery Color Studios, by Bea Smith, Avery Color Studios, Gwinn, MI (Michigan)

From Minnesota...More Than A Cookbook ©1985 Gluesing and Gluesing, Inc., by Laurie and Debra Gluesing, Shoreview, MN (Minnesota)

From the Inn's Kitchen, by Deedy Marble, Chef, The Governor's Inn, Ludlow, VT (New England)

Gateways ©1990 St. Louis Children's Hospital Auxiliary, Friends of St. Louis Children's Hospital, St. Louis, MO (Missouri)

Gatherings ©1987 Caprock Girl Scout Council, Caprock Girl Scout Council, Lubbock, TX (Texas II)

Gazebo Gala ©1983 The McMinnville Junior Auxiliary, Inc., McMinnville Junior Auxiliary, McMinnville, TN (Tennessee)

Generation to Generation ©1989 Temple Israel, Temple Israel Sisterhood, Canton, OH (Ohio)

Georgia On My Menu ©1988 League Publications/Junior League of Cobb-Marietta, Inc., Junior League of Cobb-Marietta, Marietta, GA (Georgia)

Georgia's Historical Restaurants and their Recipes ©1996 Dawn O'Brien and Jean Spaugh, by Jean Spaugh and Dawn O'Brien, John F. Blair, Publisher, Winston-Salem, NC (Georgia)

Giant Houseparty Cookbook ©1981 by Chamber of Commerce Philadelphia, MS, Philadelphia-Neshoba County Chamber of Commerce, Philadelphia, MS (Mississippi)

Good Maine Food ©1939, 1947, 1974 Majorie Mosser, by Marjorie Mosser, Down East Books, Camden, ME (New England)

Gourmet of the Delta ©1964 St. John's Women's Auxiliary, St. Paul's Episcopal Churchwomen, Hollandale, MS (Mississippi)

Gourmet Our Way ©1995 Cascia Parent Faculty Assn., Cascia Hall Preparatory School, Tulsa, OK (Oklahoma)

Gourmet: The Quick and Easy Way, by Diana Allen, Enid, OK (Oklahoma)

Granny's Kitchen, by Theone L. Neel, Bastian, VA (Virginia)

Great Beginnings, Grand Finales ©1991 The Junior League of South Bend, Inc., Junior League of South Bend, South Bend, IN (Indiana)

The Great Chefs of Virginia Cookbook ©1987 by The Virginia Chefs Association, The Donning Company Publishers, Atglen, PA (Virginia)

Great Flavors of Mississippi ©1986 Southern Flavors, Inc., Southern Flavors, Inc., Pine Bluff, AR (Mississippi)

Great Flavors of Texas ©1992 Southern Flavors, Inc., Southern Flavors, Inc, Pine Bluff, AR (Texas II)

The Great Taste of Virginia Seafood Cookbook ©1984 by the Virginia Marine Products Commission, by Mary Reid Barrow and Robin Browder, The Donning Company Publishers, Atglen, PA (Virginia)

The Gulf Gourmet ©1978 The Gulf Gourmet, Westminster Academy, Gulfport, MS (Mississippi)

Gulfshore Delights ©1984 The Environmental Studies Council, Inc., Junior League of Fort Myers, Fort Myers, FL (Florida)

The Hagen Family Cookbook, by Marilee Nelson, Noonan, ND (Great Plains)

Hall's Potato Harvest Cookbook ©1993 the Hall Family, by the Hall Family, Red River Valley, ND (Great Plains)

The Ham Book ©1987 Monette R. Harrell and Robert W. Harrell, Jr., Monette Harrell and Robert Harrell Jr., The Donning Company Publishers, Smithfield, VA (Virginia)

Have Breakfast with Us...Again ©1995 Amherst Press, Amherst Press, Amherst, WI (Wisconsin)

Heart of the Home Recipes ©1980 Capper Press, Inc., Ogden Publications, Inc, Topeka, KS (Great Plains)

Heavenly Delights, Sacred Heart Altar Society, Nelson, NE (Great Plains)

★★★★★★★★★★★★ ★★★★★★★★★★★★

Heavenly Dishes, United Methodist Women of Union Pisgah Church, Attica, OH (Ohio)

Heavenly Food II, United Methodist Women of Sunbury United Methodist Church, Sunbury, OH (Ohio)

Herbs in a Minnesota Kitchen ©1992 Janet Benskin, by Jan Benskin and Bonnie Dehn, Ramsey, MN (Minnesota)

Heritage Fan-Fare ©1992 Heritage Plantation of Sandwich, Inc., Heritage Plantation of Sandwich, Sandwich, MA (New England)

The Heritage of Southern Cooking ©1986 Camille Glenn, by Camille Glenn, Louisville, KY (Kentucky)

High Hampton Hospitality ©1970 Lily Byrd, by Lily Byrd, High Hampton Inn and Country Club, Cashiers, NC (North Carolina)

Historic Kentucky Recipes, Mercer County Humane Society, Harrodsburg, KY (Kentucky)

The Historic Roswell Cook Book ©1983 The Roswell Historical Society, Inc., The Roswell Historical Society, Roswell, GA (Georgia)

Holiday Treats from Granny's Kitchen by Theone L. Neel, Bastian, VA (Virginia)

Hollyhocks & Radishes ©1989 Bonnie Stewart Mickelson, by Bonnie Stewart Mickelson, Pickle Point Publishing, Bellevue, WA (Michigan)

Holy Cow, Chicago's Cooking! ©1993 The Church of the Holy Comforter, Church of the Holy Comforter, Kenilworth, IL (Illinois)

Home Cookin' Creations, First Baptist Church, Delta, CO (Colorado)

Home Cookin' is a Family Affair, Aldersgate United Methodist Women, Marion, IL (Illinois)

Home for the Holidays ©1991 Mescal Johnston, by Mescal Johnston, The University of Arkansas Press, Fayetteville, AR (Arkansas)

Honest to Goodness ©1990 Junior League of Springfield, Junior League Publications, Springfield, IL (Illinois)

Hopewell's Hoosier Harvest II ©1993 Hopewell Presbyterian Church, Hopewell Presbyterian Church, Franklin, IN (Indiana)

Hors D'Oeuvres Everybody Loves ©1983 Quail Ridge Press, Inc., by Mary Leigh Furrh and Jo Barksdale, Quail Ridge Press, Brandon, MS (Mississippi)

Hospitality ©1983 Harvey Woman's Club, Harvey Woman's Club, Palestine, TX (Texas)

Hospitality Heirlooms ©1983 South Jackson Civic League, Inc., South Jackson Civic League, Jackson, MS (Mississippi)

How to Make A Steamship Float ©1985 American Steamship Company, Harbor House Publishers, Boyne City, MI (Michigan)

Huntsville Heritage Cookbook ©1967 Junior League of Huntsville, The Junior League of Huntsville, Inc., Huntsville, AL (Alabama)

In Good Taste ©1983 Department of Nutrition, School of Public Health of the University of North Carolina, Department of Nutrition, Chapel Hill, NC (North Carolina)

Indiana Bed & Breakfast Association Cookbook and Directory ©1991 Tracy M. Winters and Phyllis Y. Winters, by Tracy and Phyllis Winters, Winters Publishing, Greensburg, IN (Indiana)

Into the Second Century ©1984 French Camp Academy, French Camp Academy, French Camp, MS (Mississippi)

Iola's Gourmet Recipes in Rhapsody ©1994 Iola Egle, by Iola Egle, McCook, NE (Great Plains)

Island Born and Bred ©1987 Harkers Island United Methodist Women, Harkers Island United Methodist Women, Harkers Island, NC (North Carolina)

Island Events Cookbook ©1986 Island Events Cookbook, Edited by Jolie Donnell, Telluride, CO (South Carolina)

It's About Thyme ©1988 Marge Clark–Thyme Cookbooks, by Marge Clark, West Lebanon, IN (Indiana)

It's Christmas! ©1989 Dianne Stafford Mayes & Dorothy Davenport Stafford, by Dianne Stafford Mayes and Dorothy Davenport Stafford, Carthage, MO (Missouri)

Jambalaya ©1983 Junior League of New Orleans, Inc., Junior League of New Orleans, Inc., New Orleans, LA (Louisiana)

Jarrett House Potpourri, Jarrett House, Dillsboro, NC (North Carolina)

Jubilee, Emmanuel Memorial Episcopal Church, Champaign, IL (Illinois)

Juicy Miss Lucy Cookbook ©1982 Two Girls From Filly, by Nancy Brail and Kathy Kahan, Two Girls from Filly, Longwood, FL (Florida)

The Junior League of Grand Rapids Cookbook I ©1976 The Junior League of Grand Rapids, Inc., Junior League of Grand Rapids, Grand Rapids, MI (Michigan)

Keepers! ©1983 Harvey Woman's Club, by Helene Randolph Moore, New Braunfels, TX (Texas)

Kelvin Homemakers 50th Anniversary Cookbook, Kelvin Homemakers, Dunseith, ND (Great Plains)

The Kentucky Derby Museum Cookbook ©1986 Kentucky Derby Museum Corp., Kentucky Derby Museum, Louisville, KY (Kentucky)

The Kimbell Cookbook ©1986 Kimbell Art Museum, by Shelby Schafer, Ft. Worth, TX (Texas II)

Kitchen Keepsakes ©1983 Bonnie Welch and Deanna White, by Bonnie Welch and Deanna White, Kiowa, CO (Colorado)

Kitchen Keepsakes ©1988 by The Houselog Family, Ellsworth, MN (Minnesota)

Kitchen Klatter Keepsakes, Kiwash Electric Cooperative, Inc., Cordell, OK (Oklahoma)

Kitchen Sampler ©1985 The Bessemer Junior Service League, Bessemer Junior Service League, Bessemer, AL (Alabama)

Knollwood's Cooking, Knollwood Baptist Church, Winston-Salem, NC (North Carolina)

La Bouche Creole ©1981 Leon E. Soniat, Jr., by Leon E. Soniat Jr., Pelican Publishing Company, Gretna, LA (Louisiana)

Lagniappe, Junior League of Beaumont, Beaumont, TX (Texas)

Lake Reflections ©1968-87 Circulation Services, Wayne County Extension Homemakers, Monticello, KY (Kentucky)

Lasting Impressions ©1988 St. Joseph's Hospital of Atlanta Auxiliary, Saint Joseph's Hospital of Atlanta Auxiliary, Atlanta, GA (Georgia)

Leaving Home ©1984 Louise (Lulu) P. Grace, by Lulu Muse, Seven Points, TX (Texas)

License to Cook Wisconsin Style ©1996 Penfield Press, by Juanita Loven, Penfield Press, Iowa City, IA (Wisconsin)

Light Kitchen Choreography ©1994 Cleveland Ballet Council, Cleveland Ballet Council, Cleveland, OH (Ohio)

Lighter Tastes of Aspen ©1994 Jill Sheeley, by Jill Sheeley, Aspen, CO (Colorado)

The Little Gumbo Book ©1986 Quail Ridge Press, Inc., by Gwen McKee, Quail Ridge Press, Brandon, MS (Louisiana II)

The Little New Orleans Cookbook ©1991 Quail Ridge Press, by Gwen McKee, Quail Ridge Press, Brandon, MS (Louisiana II)

Lone Star Legacy II ©1985 Austin Junior Forum Inc., Austin Junior Forum Publications, Austin, TX (Texas II)

Lost Tree Cook Book, Lost Tree Chapel, North Palm Beach, FL (Florida)

Louisiana's Original Creole Seafood Recipes, by Tony Chachere, Creole Foods of Opelousas, Inc., Opelousas, LA (Louisiana)

Love Yourself Cookbook ©1987 Edith Low, by Edie Low, Charlotte, NC (North Carolina)

Lutheran Church Women Cookbook, Lutheran Church Women, Missouri Valley, IA (Iowa)

M.D. Anderson Volunteers Cooking for Fun ©1991 M.D. Anderson Cancer Center Volunteers, M.D. Anderson Volunteer Service, Houston, TX (Texas II)

Ma's in the Kitchen ©1994 Carl R. McQueary and Mary Nelson Paulissen, by Carl R. McQueary and Mary Nelson Paulissen, Eakin Press, Austin, TX (Texas II)

Madison County Cookery ©1980 Madison County Chamber of Commerce, Madison County Chamber of Commerce, Canton, MS (Mississippi)

Magic ©1982 Junior League of Birmingham, Junior League of Birmingham, Birmingham, AL (Alabama)

The Maine Collection ©1993 Portland Museum of Art Guild, Portland Museum of Art Guild, Port, ME (New England)

Marcus, Iowa, Quasquicentennial Cookbook, QQC Cookbook Committee, Marcus, IA (Iowa)

Market to Market, Service League of Hickory, NC, Inc., Hickory, NC (North Carolina)

Marketplace Recipes Volume I ©1988 Action Advertising Inc. revised printing 1993, by Crystal Schulz Carew, Action Advertiser, Fond du Lac, WI (Wisconsin)

The Marlborough Meetinghouse Cookbook, Congregational Church of Marlborough, Marlborough, CT (New England)

Masterpiece Recipes of the American Club ©1993 Kohler Co., Amherst Press, Amherst, WI (Wisconsin)

Maurice's Tropical Fruit Cook Book ©1979 Maurice deVerteuil, by Maurice de Verteuil, Great Outdoors Publishing Company, St. Petersburg, FL (Florida)

The Mississippi Cookbook ©1972 University Press of Mississippi, University Press of Mississippi, Jackson, MS (Mississippi)

More Calf Fries to Caviar ©1988 Jan-Su Publications, by Janel Franklin and Sue Vaughn, Lamesa, TX (Texas II)

More Than Moonshine ©1983 by University of Pittsburgh Press, University of Pittsburgh Press, Pittsburgh, PA (Kentucky)

Mountain Elegance ©1982, 1991 The Junior League of Asheville, Inc., Junior League of Asheville, Asheville, NC (North Carolina)

Mountain Laurel Encore ©1984 Bell County Extension Homemakers, Bell County Extension Homemakers, Pineville, KY (Kentucky)

Mountain Recipe Collection ©1981 Ison Collectibles, Inc., by Valeria S. Ison, Hazard, KY (Kentucky)

Mrs. Appleyard's Family Kitchen ©1977 Polly Kent Campion, by Louise Andrews Kent and Polly Kent Campion, Vermont Life Magazine, Montpelier, VT (New England)

Mrs. Noah's Survival Guide, New Mexico Christian Children's Home, Portales, NM (New Mexico)

The Museum Cookbook, The Museum, Greenwood, SC (South Carolina)

Mystic Mountain Memories ©1990, 1993, Jerry and Josie Minerich, by Josie and Jerry Minerich, C & G Publishing, Inc., Greeley, CO (Colorado)

Mystic Seaport's All Seasons Cookbook ©1988 Mystic Seaport Museum Stores, Inc., by Connie Colom, Mystic Seaport Stores, Mystic, CT (New England)

The Nashville Cookbook ©1976, 1977 Nashville Area Home Economics Assn., Nashville Area Home Economics Association, Nashville, TN (Tennessee)

The Never Ending Season ©1990 Leisure Time Publishing, Missouri 4-H Foundation, Columbia, MO (Missouri)

New Mexico Cook Book ©1990, 1998 by Lynn Nusom, by Lynn Nusom, Golden West Publishers, Phoenix, AZ (New Mexico)

New Tastes of Iowa ©1993 by Kathryn Designs, by Peg Hein, Kathryn Designs, Austin, TX (Iowa)

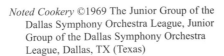

Noted Cookery ©1969 The Junior Group of the Dallas Symphony Orchestra League, Junior Group of the Dallas Symphony Orchestra League, Dallas, TX (Texas)

Nothin' but Muffins ©1991 Georgie Ann Patrick and Cynthia Ann Duncan, by Cyndi Duncan and Georgie Patrick, C & G Publishing, Inc., Greeley, CO (Colorado)

Nutbread and Nostalgia ©1979 The Junior League of South Bend, Inc., Junior League of South Bend, South Bend, IN (Indiana)

Of Magnolia and Mesquite ©1985 Su-Ga Publications, by Suzanne Corder and Gay Thompson, Su-Ga Publications, Plainview, TX (Texas)

Off the Hook ©1988 Junior League of Stamford-Norwalk, Junior League of Stamford-Norwalk, Darien, CT (New England)

Old Mobile Recipes—Tried and Proven ©1956 St. Paul's Episcopal Church, St. Paul's Episcopal Church, Mobile, AL (Alabama)

One Course at a Time ©1988 Paddi B. Childers, by Paddi B. Childers, North Myrtle Beach, SC (South Carolina)

Opaa! Greek Cooking Detroit Style ©1993 Bonus Books, by George Gekas, Bonus Books, Inc., Chicago, IL (Michigan)

The Other Side of the House ©1985 Janie Whitehurst, by Janie Whitehurst, The Donning Company Publishers, Virginia Beach, VA (Virginia)

Our Best Home Cooking, by Pearl Luttman, Red Bud, IL (Illinois)

Our Country Cookin' ©1984 Junior Social Workers, Junior Social Workers of Chickasha, Inc., Chickasha, OK (Oklahoma)

Out of this World ©1983 The Oak Hill School Parent's Association, The Oak Hill School Parent's Association, Nashville, TN (Tennessee)

Palate Pleasers, Forest Hills United Methodist Church, Brentwood, TN (Tennessee)

Palates ©1995 MVA Colorado Springs Fine Arts Center, Members' Volunteer Association Colorado Springs Fine Arts Center, Colorado Springs, CO (Colorado)

The Passion of Barbeque ©1992 Pig Out Publications, The Kansas City Barbeque Society, Hyperion, New York, NY (Missouri)

Paul Naquin's French Collection II—Meats & Poultry ©1980 Paul Naquin, by F. Paul Naquin, Baton Rouge, LA (Louisiana)

The Peach Tree Family Cookbook ©1994 Peach Tree Gift Gallery and Tea Room, by Cynthia Collins Pedregon, Fredericksburg, TX (Texas II)

Peachtree Bouquet ©1987 The Junior League of DeKalb County, Georgia, Inc., Junior League of DeKalb, Decatur, GA (Georgia)

Pearls of the Concho ©1996 San Angelo Junior League, Inc., San Angelo Junior League, Inc., San Angelo, TX (Texas)

Pennsylvania's Historic Restaurants and Their Recipes ©1986 Dawn O'Brien and Claire Walter, by Dawn O'Brien and Claire Walter, John F. Blair, Publisher, Winston-Salem, NC (Pennsylvania)

The Philadelphia Orchestra Cookbook ©1980 West Philadelphia Women's Committee for the Philadelphia Orchestra, The West Philadelphia Committee for the Philadelphia Orchestra, Bryn Mawr, PA (Pennsylvania)

Picnics on the Square ©1994 Wisconsin Chamber Orchestra, Inc., Wisconsin Chamber Orchestra, Madison, WI (Wisconsin)

Pirate's Pantry ©1976 Junior League of Lake Charles, Inc., Junior League of Lake Charles, Pelican Publishing Company, Lake Charles, LA (Louisiana)

Please Don't Feed the Alligators ©1985 Hilton Head Elementary PTA, Hilton Head Elementary School, Hilton Head Island, SC (South Carolina)

Pow Wow Chow ©1984 Five Civilized Tribes Museum, The Five Civilized Tribes Museum, Muskogee, OK (Oklahoma)

Prairie Harvest ©1981 St. Peters Episcopal Church Women, St. Peters Episcopal Church Women, Hazen, AR (Arkansas)

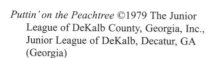

Puttin' on the Peachtree ©1979 The Junior League of DeKalb County, Georgia, Inc., Junior League of DeKalb, Decatur, GA (Georgia)

Queen Anne's Table, Edenton Historical Commission, Edenton, NC (North Carolina)

Quickies for Singles ©1980 Quail Ridge Press, Inc., edited by Gwen McKee, Quail Ridge Press, Brandon, MS (Louisiana)

Rancho De Chimayo Cookbook ©1991 The Harvard Common Press, by Cheryl Alters Jamison and Bill Jamison, The Harvard Common Press, Boston, MA (New Mexico)

Raspberry Enchantment House Tour Cookbook, Carrie Tingley Hospital Foundation, Albuquerque, NM (New Mexico)

Ready to Serve ©1984 Texas National Guard Auxiliary, National Guard Auxiliary of Austin, Austin, TX (Texas)

REC Family Cookbook ©1987 North Dakota Association of Rural Electric Cooperatives, North Dakota REC/RTC Magazine, Mandan, ND (Great Plains)

Recipes & Remembrances, Buffalo Lake Lutheran Church WMF, Eden, SD (Great Plains)

Recipes & Remembrances, by the Dotson Family, Lima, OH (Ohio)

Recipes and Reminiscences of New Orleans I ©1981 Parents Club of Ursuline Academy Inc., Ursuline Convent , Metairie, LA (Louisiana)

Recipes from a New England Inn ©1992 Trudy Cutrone, by Trucy Cutrone, Country Roads Press, Castine, ME (New England)

Recipes from Iowa with Love ©1981 New Boundary Concepts, Inc, by Peg Hein and Kathryn Cramer, Strawberry Point, Inc., Prior Lake, MN (Iowa)

Recipes from Minnesota with Love ©1981 Betty Malisow Potter, by Betty Malisow, Strawberry Point, Inc., Prior Lake, MN (Minnesota)

Recipes from the Heart, Epsilon Omega Sorority, Dalton, NE (Great Plains)

Recipes of Note for Entertaining, Rochester Civic Music Guild, Rochester, MN (Minnesota)

Red Lion Inn Cookbook ©1992 Berkshire House Publishers, by Suzi Forbes Chase, Berkshire House Publishers, Stockbridge, MA, (New England)

Renaissance Cuisine ©1981 Fontbonne Auxiliary of St. John Hospital and Medical Center, Fontbonne Auxiliary of St. John Hospital & Medical Center, Detroit, MI (Michigan)

Return Engagement ©1989 The Junior Board of the Quad City Symphony Orchestra Assn., Volunteers for Quad City Symphony Orchestra, Davenport, IA (Iowa)

Rhode Island Cooks ©1992 American Cancer Society, RI Division, Inc., American Cancer Society - New England Division, Pawtucket, RI (New England)

River Road Recipes I ©1959 The Junior League of Baton Rouge, Inc., Junior League of Baton Rouge, Baton Rouge, LA (Louisiana)

The Route 66 Cookbook ©1993 & 1999 Marian Clark, by Marian Clark, Council Oak Books, Tulsa, OK (Oklahoma)

A Salad A Day ©1980 Quail Ridge Press, Inc., by Ruth Morman and Lalla Williams, Quail Ridge Press, Brandon, MS (Mississippi)

San Antonio Cookbook II ©1976 Symphony Society of San Antonio, The San Antonio Symphony League, San Antonio, TX (Texas)

The Sandlapper Cookbook ©1974 Sandlapper Publishing Co., Inc., Sandlapper Publishing Co., Inc., Orangeburg, SC (South Carolina)

Sassafras! The Ozarks Cookbook ©1985 Junior League of Springfield, Junior League of Springfield, Missouri, Springfield, MO (Missouri)

Savannah Collection ©1986 Martha Giddens Nesbit, by Martha Giddens Nesbit, Savannah, GA (Georgia)

Savoring the Southwest, Again ©1983 Roswell Symphony Guild Publications, Roswell Symphony Guild, Roswell, NM (New Mexico)

Seasoned Cooks II, Isabella County Commission on Aging, Mt. Pleasant, MI (Michigan)

Seasoned with Love, Reorganized Church of Jesus Christ of Latter Day Saints, Springerton, IL (Illinois)

Seasoned With Love Trinity United Church of Christ, Brookfield, WI (Wisconsin)

The Second Typically Texas Cookbook ©1989 The Association of Texas Electric Cooperatives, Inc., Texas Electric Cooperatives, Inc., Austin, TX (Texas II)

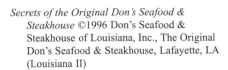

Secrets of the Original Don's Seafood & Steakhouse ©1996 Don's Seafood & Steakhouse of Louisiana, Inc., The Original Don's Seafood & Steakhouse, Lafayette, LA (Louisiana II)

The Sevier County Cookbook compiled by Patsy Bradford, Sevier County, Seymour, TN (Tennessee)

Shared Treasures ©1996 First Baptist Church Student Ministry, First Baptist Church, Monroe, LA (Louisiana II)

Sharing Our Best, Home of the Good Shepherd, St. Paul, MN (Minnesota)

Sharing Our Best, by Eileen Hardway, Martinsville, IL (Indiana)

Shattuck Community Cookbook, Shattuck Chamber of Commerce, Shattuck, OK (Oklahoma)

Ship to Shore I ©1983 Ship to Shore, Inc., by Jan Robinson, Charlotte, NC (North Carolina)

The Simply Great II Cookbook ©1995 The C. A. Muer Corp., Momentum Books, Troy, MI (Michigan)

Simply Simpatico ©1981 The Junior League of Albuquerque, Inc., The Junior League of Albuquerque, Albuquerque, NM (New Mexico)

The Smithfield Cookbook ©1978 Smithfield Junior Woman's Club, The Junior Woman's Club of Smithfield, Smithfield, VA (Virginia)

Smyth County Extension Homemakers Cookbook Volume II, Smyth County Extension Homemakers, Marion, VA (Virginia)

Somethin's Cookin' at LG&E ©1986 LG&E Employees Association, Inc., Louisville Gas & Electric Co. Employees Association, Louisville, KY (Kentucky)

Sounds Delicious! ©1986 Volunteer Council of the Tulsa Philharmonic Society, Inc., Volunteer Council of the Tulsa Philharmonic Society, Inc., Tulsa, OK (Oklahoma)

Soupçon II ©1982 The Junior League of Chicago, Inc., The Junior League of Chicago, Inc., Chicago, IL (Illinois)

Southeastern Wildlife Cookbook ©1989 University of South Carolina Press, University of South Carolina Press, Columbia, SC (South Carolina)

Southern Seafood Classics ©1988 The Southeastern Fisheries Association, by The Southeastern Fisheries Association, Peachtree Publishers, Atlanta, GA (Georgia)

Southern Secrets ©1979 E.O.S., University School of Jackson Mother's Club, Jackson, TN (Tennessee)

Sparks from the Kitchen, by Syd and Florence Herman, Manitowoc, WI (Wisconsin)

St. Joseph's Parish Cookbook, St. Joseph's Altar and Rosary, Greeley, IA (Iowa)

St. Philomena School 125th Anniversary ©1996 St. Philomena School, St. Philomena Home & School Association, Labadieville, LA (Louisiana II)

St. Mary's Family Cookbook, St. Mary's Council of Catholic Women, Bloomington, WI (Wisconsin)

St. Paul Cooks ©1986 Cookbook Publishers, Inc., St. Paul Christian Academy, Nashville, TN (Tennessee)

Stir Crazy! ©1986 Junior Welfare League of Florence, Junior League of Florence, Florence, SC (South Carolina)

Stir Ups ©1982 Junior Welfare League of Enid, Junior Welfare League of Enid, Enid, OK (Oklahoma)

Stirrin' the Pots on Daufuskie ©1985 Billie Burn, by Billie Burn, Daufuskie Island, SC (South Carolina)

Stirring Performances ©1988 The Junior League of Winston-Salem, Inc., Junior League of Winston-Salem, Inc., Winston-Salem, NC (North Carolina)

Strictly For Boys ©1980 Betty L. Waskiewicz, by Betty L. Waskiewicz, Beaufort, SC (South Carolina)

Sugar Beach ©1984 The Junior Service League of Fort Walton Beach, Fort Walton Beach Junior Service League, Fort Walton Beach, FL (Florida)

Suncoast Seasons ©1984 Dunedin Youth Guild, Inc., Dunedin Youth Guild, Inc., Dunedin, FL (Florida)

Sunny Side Up ©1980 The Junior League of Fort Lauderdale Inc, The Junior League of Fort Lauderdale, Fort Lauderdale, FL (Florida)

Susie's Cook Book, by the Clemens Family, Hatfield Quality Meats, Inc., Hatfield, PA (Pennsylvania)

Sweets...from Marina with Love... ©1983 Marina Reed Gonzalez, by Marina Reed Gonzalez, San Antonio, TX (Texas)

T. W. and Anna Elliott Family Receipts, by the Elliott Family, La Porte City, IA (Iowa)

Talk About Good III, Forsyth Library Friends, Forsyth, MO (Missouri)

Taste & See, Women Ministries of Sardinia Baptist, Westport, IN (Indiana)

A Taste of Christ Lutheran, Christ Lutheran Celebration Committee, Sharon, WI (Wisconsin)

A Taste of Georgia ©1977 Newnan Junior Service League, Newnan Junior Service League, Newnan, GA (Georgia)

A Taste of New England ©1990 Junior League or Worcester, Inc., Junior League of Worcester, Inc., Worcester, MA (New England)

Taste of the South ©1984 The Symphony League of Jackson, Jackson Symphony League, Jackson, MS (Mississippi)

A Taste of Toronto   Ohio, that is ©1994 The Toronto High School Alumni Association, The Toronto High School Alumni Association, Toronto, OH (Ohio)

Tastes & Tales from Texas...with Love ©1984 Peg Hein, by Peg Hein, Hein & Associates, Austin, TX (Texas)

A Tasting Tour Through Washington County Kentucky ©1987 Springfield Woman's Club, The Springfield Woman's Club, Springfield, KY (Kentucky)

Tea-Time at the Masters ©1977 The Junior League of Augusta, Junior League of Augusta, Inc., Augusta, GA (Georgia)

Texas Cookin' Lone Star Style ©1991 Lone Star Chapter 22, Telephone Pioneers of America, Telephone Pioneers of America-Lone Star Chapter 22, Dallas, TX (Texas II)

Thank Heaven for Home Made Cooks, Dover Christian Women's Fellowship, Dover, OK (Oklahoma)

Think Healthy, Fairfax County Department of Extension, Fairfax, VA (Virginia)

Thoroughbred Fare ©1984 Thoroughbred Fare Cookbook, by Marilyn Brown, Aiken, SC (South Carolina)

A Thyme For All Seasons ©1982 Junior League of Duluth, Junior League of Duluth, Duluth, MN (Minnesota)

'Tiger Bait' Recipes ©1976 LSU Alumni Federation, Louisiana State University Alumni Federation, Baton Rouge, LA (Louisiana)

To Market, To Market ©1984, 1993 The Junior League of Owensboro, Inc., The Junior League of Owensboro, Kentucky, Inc., Owensboro, KY (Kentucky)

To Tayla with TLC, RCRH Medical Imaging Department, Rapid City, SD (Great Plains)

Too Good to be True ©1992 Chet Beckwith, by Chet Beckwith, Baton Rouge, LA (Louisiana II)

Touches of the Hands & Heart, by Karen A. Maag, Columbus Grove, OH (Ohio)

Tout de Suite a la Microwave II ©1980 Jean K. Durkee, by Jean K. Durkee, Tout de Suite a la Microwave, Inc., Lafayette, LA (Louisiana)

Traditionally Wesleyan ©1985 The Wesleyan Business Club, Wesleyan College Business Club, Macon, GA (Georgia)

Treasured Alabama Recipes ©1967 Kathryn Tucker Windham, by Kathryn Tucker Windham, Selma, AL (Alabama)

Treasured Recipes Book II, Taneyhills Library Club, Branson, MO (Missouri)

Trim & Terrific American Favorites ©1996 Holly B. Clegg, Inc., by Holly B. Clegg, Clarkson Potter, New York, NY (Louisiana II)

Trinity Lutheran Church Centennial Cookbook, Trinity Lutheran Church, Mallard, IA (Iowa)

The Twelve Days of Christmas Cookbook ©1978 Quail Ridge Press, Inc., by Ruth Morman and Lalla Williams, Quail Ridge Press, Brandon, MS (Mississippi)

Unbearably Good! ©1986 Americus Junior Service League, Americus Junior Service League, Americus, GA (Georgia)

Up a Country Lane Cookbook ©1993 University of Iowa Press, University of Iowa Press, Iowa City, IA (Iowa)

Vintage Vicksburg ©1985 Vicksburg Junior Auxiliary, Inc., Vicksburg Junior Auxiliary, Vicksburg, MS (Mississippi)

Virginia Hospitality ©1975 The Junior League of Hampton Roads, Inc., The Junior League of Hampton Roads, Inc., Hampton, VA (Virginia)

Viva Italia ©1994 Maria Volpe Paganini, by Maria Volpe Paganini, Concord, OH (Ohio)

Wadsworth-Rittman Hospital Cookbook, Wadsworth-Rittman Hospital, Wadsworth, OH (Ohio)

Well Seasoned ©1982 Les Passees, Inc., Les Passees Publications, Memphis, TN (Tennessee)

What Is It? What Do I Do With It? ©1978 Beth Tartan and Fran Parker, by Beth Tartan and Fran Parker, TarPar Ltd., Kernersville, NC (North Carolina)

What's Cook'n?, Manitou Girl Scout Council, Sheboygan, WI (Wisconsin)

What's Cookin', by Jeanne E. Briggs, Rockford, MI (Michigan)

What's New in Wedding Food ©1985 Marigold P. Sparks and Beth Tartan, by Marigold P. Sparks and Beth Tartan, TarPar Ltd., Kernersville, NC (North Carolina)

When Dinnerbells Ring ©1978 Talladega Junior Welfare League, Talladega Junior Welfare League, Talladega, AL (Alabama)

Who's Your Mama, Are you Catholic, and Can you make a Roux? ©1991 Marcelle Bienvenu, Marcelle Bienvenu, Times of Acadiana Press, Lafayette, LA (Louisiana II)

Windsor Academy Cookbook ©1988 Ponder's Inc., Ponder's Inc., Thomasville, GA (Georgia)

Winners ©1985 The Junior League of Indianapolis, Inc., Junior League of Indianapolis, Indianapolis, IN (Indiana)

Winning Recipes from Minnesota with Love ©1992 New Boundary Concepts, Inc., by The Cooks of Minnesota, Strawberry Point, Inc., Prior Lake, MN (Minnesota)

With Hands & Heart Cookbook ©1990 Bethesda General Hospital Womens Board, Bethesda Hospital, St. Louis, MO (Missouri)

Woman's National Farm and Garden Association —Rochester Cookbook Volume II, Woman's National Farm and Garden Association, Rochester, MI (Michigan)

The Words Worth Eating Cookbook ©1987 Jacquelyn G. Legg, by Jacquelyn G. Legg, Newport News, VA (Virginia)

Wyndmere Community Alumni Cookbook, Wyndmere Community Center, Wyndmere, ND (Great Plains)

WYVE's Cookbook/Photo Album ©1990 WYVE Radio, WYVE Radio Station, Wytheville, VA (Virginia)

Y Winners...Cookbook of Champions, Fargo/Moorehead Family YMCA, Fargo, ND (Great Plains)

Trisbed *he Recipe Hall of Fame Cookbook* came about through the efforts of a host of wonderful people. In order to create this collection, we solicited the help of co-workers, family, friends, authors, editors, peers, professionals, and a great variety of cooks, both amateur and professional. To all, we are deeply indebted.

First of all we thank our devoted Quail Ridge Press staff, Cyndi Clark, Sheila Williams, Annette Goode, Shonda Chisholm, and Gordon Denman, who gave this project extra effort in the office and in their homes—and all declare they have become better cooks in the process. Indeed we all enjoyed our test-a-dish lunches, which turned our conference room into the best restaurant in town.

Thanks goes to Larry Chilnick for his ideas, direction, and determination to keep us on course . . . and on deadline.

Another good friend, food stylist, Bobbi Cappelli also offered her encouragement, and definite preferences for certain recipes (she particularly likes the Lemon Gold Cake on page 205).

A very special thanks goes to my daughter, Heather McKee Creel, who not only tried recipes and offered suggestions, but did surveys with her neighbors and friends, gave editorial advice, and reminded us what young cooks may not understand about older recipes.

And of course, as with every one of the Best of the Best cookbooks, our friend Tupper England added special all-over-America flavor with her charming illustrations. Thanks, Tup.

Accolades to our Best Club members, those individuals throughout America who have bought all the "Best" cookbooks and who graciously responded to our survey requesting their favorite choices. They seemed genuinely excited to be able to vote for their favorite recipes, and sent their enthusiastic support along with their selections.

There were editors, authors and publishers who answered phones and faxes and returned forms with signed permissions. This paperwork had to be done, and we thank each one of them for their cooperation.

And most importantly, we thank the cooks all over the country whose names may not be mentioned or even known, but who deserve special credit for creating these recipes and writing them down for others to enjoy. Each one of you deserves a part of the credit for our being able to Preserve America's Food Heritage through these Hall of Fame recipes.

Dear friends, thank you one and all.

Gwen McKee and Barbara Moseley

Index

The Great Lakes contain 6 quadrillion gallons of fresh water; one-fifth of the world's fresh surface water (only the polar ice caps and Lake Baikal in Siberia contain more). Shown here, Lake Superior at Palisade Head,

Index

Index

Index

Index

Index

BEST OF THE BEST STATE COOKBOOK SERIES

Best of the Best from
ALABAMA
288 pages • $16.95

Best of the Best from
ARIZONA
288 pages • $16.95

Best of the Best from
ARKANSAS
288 pages • $16.95

Best of the Best from
CALIFORNIA
368 pages • $16.95

Best of the Best from
COLORADO
288 pages • $16.95

Best of the Best from
FLORIDA
288 pages • $16.95

Best of the Best from
GEORGIA
336 pages • $16.95

Best of the Best from the
GREAT PLAINS
288 pages • $16.95

Best of the Best from
ILLINOIS
288 pages • $16.95

Best of the Best from
INDIANA
288 pages • $16.95

Best of the Best from
IOWA
288 pages • $16.95

Best of the Best from
KENTUCKY
288 pages • $16.95

Best of the Best from
LOUISIANA
288 pages • $16.95

Best of the Best from
LOUISIANA II
288 pages • $16.95

Best of the Best from
MICHIGAN
288 pages • $16.95

Best of the Best from the
MID-ATLANTIC
288 pages • $16.95

Best of the Best from
MINNESOTA
288 pages • $16.95

Best of the Best from
MISSISSIPPI
288 pages • $16.95

Best of the Best from
MISSOURI
304 pages • $16.95

Best of the Best from
NEW ENGLAND
368 pages • $16.95

Best of the Best from
NEW MEXICO
288 pages • $16.95

Best of the Best from
NEW YORK
288 pages • $16.95

Best of the Best from
NO. CAROLINA
288 pages • $16.95

Best of the Best from
OHIO
352 pages • $16.95

Best of the Best from
OKLAHOMA
288 pages • $16.95

Best of the Best from
OREGON
288 pages • $16.95

Best of the Best from
PENNSYLVANIA
320 pages • $16.95

Best of the Best from
SO. CAROLINA
288 pages • $16.95

Best of the Best from
TENNESSEE
288 pages • $16.95

Best of the Best from
TEXAS
352 pages • $16.95

Best of the Best from
TEXAS II
352 pages • $16.95

Best of the Best from
VIRGINIA
320 pages • $16.95

Best of the Best from
WASHINGTON
288 pages • $16.95

Best of the Best from
WEST VIRGINIA
288 pages • $16.95

Best of the Best from
WISCONSIN
288 pages • $16.95

Cookbooks listed above have been completed as of December 31, 2002. All cookbooks are ringbound except California, which is paperbound. Note: Great Plains consists of North Dakota, South Dakota, Nebraska, and Kansas; Mid-Atlantic includes Maryland, Delaware, New Jersey, and Washington, D.C.; New England encompasses Rhode Island, Connecticut, Massachusetts, Vermont, New Hampshire, and Maine.

Recipe Hall of Fame Collection

The extensive recipe database of Quail Ridge Press' acclaimed BEST OF THE BEST STATE COOKBOOK SERIES is the inspiration behind the RECIPE HALL OF FAME COLLECTION. These Hall-of-Fame recipes have achieved extra distinction for consistently producing superb dishes. *The Recipe Hall of Fame Cookbook* features over 400 choice dishes for a variety of meals; the *Recipe Hall of Fame Dessert Cookbook* consists entirely of extraordinary desserts. The *Recipe Hall of Fame Quick & Easy Cookbook* contains over 500 recipes that require minimum effort but produce maximum enjoyment. Appetizers to desserts, quick dishes to masterpiece presentations, the RECIPE HALL OF FAME COLLECTION has it all.

All books: Paperbound • 7x10 • Illustrations • Index
The Recipe Hall of Fame Cookbook • 304 pages • $19.95
Recipe Hall of Fame Dessert Cookbook • 240 pages • $16.95
Recipe Hall of Fame Quick & Easy Cookbook • 304 pages • $19.95

NOTE: All three HALL OF FAME cookbooks can be ordered as a set for $39.90 (plus $4.00 shipping), a 30% discount off the total list price of $56.85. Over 1300 HALL OF FAME recipes for about 3¢ each—an incredible value!